Job Interviews

FOR

DUMMIES®

4TH EDITION

by Joyce Lain Kennedy

WILEY

John Wiley & Sons, Inc.

Job Interviews For Dummies®, 4th Edition

Published by
John Wiley & Sons, Inc.
111 River St.
Hoboken, NJ 07030-5774
www.wiley.com

Copyright © 2012 by John Wiley & Sons, Inc., Hoboken, New Jersey

Published by John Wiley & Sons, Inc., Hoboken, New Jersey

Published simultaneously in Canada

For general information on our other products and services, please contact our Customer Care Department within the U.S. at 877-762-2974, outside the U.S. at 317-572-3993, or fax 317-572-4002.

For technical support, please visit www.wiley.com/techsupport.

Wiley publishes in a variety of print and electronic formats and by print-on-demand. Some material included with standard print versions of this book may not be included in e-books or in print-on-demand. If this book refers to media such as a CD or DVD that is not included in the version you purchased, you may download this material at http://booksupport.wiley.com. For more information about Wiley products, visit www.wiley.com.

Library of Congress Control Number is available from the publisher.

ISBN 978-1-118-11290-8 (pbk); ISBN 978-1-118-22418-2 (ebk); ISBN 978-1-118-23748-9 (ebk); ISBN 978-1-118-24207-0 (ebk)

Manufactured in the United States of America

10 9 8 7 6 5 4 3 2 1

WILEY

About the Author

Joyce Lain Kennedy is America's first nationally syndicated careers columnist. Her twice-weekly column, "Careers Now," appears in newspapers and on websites across the land. In her four decades of advising readers — newbies, prime-timers, and those in between — Joyce has received millions of letters inquiring about career moves and job searches, and has answered countless numbers of them in print.

Joyce is the author of seven career books, including *Joyce Lain Kennedy's Career Book* (McGraw-Hill), *Electronic Job Search Revolution, Electronic Resume Revolution,* and *Hook Up, Get Hired! The Internet Job Search Revolution* (the last three published by John Wiley & Sons). *Job Interviews For Dummies* is one of a trio of award-winning job market books published under John Wiley & Son's wildly popular *For Dummies* branded imprint. The others are *Resumes For Dummies* and *Cover Letters For Dummies.*

Writing from Carlsbad, California, a San Diego suburb, the country's best-known careers columnist is a graduate of Washington University in St. Louis. Contact Joyce at jlk@sunfeatures.com.

About the Technical Advisor

James M. Lemke has earned a reputation as a leader in talent strategies and processes. He is Director of Affiliate Human Resources Systems Development for Finca International, a global nonprofit financial services organization.

Jim has held executive positions with Opportunity International, Wachovia Bank, TRW, UCLA, Walt Disney Imagineering, and Raytheon. Previously, Jim spent 15 years as a human resources consultant and hiring authority. His client list included Real Networks, Southern California Metropolitan Water District, Northrop Grumman, Southwest Airlines, Jet Propulsion Laboratory, United Arab Emirates University, and the White House.

Jim resides in Buckeye, Arizona. Contact him at jamesmlemke@gmail.com.

Author's Acknowledgments

The richness of helpful information you find within these pages is due to my luck in sourcing many respected minds in the employment space. Contributors to whom I am especially indebted are individually credited in chapter pages. Applause to one and all.

Additionally, thanks a billion to the following individuals who worked long and hard to make this book happen:

James M. Lemke, above-the-title technical advising star and executive world traveler, who is indispensable to the quality of every book I write.

Lindsay Sandman Lefevere, *For Dummies* executive editor, who is godmother for this book and quite a few others.

Linda Brandon, top editor at the top of her game, who attentively shepherded this book through a myriad of publishing hoops, always making valuable suggestions.

Melanie Astaire Witt, writer and editor, who provided inordinate expertise to produce this book's first appendix of interview questions by career fields and industries.

Yevgeniy "Yev" Churinov, computer whiz and social networking guru, who contributed both technological clarity and practical production assistance to this work.

Krista Hansing, copyeditor of the first rank, who used her sharp eyes, sound judgment, and commitment to the project to make this a far better book.

Gail Ross, literary agent-attorney and longtime friend, who continues to help me make the right publishing moves.

Publisher's Acknowledgments

We're proud of this book; please send us your comments at http://dummies.custhelp.com. For other comments, please contact our Customer Care Department within the U.S. at 877-762-2974, outside the U.S. at 317-572-3993, or fax 317-572-4002.

Some of the people who helped bring this book to market include the following:

Acquisitions, Editorial, and Vertical Websites

Project Editor: Linda Brandon
    (Previous Edition: Traci Cumbay)

Acquisitions Editor: Lindsay Lefevere

Copy Editor: Krista Hansing

Assistant Editor: David Lutton

Editorial Program Coordinator: Joe Niesen

Technical Editor: James M. Lemke

Editorial Manager: Jennifer Ehrlich,
    Carmen Krikorian

Editorial Assistant: Alexa Koschier

Art Coordinator: Alicia B. South

Cover Photos: © iStockphoto.com / FMNG

Cartoons: Rich Tennant
    (www.the5thwave.com)

Composition Services

Project Coordinator: Kristie Rees

Layout and Graphics: Andrea Hornberger,
    Laura Westhuis

Proofreaders: Jessica Kramer, Toni Settle

Indexer: Ty Koontz

Publishing and Editorial for Consumer Dummies

    Kathleen Nebenhaus, Vice President and Executive Publisher

    Kristin Ferguson-Wagstaffe, Product Development Director

    Ensley Eikenburg, Associate Publisher, Travel

    Kelly Regan, Editorial Director, Travel

Publishing for Technology Dummies

    Andy Cummings, Vice President and Publisher

Composition Services

    Debbie Stailey, Director of Composition Services

Table of Contents

Introduction

*I*f you'd rather fight off an alien invasion than be grilled in an interview, take heart — you've come to the right guidebook. With the help of dozens of interviewing authorities, I make your interviewing challenge easy, successful, and even fun (steal a peek at the last chapter).

I share with you lots of new things in this fourth edition of *Job Interviews For Dummies,* ranging from the cosmic shift sparked by the rise of social media that changes what privacy means, to increasingly popular video interviewing that changes how communication occurs.

What hasn't changed is the fundamental role in the employment process played by job interviews — those crucial meetings that seal the deal on who gets hired and who gets left on the outside looking in.

Job interviews are a slice of performance art. They're staged theatrical sketches rather than X-rays of life histories. That's why theater and drama are the themes of this book, and I hope you have some enjoyable moments with the show-biz motif.

So on with the show! With the help of this guidebook, you, too, can be a ShowStopper.

What Exactly Is a ShowStopper in Job Interviewing?

In the drama of job interviewing, a ShowStopper performance is one that wins so much enthusiastic, prolonged applause that the show is temporarily interrupted until the audience quiets down.

A ShowStopper meeting causes the interviewer to mentally shout, "Bravo! More!" Your stunning impact quickly translates to a preliminary decision in your favor. If follow-up interviews, testing, and reference checking support that reaction, a job offer is on its way to you. The employer may continue to see other candidates to round out the interview process, but in reality, no one else stands a chance of landing the job after you figuratively stop the show.

Job Interviews For Dummies is packed with the essentials of performing ShowStopper interviews:

- ✔ Strategies and techniques
- ✔ Sample dialogue and research tips
- ✔ The best answers to make-or-break questions

About This Book

A guidebook of contemporary interview arts, *Job Interviews For Dummies* contains the distilled wisdom of hundreds of leading interview experts whose brains I've been privileged to pick for many years. By absorbing the guidance and tips I pass on in this guide, you can interview your way into a job by out-preparing and outperforming the other candidates.

Conventions Used in This Book

To assist your navigation of this guidebook, I've established the following conventions:

- ✔ I use *italic* for emphasis and to highlight either new words or terms I define.
- ✔ Web addresses appear in a special font to distinguish them from the regular type in the paragraph.
- ✔ Sidebars, which are shaded boxes of text, consist of information that's interesting but not necessarily critical to your understanding of the topic.

Terms Used in This Book

Is there another word for *synonym?* Would a fly without wings be called a *walk?* How is it possible to have a civil war? These one-liners from comedian George Carlin (www.georgecarlin.com) hint at the importance of words.

I use the following terminology in this guide to label specific roles and organizations:

✔ A *candidate* or *job seeker* is a person applying for a job. (Another once-common label, *applicant,* is used less today because of a federal regulation that defines an applicant as one to be counted in discrimination monitoring. But *applicant* means the same thing.)

✔ An *interviewer* is someone interviewing a candidate for a job. An *interviewee* is a candidate being interviewed for a job.

✔ A *human resources* (or *HR*) *specialist, HR manager,* or *screener* is an employer sentry who is conducting a screening (preliminary) interview.

A *hiring manager, hiring authority, decision maker, decision-making manager,* or *department manager* is a management representative who is conducting a selection interview and who has the authority to actually hire a person for a specific position. (Read about the differences in screening and selection interviews in Chapters 2 and 5.)

✔ A *company, employer,* or *organization* is the entity you hope to work for, whether private and profit-making, or private and nonprofit. *Agency* implies employment in the government (public) sector.

✔ A *recruiter* (also called a *headhunter*) is an intermediary between the employer and you. *Internal recruiters* work inside the company, either as regular employees of the human resources department or as contract employees. *Third-party recruiters* or *independent recruiters* are external recruiters, some of whom are employed as retained recruiters on an ongoing basis, while most are employed on a transaction basis as contingency recruiters and are paid only when a candidate they submit is hired.

✔ A *career coach* (also called a *career consultant)* helps job seekers gain workplace opportunities. (A *career counselor* and a career coach represent two different professions, although their work sometimes overlaps.)

✔ A *hiring professional* is any of the aforementioned professionals who is engaged internally or externally in the employment process.

Foolish Assumptions

I assume you picked up this book for one of the following reasons:

✔ You've never been through a competitive interview and you're freaking out. You need a couple thousand friendly pointers from someone who's interviewed many of the marquee minds in the job interview business and lived to write about it.

✔ You've been through a competitive interview and assume the company sank like Atlantis because you never heard a peep from those folks again. Or maybe you could have done better and actually heard back if you'd have known more about what you were doing in this interview thing.

> ✔ The most important interview of your career is coming up. You realize that now is the hour to dramatically improve your interviewing success. You need help, and you're willing to learn and work for success.

> ✔ You've been through a slew of job interviews over the course of your career and have a hunch that some important things have changed (you just don't know what exactly). You want to catch up with the help of a trusted resource.

> ✔ You want to be in the interviewing know and are sure that the authors of *For Dummies* books will give you the goods. You rely on *For Dummies* books to get the facts you need to succeed without jumping through verbal hoops until your eyes pop out of your head.

I further assume that you're someone who likes reliable, comprehensive information that gets to the point without rocking you to sleep. And I assume even further that you like your expertise with a smile now and then.

How This Book Is Organized

Before he was famous, superstar George Clooney auditioned for a television stereo commercial with a six-pack of beer tucked under his arm; he had researched the type of actor the advertiser wanted for the role, one whose attitude revealed the casual poise of a couch potato. He got the gig.

Later, Clooney explained the contribution of performance in both theatrical auditioning and job interviewing. He noted that the actor who lands the job isn't always the most talented, but the one who makes the best impression: "You get the job when you walk in the door. Because in a weird way, we're not selling acting. What we're selling is confidence."

Appearance. Performance skills. Confidence. All are winning — and learnable — traits in job interviews as well as theatrical auditions. This guidebook shows you these traits and much, much more in the following five useful categories.

Part 1: And the Interview Winner Is . . . You!

This part opens with an overview of what's happening right now in job interviewing circles, beginning with the theme of this guidebook: *Interviews are theater.* A spotlight on new topics is next, including the growing impact of screening interviews, the spread of video interviewing, and interesting interview variations in a global marketplace. The conclusion is a review of 18 formats you may encounter, from behavior-based interviews to mealtime interviews.

Part II: Backstage Researching and Rehearsing

In this part, I show you how to explore the backstage preparation that drives interview success. You learn how to research employers, understand personality tests, negotiate salary, dress like a star, overcome stage fright, look smart with questions you ask, and say all the right things to hold the door open to gracefully check back with the interviewer for progress reports on filling the job.

Part III: Actors' Studio: Casting Your Character

Are you a new graduate who's getting ready for your debut career interview and concerned about coming across as a clueless beginner? An experienced person who feels miscast and wants desperately to change careers? A job-search veteran whose presentation persona may need a touch-up? I show you how to tailor your interviews for job offers, whether you're a rookie, career refugee, or prime-timer.

Part IV: Lights, Camera, Talk! Answering Questions

How do you deal with the heart and soul of the interview, the questions? Turn to this part to find out. Here you immediately discover how to deliver a ShowStopper's response to each major question employers are almost certain to ask. I present the answers in a crisp style that puts you far ahead of your competitors.

Part V: The Part of Tens

Be ready to bag quick, surefire tips that help you put a five-star shine on your performance. You'll also learn how to avoid falling through trapdoors with the wrong answers to trick questions. As you leave the stage triumphantly, take a few minutes to smile as you read an irreverent group of statements that superstars of history may have made on a job interview, if they'd had one.

Icons Used in This Book

For Dummies signature icons are the little round pictures you see in the margins of the book. I use them to focus a searchlight on key bits of information. Here's a list of the icons you find in this book:

This icon flags news you can use that you won't want to forget.

Bravo! This icon heralds star-quality lines and moves that prompt job offers.

A bad review for a poor performance. This icon signals situations in which you may find trouble if you don't make a good decision.

Advice and information that can put you on award-winning pathways in your interview follow this icon. It lets you in on interviewing best practices.

Where to Go from Here

On the stress scale of life, job interviewing ranks with making a speech before 500 people when you can't remember your name or why you're standing in a spotlight at a podium. The spot where you start in this guidebook book depends on your present needs:

✔ When you have a job interview tomorrow, quickly read Chapter 1 for an overview, followed by Chapters 23 and 24 for an instant infusion of key know-how. Additionally, go to the company's website to glean as much basic information as you can. Don't forget to read the company's press releases.

✔ When you have a few days before you're scheduled for an interview, read Chapter 1 and then flip through the Table of Contents to the chapters dealing with your most pressing concerns. Pay attention to Chapter 12, which reveals how to stack the deck in your favor during the closing minutes of your interview.

✔ When you have plenty of time, read the book from cover to cover. Practice recommended strategies and techniques. After you master the information in these pages, you'll have a special kind of insurance policy that pays big dividends for as long as you want to work.

Part I
And the Interview Winner is … You!

The 5th Wave
By Rich Tennant

"Other than that, what would you say are your special skills and competencies?"

In this part . . .

Interviews are theater, and in this part, I start off by showing you how that's true and what it means for your role in an interview — giving you the rundown on interviews from rehearsal to curtain call.

This part also gives you the details about where interviewing stands now — the scenarios you might encounter (screening interviews, video interviewing, opportunities abroad) and the styles of interviews that stand between you and your new job.

Chapter 1

Job Interviews Are Show Biz. Seriously!

A resume or profile functions as bait to snag a job interview. The interview is the decisive event when a hiring authority decides whether you'll be offered the job.

Because the job interview is the single most important part of getting a job — and you may not have interviewed in awhile — any number of unfortunate scenarios may be sneaking into your subconscious, including fears of these confidence-disturbers:

✓ Stumbling and mumbling your way through the ordeal

✓ Being glued to a hot seat as they sweat the answers out of you

✓ Forgetting your interviewer's name (or the last place you worked)

Exhale. You've come to the right book. Take the suggestions within these pages to heart, and you'll head into every interview feeling confident, calm, and well prepared. What more can you ask?

Interviewing As Theater

When you're engaged in a selection interview, your entire future may rest on how successful you are in presenting yourself to a stranger across a desk in 15, 30, or 60 minutes. Making life-altering decisions during this micro slice of time isn't real life — it's show biz.

Like reality shows on TV, interviews are based on reality but, in fact, are staged. And as in reality shows, only one survivor beats the competition to win the prize.

The most successful interviews for you require solid preparation to learn your lines, showing your future bosses that you're smart and quick on the uptake, as well as able to communicate and not likely to jump the tracks.

At each meeting, your goal is to deliver a flawless performance that rolls off your tongue and gets the employer applauding — and remembering — you. Perfect candidate, you!

But what about all the people who tell you, "Just be yourself and you'll do fine in your interview"? That advice doesn't always work for you in the theater of job interviewing.

Why "be yourself" can be poor advice

A scene in the movie *Children of a Lesser God* features a speech teacher (William Hurt) and a deaf janitor (Marlee Matlin) duking it out in a jolting battle of wits.

In a climactic verbal battle, the janitor signs to the speech teacher, "Let me be me," to which the speech teacher replies, "Well, who the hell are you?" There is no answer.

The troubled janitor isn't the only one who has trouble with that question. The bromide "Be yourself" is very difficult to articulate with consistency. Be yourself? Which self? Who is the real you? Our roles change at various times.

Your role: Job seeker

Jerry is a father, an engineer, a marathon runner, a public speaker, a law student at night, and a writer of professional papers. Jennifer is a loving daughter, the best salesperson in her company, a pilot, a tennis player, a football fan, and a history buff.

But at this time in their lives, Jerry and Jennifer — like you — are playing the role of a job seeker. Similarly, the stranger across an interviewing desk is playing the role of interviewer.

Getting real about the job seeker role

Playing the role most appropriate to you at a given time, and playing it effectively enough to get you the job you deserve, isn't turning your back on authenticity. To do less than play the role of a hard-charging job seeker courts unemployment — or underemployment.

Why "be natural" can be poor advice

First-cousin advice to urging you to "be yourself" in a job interview is the "be natural" admonition. On the whole, isn't natural better than artificial? Not always.

Is combed hair natural? Shaved legs? Trimmed beard? Polished shoes? How about covering a cough in public? Or not scratching where you itch?

Being natural in a job interview is fine as long as you don't use your desire to be natural and authentic as an excuse to display your warts or blurt out negative characteristics.

Never treat a job interview as a confessional in which you're obligated to disclose imperfections, indiscretions, or personal beliefs that don't relate to your future job performance.

Job interviews are time-centric. Every minute counts in the getting-to-know-you game. And to really know someone in a brief encounter of 15, 30, or 60 minutes is simply impossible. Instead of real life, each participant in an interview sees what the other participant(s) wants seen. If you doubt that, think back: How long did you need to really get to know your roommate, spouse, or significant other?

If you insist on being natural, an employer may pass you over because of your unkempt beard or unshined shoes, or because you don't feel like smiling that day.

The things you've done to date — your identification of your skills, your resume and profile, your cover letter, your networking, your social media efforts — all are wasted if you fail to deliver a job interview that produces a job offer.

Because job interviewing is show biz, make the most of your critical brief encounters by learning the acting skills of storytelling, using body language, establishing rapport, and more in this modern interview guide.

New Faces, New Factors in Interviewing

Are you having trouble staking out your future because you can't close the sale during job interviews? This mangled proverb states the right idea:

If at first you don't succeed . . . get new batteries.

Recharge yourself with knowledge of the new technology and trends that are affecting job interviews. Here are highlights of the contemporary job interview space.

Curtain going up on tech trends

Classic interviewing skills continue to be essential to job search success, but more technology firepower is needed in a world growing increasingly complex, interconnected, and competitive.

The new tech trends revolutionize all components of the job search, including the all-important job interview. Here are examples of technological newcomers and how they change interviewing practices:

- **Lighting up screens:** Both live and recorded video job interviews are coming of age, requiring that you acquire additional skills and techniques to make the cut. Chapter 3 is a primer on how you can outflank your competition by presenting like a pro in video interviews.

- **One and done:** Automated and recorded phone screening services permit employers to ask up to a dozen canned screening questions and allow candidates up to two minutes to answer each question. Informed interviewees anticipate the questions and must hit their marks the first time because there are no do-overs on recorded answers. Read about this technology in Chapter 2.

- **The real deal?** Credibility issues are surfacing for multitalented job seekers (or those with a checkered work background) who, by posting various resumes and profiles online, come across as different people with different skill sets. This development can be a knock-out punch for you in a tight job market where employers have plenty of candidates on offer. Sidestep the emerging problem of identity contradictions in interviews by following the advice offered in Chapter 16.

- **Deep web woes:** Employers can hire a service to dig deep beyond the usual suspects (Facebook and Twitter) to check out your online history. The service rakes through closed databases in the deep web, leaving virtually no secrets unrevealed. If the deep web reveals negative information, you may get a chance to defend yourself in an interview — or you may never know why you struck out. See Chapter 16 for more information on this 21st-century sleuthing tool.

Expect new kinds of interviewers

If the last time you trod the boards of job interviewing you went one to one with a single interviewer, usually a white man or woman, get ready for a different set of questioners, like these possibilities:

- ✔ A veteran team of six managers — individually or collectively
- ✔ A hiring manager (especially in technical and retail fields) who is two decades younger than you
- ✔ Someone of another color or heritage

Turn to Chapter 5 for a broader picture of group interviews, and to Chapter 15 for a good tip on interviews with younger bosses.

Showcase your ability to start fast

Because you can't count on being on the job more than a few years — or, in contract assignments, a few months — the hiring spotlight lasers in on competencies and skills you can use from Day One. The question is, *What can you do for our company immediately?*

You can come across as ready to blast off if you do enough research on the company's goals (increase revenues, reduce costs, acquire new market share, land larger accounts, create a technical breakthrough), think about how you can help the company reach those goals, and remain ready to speak the insider jargon of the industry.

If the job you're applying for isn't at the professional or managerial level, research the nature of the company's business, assume that it wants to make or save money, and stock up on a few good buzzwords used in the industry.

Scope out more ways to show your launch speed in Chapter 6.

Overcome job-hopping objection

The current employer-driven job market makes it easy for companies to buy into the "job-hopper objection" and, as a matter of policy, turn away unemployed candidates and people who've held three jobs in five years. Unfortunately, many of these automatic rejects have been trapped in a cycle of frequent layoff's, part-time work, temp assignments, seasonal employment, contract jobs, freelance gigs, and company shutdowns.

Some companies refuse to hire so-called job hoppers, claiming that they'll quit before employers can get a return on their training investment — or that, if the unemployed candidates were any good, they'd be on someone's payroll.

What's a sincere, hard-working person to do? Try this quartette of basic rebuttals:

- ✔ **Say varied experience beats repeated experience.** Explain how your dynamic work history makes you a far more vibrant and resourceful contributor than if you'd been stationary for four years.

- ✔ **Briefly explain departures.** Give a reasonable, short, even-toned account of why you left each job. (It wasn't your fault.)

- ✔ **Review your accomplishments.** You can't change the amount of time you were on certain jobs, but you can divert the focus to your accomplishments and contributions. Employers are impressed by candidates who are good at what they do, even if they had only a short period of time in the role.

- ✔ **Confirm interest in stable employment.** Forget the "loyalty" chatter. Make a point of your intense interest in a stable opportunity where you can apply all your considerable know-how for the employer's benefit.

Chapter 19 offers more suggestions on how to maximize the value of your experience.

Cut out the loyalty oath

Answers to certain questions are pretty much the same year after year, but watch out for one humdinger requiring a new response: Why do you want to work here? The old "I'm looking for a home and I'll be loyal to you forever" statements don't play as well as they once did.

Many employers now solicit contract employees — no muss, no fuss in getting them out the door when a project's finished or when a decision is made to outsource the work.

 Rather than pledge eternal fidelity, talk about your desire to do the work. Talk about how you are driven to funnel substantial amounts of productivity into the job quickly. Talk about wanting to use your superior technology skills. Talk about your interest in work that excites you, work that matters.

But fidelity? Pass on that as a theme song; it won't make the charts today.

Stock up on what you *should* say instead of talking about loyalty in Chapters 16, 17, 18, and 19.

Learn new lines for small-business jobs

Have you grown up professionally in a large-company environment? If so, carefully consider the answers you give when applying to small companies. Such a move can happen sooner than you think if you're forced into an involuntary change of employment. Prime-timers in countless droves are discovering that the small company sector is where the action is for them.

Emphasize different aspects of your work personality than the ones you emphasize when interviewing for a big company. Interviewers at big companies and small companies have different agendas.

Among the reasons owners of small ventures reject former big-company people are these stereotypical perceptions: People who come out of Big Corporate America often are thought to be

- Unaware of the needs of small business

- Too extravagant in their expectations of resources and compensation

- Too spoiled to produce double the work product their former jobs required

- Unwilling to wear more than one job hat at a time

- Deadwood, or they wouldn't have been cut loose from the big company

Chapters 15, 17, and 18 can help you with this issue.

Get ready for the global job interview

For professional jobs, the basic format of interviews globally is Western style, accomplishment oriented, but cultural interviewing differences among nations still matter. Newcomers to the United States may be surprised to learn, for example, that they aren't expected to dress in pinstriped suits to interview for a technology job, nor are they encouraged to speak extensively of family and other personal issues.

Americans who hope to work overseas for the first time may be surprised at such local customs as those of China, where interviewees are expected to nod, showing that they're listening and understanding the Chinese speaker who is communicating in English, or of certain European countries, where a female candidate may be asked directly, "Are you pregnant?"

Chapter 4 tackles the emerging body of buzz about international interviewing.

Polish your storytelling skills

Behavior-based interviewing is said to predict future performance based on past performance in similar situations. The behavioral interviewing style isn't new, but it seems to be more popular than ever.

Advocates of the behavioral style claim that it is 55 percent predictive of future on-the-job behavior, compared to traditional interviewing, at only 10 percent predictive. The reasoning is, "If you acted a certain way once, you'll act that way again." Solid proof of this claim is hard to come by. But for you as a job seeker, it doesn't matter the least bit whether the claim is true or false. The behavioral style is such a big deal with employers today that you need to know how to use the style to your advantage.

It works like this: Interviewers ask candidates to tell them a story of a time when they reacted to a certain situation. *How did you handle an angry customer? Describe an example of a significant achievement in your last job.* The more success stories you can drag in from your past, the more likely the interviewers using this approach will highly rate your chances of achieving equivalent success in the future.

Read more about behavior-based interviewing in Chapter 5.

Focus on fitting in

"We chose another candidate who is a better job fit" is another familiar reason that seems to be heard today more often than before when explaining to a disappointed job seeker why someone else got the job.

In the workplace, "fit" essentially refers to how an individual fits into a company's culture. Company culture is expressed in the values and behaviors of the group, which forms a kind of "tribe" or, to use an analogy from high school, an "in crowd."

The culture typically flows from company or department chieftains: If the boss wears long sleeves, you wear long sleeves; if the boss shows a sense of humor, you show a sense of humor; if the boss works until 6 o'clock, you work until 6 o'clock.

When you're given the not-the-best-fit-for-the-job rejection, the reason is

- A convenient short and legally safe answer
- A cover story
- A belief that the hiring decision makers perceive you won't fit in well with the "tribe"

When the reason really is the fit issue, decision makers may think that you can do the job but that you won't do it the way they want — and, furthermore, they just don't feel at ease with you.

Instead of losing sleep over a fit-based turn-down, move on. Do better preinterview research (see Chapter 6). At least you won't waste time on companies well known for being a fortress of round holes when you're a square peg.

Seven Concepts to Make You a Star

You've heard it said over and over that you have only one chance to make a first impression. It's especially true for job interviewing, so make that first impression pay off. Read these seven super tips to make the hiring gods choose you at job interviews.

Go all out in planning ahead

Preparation makes all the difference in whether you get the best offers as you face intense scrutiny, field probing questions, and reassure employers who are afraid of making hiring mistakes. You must show that you're tuned in to the company's needs, that you have the skills to get up to speed quickly, and that you're a hand-in-glove fit with the company.

Fortunately, never in history has so much information about companies and industries been so easily accessible, both in print and online. Chapter 6 gives tons of tips on researching your audience.

Distinguish screening from selection interviews

As hiring action is increasingly concentrated in smaller companies, the separation between screening and selection interviews fades: The same person may do both types. But traditionally, here's how the types, which I cover in Chapter 5, differ.

Screening interviews

In large organizations, interviewing is usually a two-stage process. A screening specialist eliminates all candidates except the best qualified. The screening interview is usually conducted by telephone or video interviews instead of face-to-face in the same room. Survivors are passed to a manager (or panel of managers) who selects the winning candidate.

Screeners are experienced interviewers who look for reasons to screen you out based on your qualifications. Screeners can reject, but they cannot hire. They won't pass you on to hiring managers if your experience and education don't meet the specifications of the job.

When you're being interviewed by a screener, be pleasant and neutral. Volunteer no strong opinions. Raise no topics, except to reinforce your qualifications. Answer no questions that aren't asked — don't look for trouble.

But do remember to smile a lot.

Selection interviews

By the time you're passed on to a hiring authority who makes the selection, you're assumed to be qualified or you wouldn't have made it that far along the channels of employment. You're in a pool of "approved" candidates chosen for the selection interview.

At a selection interview, move from neutral into high gear if the person doing the interview will be your boss or colleague. No more bland behavior — turn up the wattage on your personality power. This is the best time to find out whether you'll hit it off with the boss or colleagues, or fit into the company culture.

Verify early what they want and show how you deliver

Almost as soon as you're seated in a selection interview, ask the interviewer to describe the scope of the position and the qualifications of the ideal person for it.

Although you've already done this research when you're going for ShowStopper status, use this question to confirm your research. If you're wrong, you must know immediately that you need to shift direction.

(*Insider's note:* This super tip was shared with me by several career management hall-of-famers, including the late Bernard Haldane.)

How can you adapt the tell-me-what-you-want tip when you're dealing with multiple interviewers? That's easy: Direct your question to the senior panel member and wait for an answer. Then gaze around the group and ask, "Does anyone have something to add to the ideal person description?"

Confirming your research (or gaining this information on the spot) is the key to the entire interview. You now know for sure the factors upon which the hiring decision is made and how to target your answers.

Connect all your qualifications with a job's requirements

If a quick glance at your notes reminds you that the interviewer missed a requirement or two listed in the job posting when describing the position's scope and the ideal person for it, help the interviewer by tactfully bringing up the missing criteria yourself. Keep it simple:

I see from my notes that your posting asked for three years of experience. I have that and two years more, each with a record of solid performance in . . ..

You want to demonstrate that you take this job possibility seriously, an attitude that the employer will applaud. Winning job offers by targeting your interview performance to a company's requirements is a logical follow-up to the resume targeting strategy that I explain in my book *Resumes For Dummies,* 6th Edition (John Wiley & Sons, 2011).

Memorize short-form sales statements about yourself

Almost certainly, you will be asked to respond to some version of the "tell me about yourself" question (see Chapter 16). You're not helping your hiring chances if you respond with a question that a 13-year-old might ask: "What do you want to know?" That naive approach makes you sound unprepared.

Instead, commit to memory a short-form sales statement (two minutes max, and preferably less than one minute) that describes your education, experience, and skills, and matches your strengths to the jobs you seek.

Some people call such a statement a "commercial," while others prefer the terms "elevator speech" or "profile summary." Whatever you call it, after briefly reciting the facts of your background, make your statement sizzle by adding a couple personality sentences about such traits as your curiosity, commitment, and drive to succeed.

The "personal branding brief" is another version of the short-form sales statement. Used chiefly by professionals, managers, and executives, it's incorporated into all self-marketing opportunities, including job interviewing.

In personal branding, you become known for something — Jon Stewart for political satire and Serena Williams for tennis, for example. You don't have to be famous to pursue personal branding, but you do have to be consistent in your efforts to develop your brand.

Your goal is to perfect a *branding brief* that tells your "story" — one that rolls off your tongue — in about 20 to 30 seconds, or in 100 words or less:

> *After I graduated from San Diego State University, I worked in the insurance industry until I took a break to start a family. That accomplished, I went back for refresher education. Now, thoroughly updated, I'm looking for a new connection in either the insurance or financial fields.*

Learn much more about the pursuit of personal branding from renowned personal branding expert Dan Schawbel (`www.danschawbel.com`), who literally wrote the book (the best-selling book) on the topic, *Me 2.0: 4 Steps to Building Your Future* (Kaplan Publishing).

The difference between a commercial and a branding brief is length and content. A commercial is longer and includes more details than a cut-to-the-chase branding brief.

Win two thumbs up from the hiring manager, and you're in!

Likeability is a huge factor in choosing and keeping employees, as I note later in this chapter. Given a choice of technically qualified applicants, employers almost always choose the one they like best. For your purposes, remember this:

> *We like people who are like us.*

How do you encourage the interviewer to think, "You and me against the problem" rather than "You against me"?

Beyond exchanging pleasantries, establishing mutual interests, connecting with eye contact, and other well-known bonding techniques, watch for special opportunities:

✔ Suppose your interviewer looks harried, with ringing telephones and people rushing about interrupting your talk. Flash a sympathetic smile and commiserate: *It looks like you're having one of those days.* The subtext of your comment is, *I understand your frustrations. I've been in a similar place. You and I are alike.*

✔ Or suppose you're showing a work sample. Ask if you can come around to the interviewer's side of the desk to discuss your sample. You are looking at it "together."

Forget about age, color, gender, or ethnic background. Do whatever you reasonably can to make the hiring manager believe the two of you are cut from similar cloth.

To rewrite the famous 20th-century Broadway wit and playwright Damon Runyon:

> *The part goes not always to those we like, nor the hiring to our twins, but that's the way to bet.*

Try not to talk money until you know they want you

When the salary question comes up at the beginning of an interview, say that money isn't your most important consideration — nor should it be at this point.

Admittedly, stalling salary talk until a better time is much more difficult today than it was a decade ago. But you should be holding out for the market value of the new job, not settling for an inadequate figure of your present or previous employment.

Only when you know the scope of the position and its market value — and that the company wants to hire you — are the stars in alignment to bargain in your best interest.

Read Chapter 8 for in-depth guidance on salary negotiation.

Take Home an Oscar from Any Interview

Rookie? Prime-timer? Clerk? Chief executive officer? No matter. You can do exceptionally well by following certain performance routines that succeed in any interview scene. Some of these suggestions are basic and familiar, but most people who haven't been on the interview tour for awhile can use the reminders.

Play the likeability card

When you're up against a rigid requirement that you absolutely can't meet and that you're pretty sure is going to mean curtains for you in the interview, try this last-ditch compensatory response:

Let's say that you were to make me an offer and I accept. What can I do when I start to further compensate for my lack of [requirement] as I work hard to relieve your immediate workload?

Essentially, you're counting on your likeability. You're asking the employer to revert to the philosophy of hiring for attitude and training for skill. You're using the likeability qualification to plug your requirement gap.

As legendary recruiting guru Paul Hawkinson observes: "Likeability is a factor that can turn the tide in your direction. Although skill level and applicable experience trump at the beginning of the interview process, I've seen dozens of less-than-qualified people hired because the employer *liked* them better than the perfect candidate with the personality of a doorknob."

Everyone likes to work with agreeable, sunny people. People rarely hire someone they don't like.

Soak up moves that make interviewers see you as an agreeable and calm person in Chapter 10.

Style your body language

Interviewers observe everything about you: not only your dress and interview answers, but your body language, facial expressions, posture, carriage, and gestures. If you're a rookie, think dignity. If you're a prime-timer, think energy. In between? Watch political candidates on TV for hints of what looks good and what doesn't.

Confirm that your body language is sending the "Hire me!" message with tips in Chapter 10. Chapter 9's up-to-date data on dress and appearance add even more nonverbal firepower to your candidacy.

Be a treat: Act upbeat

Steer clear of negative words (such as *hate, don't ever want, absolutely not,* and *refuse*). And avoid such risky topics as the knock-down, drag-out fights you had with that bonehead you used to work for — never knock the old boss. Your prospective new boss may empathize with your old boss and decide to never be your boss at all.

Chapters 7 and 14 throw more light on avoiding a maze of negativity and looking as though you're a serial complainer who will never be satisfied.

Start your interview on the right foot

Here are four tips to help you make a good impression right off the bat:

- ✔ Find out in advance what to wear (see Chapter 9) and where the interview site is located. Make a trial run, if necessary.

- ✔ Be on time, be nice to the receptionist, read a business magazine while you're waiting, and — surprise, surprise — don't smoke, chew gum, or otherwise look as though you lack couth.

- ✔ Develop a couple icebreaker sound bites, such as comments about a nice office, attractive color scheme, or interesting pictures.

- ✔ Don't sit until you're asked or until the interviewer sits. Don't offer to shake hands until the interviewer does.

During the interview, frequently use the interviewer's name (but never use a first name unless you're old friends). And remember to make a lot of eye contact by looking at the bridge of an interviewer's nose. (Divert your gaze occasionally, or you're perceived as more creepy than honest.)

Track down more suggestions for making yourself a memorable candidate in Chapter 11.

Remember that you have a speaking part

Communication skills are among the most desired qualities employers say they want. Answer questions clearly and completely. Be sure to observe all social skills of conversation — no interrupting, no profanity. Just as you shouldn't limit yourself to one- or two-word answers, neither should you try to cover your nervousness with surround-sound endless talking. Aim for a happy medium.

Take in Chapter 16 for a savvy start on how to talk about yourself.

Revisit the dramatic pause

In face-to-face live interviews, allowing a few moments of silence to pass, perhaps pausing to look at the ceiling or glance out an open window — taking time to think — can make you look wise and measured in your response. Pauses can raise the ante by reflecting disappointment in a salary offer. Pauses can suggest that you're reluctant to travel 50 percent of the time but that you're a team player and will consider the requirement.

Surviving a snippy interviewer

Short of taking out a restraining order, what should you do when an interviewer's manner is offensive?

That depends on who's doing the talking. When the interviewer is the person who would be your boss, be certain that you're not misunderstanding intent. If conversation really is disrespectful, bail out unless you want to spend most of your waking hours dealing with a difficult person. Show class. Just say, "Thank you for your time. I don't think this job is a good fit for me." (*Payback:* It may leave the interviewer regretful that you're the good one who got away.)

But when the interviewer is doing preliminary screening, give the employer the benefit of the doubt by assuming that the interviewer doesn't represent the entire company and will be working five floors below you in a subbasement. Here are a few coping techniques:

✔ Smile and make a light remark: "Oh, do you think so? That bears watching."

✔ Respond with a two-second nonanswer, and then quickly ask a question: "That's an interesting observation. It reminds me to ask you, what role would the person in this position play in the new company product launch?"

✔ Pretend the rude remark is a dropped call that you didn't hear, pause, and talk about your accomplishments or skills.

✔ When an interviewer keeps interrupting or contradicting you, look puzzled and ask for clarification. "Perhaps I'm not following you correctly. Can you please restate the question or explain what you mean by — *?*"

When all else fails, remember the words of English writer Joanne Kathleen Rowling, author of the Harry Potter books: "Yet, sadly, accidental rudeness occurs alarmingly often. Best to say nothing at all, my dear man."

A pause is effective body language and works great in live, face-to-face interviews. But today's interviewer may call on a telephone or use online video interviewing, and dead air time can make you appear dull-witted rather than contemplative.

Moral: Exercise judgment in using the reflective pause as a communications tool. (When you just don't know the answer immediately, that's another story; stall by asking for clarification.)

Rely on Chapter 3 for details on video body language and Chapter 8 for salary negotiation.

Agree to take pre-employment tests

No one likes those annoying pre-employment tests. Job seekers keep hoping they'll drop off the face of the earth, but they're with us still. When you want the job, you're going to have to suck it up and test when asked. No test, no job.

Race to Chapter 7 for survival clues when you hope to be the last one standing after test time.

Flesh out your story beyond a college degree

Education is a fulcrum for movement throughout your career, but relying on it alone to pull you through a competitive job search is a mistake. The mistake grows larger with too many mentions of an illustrious alma mater, assuming that the school's marquee power is a hall pass to move forward.

For example, a couple mentions of Harvard in an interview are plenty; interviewers get it the first time. They wonder whether the Harvard background is the singular "accomplishment" a candidate offers.

Instead, spell out your accomplishments with true examples — what you learned and what you can do with your degree that benefit the employer.

In marketing a three-dimensional you, think of your education as one dimension, your experience as a second dimension, and your accomplishment record as a third dimension. All are important.

Wait. Back up. If the interviewer is also a Harvard grad, three mentions is perfectly okay. And if three is good, maybe four or five is better.

Chapter 5 is headquarters for storytelling tips; Chapters 16–20 show you how to fill in the blanks for your campus experience and beyond.

Bring a pen and notebook with you

Making a note here and there is advisable, as long as you don't attempt to record a transcript. To illustrate, you need to jot down reminders to get back to the interviewer when you can't answer a question from memory.

Brownie point: Writing down what someone says is flattering to the speaker.

Winning candidates are memorable

Comparing TV reality talent show winners to job interview candidates, Phoenix career coach Joe Turner (www.jobchange secrets.com) says it's the total package that counts. "You don't have to be the best singer or dancer — just the *most remembered* decent performer. Same for the job interview. You don't always have to be the best candidate with the top skills. You do have to find a way to be the *most remembered* hirable candidate."

Fighting back on interview exploitation

You can lose your intellectual property through abuse of the job interview.

In the so-called *performance interview* for professional and managerial jobs, candidates are required to prove themselves with projects that demonstrate on-the-job skills, problem-solving capabilities, and communications abilities.

The employer asks for a proposal of how you would handle a company project or requests that you design a process the company can use. You're told to be ready to "defend your ideas" at the interview.

Unfortunately, sometimes the free-sample demand is incredibly time-consuming (say, 80 hours) and costly ($200 and up in materials and research). You do your best, but suppose you don't get the job. In an example of shoddy ethics, your work samples may be given to the victorious candidate, who then steals your viable creative ideas. In the following sections, I give you a few examples from stung readers of my newspaper and web column.

Portfolio scam

When applying to an advertising agency for a copywriting job, the owner asked me to leave my portfolio for review. He kept the portfolio and called on all the clients whose work was shown in the portfolio! Since then, I always respond to requests to leave or send my portfolio with this statement: "I need to be there to clarify the work shown. I will be glad to bring it, and we can discuss my work at your convenience."

State government rip-off

When I applied for a significant and highly symbolic job with my state government, I was informed I had been selected but had to go through the formality of an interview with a key aide to the governor. As requested, I took materials and a plan for approaching the job's goals to the confirmation interview. A long, official silence followed before a form letter arrived *stating that a less qualified professional, to whom I was a mentor, had won the position. The victor showed me the state's plan of action: mine.*

Consulting caper

My husband, an expert in human resources, spent two long days interviewing in a small town with the owner of a family company and his son. He gave them an unbelievable amount of advice and information to help their meager HR program, process management, and integrated product development. All we got out of that was reimbursement for a 200-mile car trip, a bad motel, and meals. That was our first realization of how small businesses, in particular, get almost-free consulting work.

Training trickery

I was a candidate for a city's new training division chief. I had to spend several hours in the city's computer labs designing programs and leaving them on CDs. I knew that, with my education and experience, I had done well.

A long-term firefighter with zero training experience got the job with the city and used my materials for new employees!

Protecting Yourself

How do you avoid abuse without taking yourself out of the running for a job you want when you're not sure about the real interview agenda? Here are two ideas:

✔ You can copyright your plan and place a valid copyright notice ©, along with the publication date and your name, on its cover as an indication of your underlying claim to ownership. For free information, contact the Copyright Office online at www. copyright.gov, or by mail at Registrar of Copyrights, Copyright Office, Library of Congress, 101 Independence Ave. SE, Washington, DC 20559.

For easier reading, see an excellent guide, *The Copyright Handbook: What Every Writer Needs to Know, 11th Edition,* by Stephen Fishman (Nolo Press; www. nolo.com).

✔ You can bluff, hoping to create a theft deterrent by slapping a copyright notice and "Confidential — Property of (Your Name)" on your plan's cover.

When you're desperate or really, really, really want the job but don't have the time, inclination, or money to respond in full measure, offer something like this:

I'm glad that you see I have the brains and talent to bring value to your company. I'm happy, too, that you have the confidence in my work to ask me to handle such a potentially important solution to your marketing challenge. With my background, I'm sure I can do an outstanding job on this assignment. But you do realize, I hope, that such an important project would require 80 to 100 hours of intensely focused work. I'd enjoy doing it, but, quite frankly, I have several other job interviews scheduled that I really can't shift around. Do you think a sample of substantially smaller scope would serve as well for your purposes?

With a statement like this, you

✔ Remind the interviewer that you're a top candidate

✔ Promise superior results

✔ Bring a reality check to a sensitive interviewer about what's being asked of you

✔ Let the interviewer know others are interested in you

✔ Propose to do much less work until a job offer crosses your palm

You can, of course, flatly refuse to part with advance goodies. In a seller's market, you'll probably be considered anyway. But in a buyer's market, the likelihood is that you'll be passed over when you decline to turn in a hefty free sample.

Keep your ears up and your eyes open

Don't just sell, sell, sell. Take time to listen. When you're constantly busy thinking of what you're going to say next, you miss vital points and openings. So work on your listening skills. When you don't understand an interviewer's question, ask for clarification.

Observe the interviewer's moves. Watch for three key signs: high interest (leaning forward), boredom (yawning or displaying a glazed look), or a devout wish to end the interview (stacking papers or standing up). After assessing where you stand with the interviewer, take the appropriate action:

✔ High interest suggests you're stopping the show and should continue.

✔ The remedy for boredom is to stop and ask, *Would you rather hear more about (whatever you've been talking about) or my skills in the ABC area?*

✔ When the interviewer is ready to end the meeting, first ask whether the interviewer has any reservations about your fit for the job; if so, attempt to erase them.

Then go into your interview closing mode (see Chapter 12). Gain a sense of timing and keep the door open for follow-up contact by asking three questions: *What is the next step in the hiring process? When do you expect to make a decision? May I feel free to call if I have further questions?*

Building Lifetime Confidence

This first chapter serves as an overview for the entire book. The pages that follow are wide and deep, with details that can help you gain a lifetime of confidence in your ability to sail through the drama of interviews and secure the best job offers.

Chapter 2

Tryouts: Getting Past Screening Interviews

··

In This Chapter

▶ Making the cut when the casting call is a zoo

▶ Calling your screen shots with top tips

▶ Dialing for effective phone screeners

··

*N*ot understanding how screening practices work in today's recruiting industry is keeping many good people on the sidelines when jobs are handed out.

Under the watchful eye of James M. Lemke, this guidebook's technical advisor and headliner in the human resource trenches, this chapter gives you the fundamentals of modern screening practices, to help you survive being "screened out." (Additionally, see Chapter 5 for the big picture on different types of interviews and how they relate to each other.)

Two Basic Steps in Job Interviewing

Most employers that are large enough to have a human resources department split the hiring function into two steps: screening and selection.

> ✔ *Screening interviews* are Step 1 in choosing someone for a job. Designed to narrow the candidate pool for the managers who make the hiring decisions, screening interviews weed out unqualified candidates. If you don't get past Step 1, you're out of the running.
>
> A screening interview is typically conducted by an employee in the employer's human resources department (often a support person or a junior recruiter) or by an outside recruiting contractor.

> Your goal in a screening interview is to show that your qualifications fill the employer's bill. It's not to quiz the interviewer about job suitability for factors important to you, but to keep yourself in the running for the job.
>
> ✔ *Selection interviews* are Step 2 in choosing someone for a job. Selection interviews provide a wider and deeper evaluation of qualified candidates who survive screening interviews. (Selection interviews are also called "hiring interviews.")

A selection interview is typically conducted by one or more managers to whom the new hire will report. Sometimes it includes potential colleagues as well.

Asking questions about the company is appropriate in a selection interview. (Find questions to ask about the company in Chapter 11.)

Hot News about Screening Interviews

In a frigid job market, job seekers experience a heat wave of screening interviews.

As one example, global talent management firm Ol Partners (`www.ol partners.com`) recently surveyed l84 organizations throughout North America and found that 54 percent are more frequently screening potential employees via phone interviewing than they did in the past.

The uptick in a rush to discard unqualified candidates makes sense. It can be explained by digital traffic jams caused by the mobs of people who "spray and pray." The spray-and-pray theory is that if you apply for every open job within reach, qualified or not, you're sure to land one. (This hope is misplaced, akin to counting on the lottery as a retirement plan.)

As a consequence of the continuing resume floods caused by too many unqualified candidates, employers have developed an understandable preference to cut to the chase as a strategy to save both time and money. That's why when you apply for a job, if and when you're contacted by the employer, your first acknowledgment is likely to be made by a screener.

Screeners can't hire you. But they can keep you from being hired. Give a screener enough information about your qualifications to satisfy the job's requirements. Engage! Go all in to help the screener connect the dots from the job to you.

Confusing term

To keep terms confusing, if not amusing, screening interviews are sometimes called "screeners." The people who conduct them are also sometimes called "screeners." Hey, I didn't make this up!

Learning Your Lines for Screening Questions

Screeners usually aren't concerned with evaluating your personality or thought processes. They have one basic responsibility before putting you on an approved list and waving you up to the next interviewing level: to be sure you qualify. They do so by zeroing in on your experience, education, job-related skills, and track record.

In looking for reasons to rule you in, or to rule you out, screeners quiz you on questions that prove you can do the job — or can't do the job. Here are the kinds of job-related root questions to mentally gear up for:

- ✔ What is your experience? Can you describe your past/current day-to-day routines and duties? (See Chapter 19.)

- ✔ What are your skills, particularly your technical skills and competencies? (See Chapter 18.)

- ✔ What is your education, training, and certification? (See Chapter 20.)

- ✔ Where do you live? (Is your geography convenient or inconvenient? Relocations are a tough sell.)

- ✔ What is your salary requirement? (If your requirement is too low for the job's predetermined range, employers think you'll move on as soon as possible; if it's too high, they think they can't afford you.)

Additionally, screeners may send zingers your way to probe inconsistencies on your resume (work history gaps) or ask questions designed to highlight lies in your resume.

Short Script of Screening Styles

Screening interviews come in three basic models:

- **Human screening:** A person asks specific job questions. Usually the interviewer follows a script and has no specific knowledge of the related position. Successful applicants are passed on to a hiring manager for the next step, a selection interview. Most screening interviews are conducted by telephone, whether mobile or tethered to land lines. These interviews aren't typically recorded.

- **Automated phone screening options:** A phoned set of preset questions is asked of all comers. Answers are recorded and often shared among company hiring managers.

- **Online screening questionnaire:** Questions in this model are attached to a job posting. From the company's perspective, this step is considered not an interview, but a "prescreening."

An organization's automated tracking system ranks a job seeker's responses based on how its recruiter weighted each question.

For instance, if 100 people respond to a job posting, only the highest-ranked job seekers would be considered viable for further consideration. The next step usually is a phone screen, either automated or human.

Sounding Qualified on the Phone

Even though talking on the phone gives a casual impression, you need to present yourself as a qualified professional for the job you want.

Mobile phones are wireless and include cell phones, smartphones, and feature phones. Although mobile phones have become the norm in a mobile world, they still suffer from too many can-you-hear-me-now moments to be your first choice for a life-altering event like a screening interview.

Generally, wired land-line phones of good quality remain the most reliable for excellent audio quality.

Because most people don't prepare for screening phone interviews as rigorously as they prepare for face-to-face meetings, the casualty fallout is heavy. The telephone "screen call" can come at any time, day or night.

If surprises aren't your thing, stick to the steps I outline in the upcoming sections.

Stock your back-stage office with essentials

Stash one phone in a quiet room stocked with all your interview essentials. Must-haves include

- ✔ Your current resume (preferably customized to the job you're discussing)
- ✔ A list of your professional accomplishments
- ✔ Background information on the employer
- ✔ Questions about the company and position
- ✔ Outlines of brief stories that illustrate your qualifications and problem-solving abilities
- ✔ A calendar, with all scheduled commitments and open dates
- ✔ A notepad, pen, and calculator
- ✔ Water and tissues

Make phone appointments

Screeners sometimes purposely try to catch you with your guard down, hoping surprise strips away the outer layers of your preparation and hoping you'll blurb out genuine, unrehearsed thoughts and feelings. They may see unanticipated calls as useful for measuring your ability to think on your feet.

But you want to avoid giving answers from a brain frozen on standby status, right? Whenever possible, don't answer stuff on the fly when a call comes in. You won't be prepared and you won't do your best. Schedule an appointment for your phone interview. Say that you're walking out the door to a meeting across town and will call back as quickly as you can.

> *Thank you for calling. I appreciate your attention. I'm very interested in speaking with you about my qualifications. Unfortunately, this is not a good time for me — I'm headed out the door. Can I call you back in an hour or two? Or would tomorrow be better?*

If a recruiter insists on calling you back rather than the other way around, do what you would do for any other interview: Be ready early as a reminder to interview as a professional. Change out of your jeans and into the type of dress you'd wear in a business meeting. Most importantly, treat the call as an overture to an in-room meeting that you're going to snag by doing an excellent job on your screener.

Phone interviewing when you're at work

When your current employer doesn't know that you're looking for a new job, close the door and speak to the interviewer for only a couple of minutes. Ask the caller if you can set up an in-person interview right then — or if you can talk in the evening when you're at home.

Project your winning image

When the call comes, heed the following suggestions, most of which come from Mark S. James, a leading executive career coach (www.hire consultant.com).

- ✓ **If you have a home office, use it.** An office just feels more businesslike. You may find it helpful to face a blank wall, to eliminate distractions of gazing out a window or spotting dust on your favorite painting.

- ✓ **Gather essential information.** At the start of the conversation, get the caller's name, title, company, e-mail address, and phone number. Read back the spelling.

- ✓ **Market yourself.** Assume the role of "seller" during the interview. If you sell your skills and abilities effectively, the listener sees value in bringing you in for an interview.

- ✓ **Strike the right tone.** Be enthusiastic, but don't dominate the conversation.

- ✓ **Have an answer ready.** Be prepared to answer the "tell me about yourself" request early on; keep your answer to two minutes. (You find strategic techniques for handling this key question in Chapter 16.)

- ✓ **Don't rush or drone on.** Speak clearly and be aware of your pace — not too fast, not too slow. Don't ramble. Keep your answers short and succinct; if the interviewer wants more information, she'll ask for it.

- ✓ **Use check-back phrases.** After answering a question, you can add such follow-on phrases as, *Does that answer your question? Have I sufficiently answered your question about my managerial experience? Is this the kind of information you're seeking?*

- ✓ **Be a champion listener.** Prove that you're paying attention by feeding back what the interviewer says: *In other words, you feel that . . . .* Interject short responses intermittently to acknowledge the interviewer's comments: *That's interesting . . . I see . . . great idea.*

- ✓ **Get specific.** Describe your ability to benefit the company by using specific dollar amounts and percentages to explain your past accomplishments. Let them know *how* you did it.

✔ **Divert important questions.** Tickle interviewers' interest by answering most of their questions. Then when they ask a particularly important question, give them a reason to see you in person. Tell the interviewer that you can better answer that question in person:

That's an important question — with my skills (experience) in this area, it's one that I feel I can't answer adequately over the phone. Can we set up a meeting so that I can better explain my qualifications? I'm free on Tuesday morning — is that a good time for you?

Decide beforehand which questions can best be put off. You can use this tactic two or three times in the same conversation.

✔ **Punt the salary question.** Phone screeners often ask you to name an expected salary. Play dodge ball on this one. You don't know how much money you want yet because you don't know what the job is worth. (You find more techniques to avoid premature salary talk in Chapter 8.)

✔ **Push for a meeting.** As the call winds to a close, go for the prize:

As we talk, I'm thinking we can better discuss my qualifications for (position title) in person. I can be at your office Thursday morning. Is 9:30 good, or is there a better time for you?

Another statement:

(Interviewer's name), based on the information you have given me, I am very interested in pursuing this work opportunity and would like to schedule a time for us to meet in person. What looks good for you?

When the interviewer agrees but can't set a specific time, simply suggest when you are available and ask when would be a good time to follow up. Remember, what you want is an in-person meeting. Assume you'll get it and give the interviewer a choice as to the time.

✔ **Say thanks.** Express your appreciation for the time spent with you.

✔ **Write a thank-you letter.** Just because the interview was via phone doesn't negate the wisdom of putting your thanks in an e-mail.

Make it a sales letter restating the qualifications you bring to the position.

Scriptwriting lingo

You may see and hear terms like *job seeker, candidate, prequalification,* and *prescreening* and wonder whether the words are used interchangeably. Yes, no, and sometimes. Jim Lemke, this guidebook's technical advisor, gives a long-story-short answer:

"These terms are used by employers to avoid the A-word *(applicant).* The federal government requires all employers to track racial, ethnic, and gender statistics of all applicants, so if you are not classified as an applicant (but as a candidate or job seeker), the employer is saved a ton of work."

Nose-to-nose screening

In addition to questionnaires, phones, and computers, sometimes you'll score an in-person screening interview, typically at job fairs and shopping malls.

A creative and proactive technique is called the "job search pop-up" or "job search ninja" technique, in which you stand outside stores and restaurants for half an hour before opening time and try to talk to managers as they start their day. Your opening pitch is something like this: "Good morning! I'm (name), a hardworking person seeking a (type of job). I have exceptional references and useful experience. Can we talk briefly about my working here?"

Acing Automated Phone Screens

An automated screening interview in which you use a phone to answer a fixed list of questions posed by a faceless recorded voice is becoming ever more common. How successful is the technology? The answer depends on who you ask.

- ✔ Recruiting professionals say they like automated phone screening because they don't have to play phone tag with candidates, they can schedule blocks of time to listen to all the interviews one after another and forward the best to hiring managers, and they can listen at any hour of the day or night.

- ✔ Interviewees say they don't like automated phone screening because answering canned questions is cold, rigid, and impersonal. They find it uncomfortable to realize that their recorded performances can live on and on and on. They much prefer live, reactive, and unscripted responses by someone on the other end of a phone call.

Particulars vary among automated interview vendors, but here's a typical routine:

For each position to be filled, the recruiter records up to 12 interview questions. Each question allows a maximum of a two-minute answer.

Automated phone screening systems often work on a "one-and-done" rule. That is, once you have recorded your answer to a question, you cannot rerecord your answer even if you immediately realize that your original answer was weak or wrong. Double-check your understanding of whether the one-and-done rule applies to your interview before you begin recording.

How do you know when you're selected to interview by recording? An employer sends an interview invitation to you by e-mail or includes an "interview now" button in a website job posting.

To learn more about how to survive an automated phone screener, visit vendor websites. For the names of specific companies providing this type of screener, Google "automated phone job interviews."

Pushing the Right Buttons: Computer Screens

Questionnaires and phone screens aren't the only screening game shows in town. Computer-assisted screens are still around, substituting meetings with a PC or app that takes you directly to a screening website, especially for jobs with high turnover, such as food service and retailing. Here's what you can expect keyboard style.

Most computer programs frame questions in a true/false or multiple-choice format, but some ask for an essay response.

A preset time limit for each question is the norm for digital digging, so be ready to keyboard your answers in a timely manner.

Encourage a friend to try a computer interview you plan to take so you can look at the questions before diving in. Make notes of the questions and reflect on your own upcoming responses before you hit the keyboard.

Additionally, if you've never participated in a computer-controlled interview, practice on the employers you least want to work for and save the best for last, when you know what you're doing.

After you run through your computer lines, the computer compiles a summary of your answers, which the interviewer uses to decide whether you flunk the first cut or advance to the next round of interviewing.

Newer computer software allows candidates to type in comments they would like to have considered — eagerness to enter or reenter the workplace, a history of unemployment due to a sick but now recovered family member, an emphasis that you're no stranger to hard work or that you never leave home without enthusiasm. Inject any comment you would have said to a human interviewer.

Screening Survival Skills Are Now a Must-Have

The goal of the screening interview is to land the selection interview. The goal of the selection interview is to land the job.

According to an old baseball truism, you can't win if you don't score, and you can't score if you don't get on base.

Moving beyond screening interviews is all about getting on base.

Sticky wicket screen plays

Be sure you're well rehearsed for potential knock-out questions that may come by phone or computer:

✔ Are you willing to relocate at your own expense?

✔ Do you have reliable transportation?

✔ Did you graduate from an accredited college?

✔ Do you have reliable child care arrangements?

✔ Would you consider a commute of more than 25 miles?

✔ Are you willing to travel 50 percent of your workweek?

Screening may also include integrity testing. Employers want to know whether you will steal from them or otherwise turn in an ethically challenged performance. Key: Avoid absolutes, like *always* or *never*. Recruiters are not going to believe that you have never lied, even a teensy, tiny white lie. Learn more by browsing online for "integrity testing for employment."

Chapter 3

21st-Century Video Interview

In This Chapter

▶ Identifying three digital roads to video face-time

▶ Prepping for your close-up video interview

▶ Separating video resumes and video interviews

As smaller recruiting staffs face larger numbers of job applications, employers are turning to video interviews to cut costs when identifying viable candidates.

Overall, video technology is still most often used for initial screening, as described in Chapter 2, or for distance meet-ups when the cost of travel is prohibitive.

But for lower-level jobs — such as internships, commodity jobs, and some technical positions — the online job video may be the entire interviewing package.

The 21st-century transition of the job interviewing process to video screens — one that's evolving minute by minute — adds a whole new layer of techniques you'll want to master for successful job hunting.

This chapter describes the essentials of nailing the video interview, whether it's used as a screening or selection event.

Casting Calls for Video Shoots

When you're targeting a managerial or professional job, a job offer is unlikely to be extended until the candidate and the person with hiring authority have gone nose-to-nose in the same room.

The video look-over, which may include multiple screening interviews, is usually aimed at reducing in-person meetings to a single event. Having said that, remember that nothing is fixed in bronze in today's rapidly developing online video interviewing industry. After a round of phone and video interviews, job offers are occasionally extended to candidates who've never set foot inside the employer's office.

Not all video interviewing models are the same, and some employers may use more than one model. Regardless of the model, interviewing skills are front and center in a video version. This section describes the three basic video models.

Working with third-party vendors

Private video interviewing firms like HireVue, the first company of its kind, are fast climbing the pop charts of talent-management technology. Launched with a single Salt Lake City office in 2004, the video interviewing industry is estimated to number more than two dozen vendors in 2012. (Check out www. talentmanagementtechnologymegalist.com.)

Here's how it works: The typical method is for a third-party vendor to send the job applicant a webcam, with detailed directions on how to use it. Additionally, the vendor's website usually has detailed instructions, an 800-number to call if there are problems, and sample interviews.

Assuming you're the job seeker, once you receive an interview invitation, you log in to a server to get the interview questions, which appear on your computer screen or are spoken by an announcer or company spokesperson. You have about 30 seconds to read each question and a given amount of time (usually two to three minutes) to answer on camera.

Once your interview begins, there's no turning back. The interview is recorded, and you can't edit your answers, even if you quickly realize you gave a mother-of-all-jokers answer. The questions keep coming — usually about seven to ten of them. For instance, "Can you give an example of why your past work history qualifies you for this position?"

Chatting through Skype

You can interview live using Skype, an online phone and video Internet service. But you need a computer, a webcam, and a decent broadband connection.

Skype started in 2003, and its name is short for "sky peer-to-peer." Free to use in its basic version, with an easy registration process, Skype is the best-known service of its type. Skype is now the preferred method many employers use to conduct long-distance screening interviews, although a number stick to "old-fashioned" phone screeners for simplicity. Comments by interviewees who've tried video chat interviewing range from enthusiastic to grumbly:

> *I really liked the video interview a lot better than the phone-based interview —*
> *it was a much friendlier and warmer exchange.*

> *A webcam isn't the most flattering piece of technology. It can make you look*
> *as attractive as Jason in* Friday the 13th.

Before you make your first screen appearance on the interview scene via video chat on Skype, take the following steps:

- ✔ Download the Skype software a week or two in advance. Cultivate a first-name basis with it. Set up practice training calls with your friends so you'll look comfortable and polished when real interviews come your way.

- ✔ Create a professional username; this isn't the scene to joke around.

- ✔ On the morning of a real interview, conduct a quick test of the technology to ensure that your camera and microphone are working like a charm.

Videoconferencing services

Videoconferencing is conducting a conference between two or more participants at different sites by using computer networks to send audio and video data.

A two-person videoconferencing system works much like a video telephone. Each participant has a video camera, microphone, and speakers mounted on a computer. Similar to video chatting, as the two participants speak to one another, their voices are carried over the network and delivered to the other's speakers, and whatever images appear in front of the video camera appear in a window on the other participant's monitor.

Some videoconferencing services invite job candidates into an office, college career center, or other permanent set and may utilize traditional high-end equipment.

The development of multipoint videoconferencing technology allows three or more participants to sit in a virtual conference room and talk as if they were sitting next to each other.

Determining Video's Upside and Downside

Certain advantages and disadvantages of video interviewing are obvious, but others are sure to turn up as employers and job seekers gain more experience using the technology. First, a look at the pros:

- ✔ **Time savings:** In certain situations, you may get a job faster because of video interviewing. Recruiters and hiring managers can conduct first-round interviews more quickly online using video interviewing than they can scheduling in-person interviews. Video interviewing is a time-saver particularly when you can't easily break away from your present job to travel to an interview or when several groups of company executives must weigh in on your hiring but are in different locales; video interviewing allows several locations to connect at once.

- ✔ **Convenience:** When you're currently employed, you don't have to miss work to interview if you can respond at your convenience.

- ✔ **Distance-jumping for short-term employment:** Video interviewing is a boon to prospective interns and contract workers who want jobs far away; a company isn't going to fly you in for a three-month summer internship or contract gig, but it may hire you on the basis of an online video interview.

- ✔ **Modernity:** Not many candidates have used video interviewing yet. If you can show that you take technology in stride (especially if you're over 40), you get bonus points. You look like a good fit in forward-looking companies.

But nothing is perfect. Take a look at some of the drawbacks that video interviewing presents:

- ✔ **Lag time:** A lag time occurs when data is compressed and sent from one location to another. You have to remember to allow for the delay and not step on the interviewer's lines. Additionally, the interviewer may inadvertently cut you off midsentence.

- ✔ **Connectivity:** Sometimes the connection isn't great, and you have to strain to hear what people are saying.

- ✔ **Lighting:** If the lighting is goofy, you may look purple or pale as a corpse.

- ✔ **Performance pressure:** When it's your turn to speak up, you have very little time to look away, down, up, or sideways to process your thoughts. When the "green light" goes on, the pressure on you is somewhat like a contestant at a quiz show: Talk or walk.

> ✔ **Learning curve:** Being judged in front of a camera takes some getting used to. Glimpses of awful screen tests of actors who later became famous confirm the point. While camera success may be ducks-to-water for a few people, more typically, candidates start out feeling unnatural. Time and practice make them less so.

Rock the Video Job Interview

The *content* of a video interview is much the same as an in-person interview. But the *execution* differs. Consider these sample reactions:

> ✔ A candidate, a cool 20-something manager who isn't easily thrown off center, told a magazine that his video interview was "kind of nerve-wracking" and a totally different feeling from sitting in front of someone for a live interview.

> ✔ An employer reported on a comments board that a lot of things don't come across the camera and that certain factors are accentuated: "Posture, dress, comfort with uncertainty, facility with technology — all those things get highlighted and bolded during a web interview."

Online, you can't use handshakes and ingratiating small talk as you enter and leave an interviewer's office to help imprint favorable memories of you. To compensate, include a memorable statement — a sound bite. Somewhere near the end of the interview, an experienced candidate says something like this:

> *Of the many things I've accomplished in my career, (name a top achievement) stands out as the most significant. Do you see a strong connection between my favorite accomplishment and what it will take to be very successful in this position?*

An entry-level candidate can aim to become unforgettable by saying something unexpected like this:

> *I know that many employers consider my generation to be lacking in writing and critical thinking skills and are not pleased that some of us write company e-mail as if we were texting cell-phone messages with our thumbs. That's not me. I'm good with technology, but I'm old fashioned. I spell my words correctly and include all the letters. And I believe you will be happy to know that I use my head when I write — not just my thumb. When can we get together and speak face-to-face?*

Getting ready to video interview

As with all interviews, don't walk in cold and sit down before a camera unprepared. The following suggestions brief you on what you need to know.

Time limits

Find out whether you're on a clock for the interview. If the interview is scheduled for 30 minutes, consider it a rigid cut-off and don't plan on overtime.

Advance work

Send materials for show-and-tell in advance of the interview, in case the interviewer wants to ask questions about an updated resume or project; you can't slide materials through the screen.

Content review

Review potential questions that you're likely to be asked. (See Chapters 16–22 and 24.) Be ready to relate your qualifications to the job's requirements. Memorize examples of accomplishments that illustrate what you can bring to the company.

Note taking

Making a few notes during an in-person interview is flattering to the interviewer. But the jury's still out about whether you should take a notebook to video interviews and jot down points that will help you respond with clarity. The criticism of note taking is that it is more pronounced and disruptive onscreen than it is face-to-face. Others disagree, saying that glancing at your notes may make you seem more conscientious.

On balance, I vote with the note-taking school. I think it's okay to refer to your notes (and resume) and hopefully be seen as a thorough person who covers all the bases.

Technical check

When you're not interviewing at home, arrive 15 to 30 minutes early at the interview site to deal with any technical issues that may arise. Request an overview of the interviewing event and a refresher on the use of the equipment. Ask the technician how loudly you should speak into the mike and how to use the picture-in-picture feature that shows you in action.

When you're using your own video equipment, check your camera angle (set it at eye level) and speakers (place them out of view). Improve the quality of the audio by wearing a lavalier microphone clipped to your collar or tie rather than relying on the uncertain audio quality of your webcam.

Each morning before a real interview, double-check your Internet connections. Arrange to keep the other Internet traffic to a minimum during Skype sessions; make sure no one is surfing, playing online games, or watching streaming video in another room (these all compromise the bandwidth you need for Skype).

Appearance

To avoid a contrast issue, you can't go wrong with solid colors that aren't too dark (black) or too light (white, yellow). Blue works well. Although you may see an anything-goes range of colors on high-definition or digital TV, you can't count on the technology for the average computer monitor being that advanced.

Additionally, busy patterns distract from your face. So do definitive stripes and plaids. Watch TV newscasters to form your own wardrobe preferences. Otherwise, wear the clothing you would wear to a same-room interview. (See Chapter 9.)

Background

Plan for an uncluttered look. Eliminate such distractions as too many books or magazines, wall hangings, memos taped to the wall, stacks of laundry, posters from your favorite band, and so forth. Avoid background motion — second hands ticking on a clock, barking dogs racing back and forth, cats leaping into camera range, or kids walking in and out of camera range, for instance.

Lighting

Eliminate any bright light (as from a window) behind you — it will darken your face.

Dress rehearsal

Arrange test interviews with friends. Can you hear each other? Can you see each other? Is the framing of your screen about right (head to waist), or is the focus on your face so tight that every pore looks like a moon crater?

Go beyond merely conducting test interviews with friends — record your performances to see for yourself how you're coming across on camera. In addition to paying attention to the quality of your answers and how you look overall, be on the lookout for awkward or off-putting behaviors, such as the following actions:

- Swinging your leg
- Tapping your foot
- Fiddling with your hair

- ✔ Leaning back
- ✔ Crossing your arms
- ✔ Looking dour
- ✔ Slumping or slouching
- ✔ Reacting in slow motion

This tip, more than any other, will improve your interviewing performance.

During the interview

You're almost prepared to command the screen. Now review these finer points gleaned from others who have gone in front of the cameras before you.

Movements and posture

Calmness is classy and shows confidence. No way should you check your personality at the door, but do try to be fairly still. Smoooooth. Avoid overly broad gestures — you're not directing traffic. Ration your gestures to underscore important information.

Pause and think before answering a question, to seem thoughtful and unflappable.

Look interested when you're seated by leaning slightly forward with the small of your back against your chair.

Microphones have an irritating habit of picking up all the noise in the room. Don't shuffle papers or tap a pen. Noises that you may not notice in a same-room interview can become annoying in a video interview.

Occasionally glance at the picture-in-picture feature on the monitor to check your body language and hope you don't catch yourself scratching, licking your lips, or jangling your keys. Hunching your shoulders and other bad-posture poses make you look even worse on those small screens than they do in person.

Facial expressions and speaking

The first thing you say is, "Hi, I'm Bill Kennedy. Nice to meet you." (And if you're not Bill Kennedy, use your own name.) Speak normally, but not too fast. When nervous, some people don't stop for air, and their best lines are left on the cutting room floor, unheard or not understood.

Be conscious of a sound delay. A couple seconds will lapse between when the interviewer speaks and when you hear the statement or question (you observe this audio pause on TV when a foreign correspondent is on another continent). At the end of an interviewer's words, pause *(One-Mississippi Moment)* before you reply.

Look directly at the camera as often as possible when speaking — this is how you make eye contact. You can look around occasionally, but avoid rolling your eyes all over the room as though you can hardly wait to make your getaway. Some people look down at the desk. Don't, especially if you have a bald, shiny spot on the top of your dome. And don't bend over a microphone; imagine that the interviewer is sitting across the table from you. (Remember to use a lavalier microphone and eliminate that temptation.)

The three most important things to remember in a video interview are (1) smile, (2) smile, and (3) smile. Have you noticed that, even when reporting disasters of nationwide proportions, TV anchor people don't always wipe the smile off their faces? Why do you suppose that is? *Smile!*

Virtual handshake

Unless your interview space is on fire, it's not your prerogative to end the interview. Always allow the interviewer to indicate when time's up.

Since at the end of a video interview you can't shake hands through a monitor, deliver a sign-off statement indicating you understand that the interview is over. You can say something as simple as "Thank you for interviewing me. I enjoyed it. Let's talk face-to-face very soon."

For other sign-off ideas, review Chapter 12. When you're in a professional setting, push the mute button and leave the room. When you're at home, mute the mike and close the camera.

Not the Same Thing — Video Interview vs. Video Resume

Video interviews and video resumes are sometimes lumped together in discussions of video technology. They shouldn't be. They're two different documents with different purposes.

The differences between the digital siblings are based on the following four factors:

> ✔ The stage at which video enters the hiring process
>
> ✔ The length of the video
>
> ✔ Who controls the video's content
>
> ✔ Who pays the video's costs

A *video resume* — which is offered in a message of voice and motion — is an employer's first look at a specific job seeker. The resume typically lasts between one and three minutes. The job seeker controls the content. The job seeker pays for the video.

A *video interview* — also presented in a message of voice and motion — is an employer's second look at a specific job seeker that ordinarily takes place only by invitation after the employer evaluates the applicant's fixed online or on-paper resume. A video interview may replace a phone screening interview prior to an invitation for an on-site interview. The duration of a video interview varies. The employer controls its content. The employer pays for the video.

Weighing In on Video Resumes

I surveyed 20 established career management experts nationwide for their experience-based opinions about the value of video resumes to job seekers. Eighteen respondents — nearly all — said that replacing fixed resumes with video resumes is a dim-bulb idea.

Checking out the objections

In a nutshell, the two chief objections to video resumes are the issues of time and discrimination. Here's a quick look at each issue.

The time vampire issue

Addressing the time issue head-on, Barbara Safani, a leading resume authority and president of Career Solvers (www.careersolvers.com), says that, in today's pressure-cooker world, no one really wants to see your video resume because we want our information fast!

"Everyone needs to be a master scanner just to keep up with the incredible amount of information flying by," Safani observes.

Hiring systems take less than a minute to slice and dice data on traditional resumes to determine a match between a candidate and an open job. But as Safani explains, "There's currently no good way to parse a candidate's information and accomplishments on a video resume."

Video views at virtual job fairs

A *virtual job fair*, also known as an *online job fair*, is a digital version of a traditional job fair. Employers and job seekers meet on the Internet to discuss employment opportunities by way of specialized websites. Like a traditional job fair, online job fairs are live, fully interactive, and held at specific times.

Video interviews — as well as live chat via text and voice — allow recruiters and job seekers to discuss opportunities. A recruiter with a hot prospect can conference in a hiring manager on the spot.

Video job fairs have grown in popularity and are used by large companies and some colleges.

"With few extra professional minutes to spare in sizing up candidates' qualifications for a job, why would anyone want to look at video resumes from 500 applicants?" Safani understandably asks.

CareerXroads is a company that holds dozens of events each year with hiring authorities across America. Gerry Crispin, a principal of CareerXroads, applauds the growth of video interviews but boos the video resume:

"Not a single firm I know would spend time on a video resume of a prospect or candidate who has not already been previously evaluated. Not one."

The video resume time issue also carries a cost issue for job seekers. Crispin worries about candidates not only wasting their money paying to record video resumes, but also losing job-search time while learning how to project themselves to an imaginary audience of recruiters.

The potential discrimination issue

Video resumes increase the risk of even the best-trained managers sliding into discriminatory practices, according to Donald Asher, a top-shelf career consultant and author of *Cracking the Hidden Job Market: How to Find Opportunity in Any Economy.*

Asher says, "Video resumes could so easily be used to discriminate against candidates on the basis of race, age, gender, 'looks,' and sexual orientation."

Michael Forrest agrees. Forrest, now retired, was president of a major job board, head of the National Associate of Colleges and Employers, and dean of a famous MBA executive program. Forrest's view:

"Pictures — motion or not — have been a great big 'no!' in the human resources world for decades, as the practice assures both discrimination and reverse discrimination. The attorneys will have a field day."

Learn about videos by viewing videos

A number of free online videos present show-and-tells on the details of delivering a golden performance in the interviewing arena. Open your curtain by browsing for "How to Ace a Job Interview on Skype," by Barbara Kiviat for Time.com. Staging directions alone are worth the look.

Seeking exceptions

Consider making a video resume only when you're in an occupation that requires presentation skills, such as acting or sales.

Viewing the bottom line

Of the 20 career management experts I surveyed for their takes on the value of video resumes, 2 were on the fence and responded with the thought that video resumes may be more widely acceptable "tomorrow maybe."

In short, the video resume is not an idea whose time has come. But the video interview is an idea whose time is now.

Keep Smiling: You're on Camera

Regardless of model or format, learning to look and sound good on camera is a challenge, according to candidates who've been through the experience. (If it were easy, anyone could be on television presenting the news.) I anticipate that community colleges will pick up the pace in offering students the opportunity to enroll in video interviewing training courses and workshops sooner rather than later. In the meantime, I emphasize these two tips:

- ✔ Become familiar with a webcam (set at eye level), a microphone, and video chat software. Schedule regular online visits with friends and family, during which you learn how loudly to talk and how to watch the picture-in-a-picture on your computer monitor to see if you're guilty of overacting. Keep doing this until you feel comfortable.

- ✔ Periodically search the Net for evolving video job interview advice about everything from correct lighting to clothing.

The content of an online job screening interview is virtually the same as that of an in-person or phone screen. But the mechanics . . . oops, the electronics . . . are changing the interview picture as you read this.

Chapter 4

Interviewing on the Global Stage

. . . .

In This Chapter

▶ Looking at interviewing makeovers around the globe

▶ Spreading Western employment practices to other cultures

▶ Getting guidance for continuing cross-cultural differences

. . . .

The United States. Germany. France. The United Kingdom. Kenya. United Arab Emirates. South Africa. China. India. Australia. Russia. Mexico. Norway. Spain. Turkey. Japan. Philippines. Brazil. These countries and many more far-off places may be a workplace destination for someone on the wing — perhaps you.

A flow of workers has always moved among the world's developed nations. But today's employment practices make international exchange of talent more vigorous — speeded up with Internet job searches and technology-rich smartphones.

A Changing Face of Global Interviewing

Old-style job interviewing for foreign nationals is getting an update, too. Interviewing styles are no longer as tightly bound to the customs of individual and disparate nations as they were only 20 years ago.

Back then, job interviewing customs between cultures could be strikingly dissimilar. Day and night! Now interviewing mannerisms are becoming more alike across the globe. Why? In a word, modernization.

Western-style employment practices, sparked especially by American-based multinationals, are narrowing variations in how candidates are interviewed and evaluated in many countries. Employers everywhere want all job seekers to have technical knowledge in their fields, and they look for cross-cultural adaptability.

The interviewing strategies I present throughout this book are widely applicable for mobile professionals in the global workforce. So says Jim Lemke, this book's technical reviewer and a hiring executive with a recent decade of international experience.

Lemke explains, "Multinational corporations are looking to expand in developing countries and need bright young professionals with Western training who have the required work qualifications and who know how to present themselves."

Ron Krannich agrees that interviewing conventions are on the move. President of Impact Publications (`www.impactpublications.com`), an international publisher of career and travel books. Dr. Krannich observes that, with the exception of small and medium-size companies, especially companies that don't operate in the world's major cities, today's employee-selection interviews are looking more alike than unalike.

Dr. Krannich says, "The world's employers increasingly expect to see the 'sales' model that Americans use in job interviewing. I use the term to mean confidently emphasizing positive accomplishments rather than making neutral or negative statements.

"But here's an important caveat: Be careful not to come across as overly aggressive in nations your research shows are traditionally more accustomed to low-key interviewing styles."

Looking at Remaining Cultural Norms

Although poles-apart interviewing styles are in decline, that trend doesn't mean they've disappeared entirely. They haven't.

Handshakes are an example. In the United States, a healthy grip as you pump hands is considered a friendly and straightforward gesture for women as well as men. But in Muslim countries, including Turkey, United Arab Emirates, and Kuwait, unmarried men and women do not touch. This cultural issue presents a dilemma for a Saudi woman candidate being interviewed by a male in America.

Eye contact is another point of difference between cultures. When interviewing in the United States, candidates are expected to make a lot of eye contact, showing honesty and sincerity. Failing to look your interviewer in the eye can be perceived as a sign that you're evasive or you're lying. In Latin America, too much eye contact may suggest a lack of respect or a challenge to authority.

If you're a professional worker who hopes to add far-off places to your resume, it's never too early to begin planning your moves. You've got plenty to plan in your efforts to convince a foreign interviewer that you "get" the host country's culture and that you fit right in.

Interviewing across Cultures

To jump-start your understanding of cross-cultural interviewing norms, here are generalized observations about conditions you may encounter in far-off interviews. The following verbal snapshots are a starting point for your further research aimed at understanding specific mores in individual nations, regions of the country, and individual companies:

- ✔ **Important protocol variations:** Find out in advance how much interviewing formality to generally expect in a particular nation before moving on to pinpoint research about the region and the company. The tone of the interview may be more or less formal than you'd expect at home.

  Joking in an interview is risky enough in your own country. In another land, you may seriously offend if the interviewer interprets your humor as a sign that you won't take the work seriously or that you're a superficial clown.

- ✔ **Personal questions and privacy:** In the United States, laws discourage privacy-penetrating questioning that may lead to discrimination (see Chapter 22). However, employers in a number of nations have no qualms or legal restrictions about asking personal questions of candidates. Understand in advance that you may be expected to answer questions about your age, health, or marital status.

- ✔ **Critical language skills:** Language fluency is a main component of cross-cultural adaptability for professional employees. An inability to speak the language or understand accents is going to prove an almost insurmountable obstacle to being hired.

  English is the lingua franca of international commerce, and in some countries, you may be able to stick with it to be hired. In most cases, though, you'll get greater approval by speaking the local language, bad grammar and mispronounced words notwithstanding.

- ✔ **Self-promotion American style:** Americans are taught to "sell and not tell" when interviewing for employment, to emphasize accomplishments and minimize shortcomings. But in some cultures, being too assertive in tooting your own horn is perceived as being nervy, brash, and brazen.

  In those cultures that prefer an understated performance, employers may want you to volunteer only the skeleton facts of your education and work history, such as previous schools, previous employers, years of employment, job titles, and responsibilities.

> ✔ **Appropriate dress and grooming:** Although local conventions in dress and appearance continue to impact how candidates dress for interviews in a number of countries, most professionals now dress in suits or other business wear. The default mode is conservative.

Tracking Down Country Research

Develop a job search plan for each country of interest. The plan needs to include foundation research for most interviews (see Chapter 6). Add to that base and customize it with information about cultural subtleties for each target country, region of the country, and potential employer of interest. Because hiring customs in the world's nations are still evolving, seek the latest data by researching online and by networking your way to people in each target country.

International websites

The following websites provide information for your cross-cultural job search:

- ✔ **Going Global** (www.goinglobal.com): Visit this site to find country-specific annually updated interviewing advice for 30 countries. A sample content page for each country is free; you can download the complete guide for a country for a modest fee. You may be able to read everything free at a library or college career center.

- ✔ **Job-hunt.org** (www.job-hunt.org/international.shtml): Discover links to resources for international job postings where you can dig up country-specific interviewing intelligence.

- ✔ **Monster.com** (www.monster.com/geo/siteselection): Choose from a number of job search engines aimed at international jobs.

- ✔ **The Riley Guide** (www.rileyguide.com/internat.html): You can learn a lot from this link to international job resources, including how to execute an international job search.

- ✔ **Transitions Abroad** (www.transitionsabroad.com): Check out this site for articles and books about working, studying, traveling, living, and volunteering in countries other than your own.

Questions that probe expat expectations

Employers of expatriates of any nation are likely to ask questions about your ability to adjust and function in a foreign setting. Can you be happy in an unfamiliar place without becoming homesick? What if your spouse and children hate the place and flee back home? If you can't stand the climate, will you pack up and leave within several months? Survival questions to expats may be direct or inferred. Consider the following examples.

Do any factors limit your ability to take on this assignment, such as your health or your family situation?

Are you realistic about living overseas and working under different conditions? What about in developing nations, where the living isn't as easy and convenient as back home?

How do your spouse and children view this assignment — are they on board?

International social networking

Tapping into personal and professional online networks to discover the rules of the road in foreign interview rooms is easy — a bit time-consuming, but easy. Here are a few suggestions about tracking interviewing conventions the digital way. If you were a marketing professional who wanted to work in Denmark, for example, you'd take the following steps.

1. **Start with contacts you already have.**

   Your contacts know people you don't know, and their contacts know people they don't know, and so on. Send a brief e-mail message to each contact, stating your desire to prepare for a job interview in Denmark. Say that you'd appreciate any of the following kinds of assistance from the recipient:

   - To help you directly or to forward your message to a personal contact who can help you in your quest for knowledge about the interviewing protocols and customs common in Denmark.

   - To help you arrange a more substantial informational interview with a resident of Denmark who, like you, is a professional or businessperson. In an online informational interview, whether by e-mail or through Skype (with a video cam), ask a series of questions that you write out before the interview. Remember, you're exploring only typical job interviewing in Denmark at this informational interview — you're not investigating every aspect of the job or employment there. You can, of course, arrange for a follow-up interview if your Denmark contact is agreeable.

2. **Check out professional member organizations in the field of work you seek.**

   Post your request for current information about interviewing protocols in Denmark for your profession on a forum, chat room, or blog. You probably have to be a member of the organization to access the organization's site.

3. **Try popular business-oriented social network tools.**

   Conduct a keyword search on a site such as LinkedIn (`www.linkedin.com`), Facebook (`www.facebook.com`), or Twitter (`www.twitter.com`). Use a term that's relevant to your objective — say, "Denmark corporate marketing" or "Denmark human resources" or "Denmark manager" — to see whether you can connect with social media users who may be able to provide the latest interviewing information.

Preparing for the Global Job Interview

Whether your interview takes place in a cosmopolitan city, a little-known town on the slopes of a mountain, or your home bedroom on a smartphone, the secret to your global search success is preparation and practice. In addition to getting the country-specific environment right, you have to sell yourself as an ideal candidate for the position you seek.

Chapter 5 catalogs the types of interviews you may encounter as you move on up in your life.

Chapter 5

A Chorus Line of Interviews by Type

A ction/adventure. Comedy. Mystery. Martial arts. Musical. Romance. Suspense. Thriller. You know the old saying: "Variety is the splice of life in filmmaking." (Yes, you can groan now.)

Variety, in today's job market, is similarly rich in job interviewing dramas. Do yourself a favor by becoming familiar with the various shapes, forms, and fashions of interviews.

This chapter helps you accomplish that as it spotlights the most common styles of job interviews today. For convenience, I divide them into four clusters describing the

✔ *Objective* for the interview

✔ *Interviewer number,* from one to dozens

✔ *Technique and interview forms* that shape your participation

✔ *Location* where the interview takes place

Mastering Interviews by Objective

Interviewers set up different kinds of meetings for different reasons, as the leading player in the following story illustrates:

A woman with a dog was leaving a movie theater when a reporter stopped her and said, "I'm sorry to bother you, but I was amazed that your dog seemed to get into the movie so much. He cried at the right scenes, yawned during the ho-hum spots, and laughed his head off at the funny parts. Don't you find that amazing?"

"Yes," the woman replied. "I find it quite amazing, considering that his objective in coming here was to find out whether the movie was as bad as the book!"

You can read about interview objectives in the upcoming sections.

Screening interview

Interviewing is a two-stage process in large organizations. The two stages are *screening* and *selection.* Screening precedes selection.

The purpose of screening — or first-cut interviews — is to weed out all applicants except the best qualified. (Head to Chapter 2 for more on today's beefed-up emphasis on screening job seekers.)

Live (in-person) interviews to screen applicants typically are held at the employer's worksite, independent employment services, college career services, and job fairs.

But interviewers increasingly rely on technology — such as telephone and webcam (video online) interviews — to screen applicants. They use the technology as cost-cutting moves to knock out underskilled and overpriced candidates before their companies invest too much time and money in dead ends.

The *screener,* usually an employee of the employer inside the human resources department or an outside, third-party (independent) recruiter, quizzes all comers and passes the survivors to a person who makes the final selection.

The *selector,* the person who makes the selection — that is, the person who has the final say on hiring— is usually the department manager or the boss to whom the victorious candidate will report.

Selection interview

The selection interview (sometimes called the decision interview) typically is a live interview (face to face). You meet with a supervisor, department head, or another person who has the authority to hire you. (Sometimes the selection decision is made by more than one person, as I explain in the later section "Group interview.")

Because this final interviewer will be your potential boss, you, too, will be making judgments during the interview.

Selection interviewers are rarely pros at interviewing and often just go with their intuition, hoping the task is over as quickly as possible so that they can get back to their "real" work.

Because the selection interview may take several detours, be ready to ask leading questions to (1) get the interview back on track and (2) set up an opening to describe your qualifications for the position.

Even if the questioner seems like a long-lost buddy, don't relax. Your interviewer is trying to decide which candidate is the best investment for the company — because a wrong choice can cost the company thousands of dollars in training time, correcting mistakes, and firing to hire again.

Selection interviewers are looking for

- ✔ **Strong presentation of personality:** How you blend with other employees, as well as your general likeability and motivation to work

- ✔ **Specific details of your competencies and skills:** How your qualifications allow you to do the job better than other candidates

- ✔ **Specific details of your job experience or education:** How you've not only done — or been trained to do — a similar job, but how you'll apply that background to the new job

- ✔ **How you handle specific job scenarios:** How your mind works under variable or stressful conditions, and how you solve challenges

Assuming that the person conducting the meeting will be your boss or a colleague with whom you have to get along, the selection interview is where you move from neutral behavior into high gear. This is the forum where you reveal the best of your personality!

And the selection interview is where you take note of how you and your potential boss blend. If your gut instinct tells you the blend is oil-and-water, think twice before saying yes to this job if it's offered.

Even when every other factor about the job is tempting, your work life will be a happier place when you and your future boss are "using the same software."

In a classic Western spoof, *Blazing Saddles,* actor Harvey Korman plays a gang leader recruiting bad guys to ruin a town. Interviewing funnyman Cleavon Little, who applies to be his sidekick, Korman initially worries that the two of them are not "using the same software."

Korman asks Little to describe his qualifications as a villain. When Little tells the gang leader that his past work was stampeding cattle, Korman is about to blow him off with a comment that stampeding cattle isn't a big thing in gangland. Little smirks knowingly, then says, "Through the Vatican?" Right then, Korman decides that Little and he are two villains of a kind, shouting "Kinky!" and hiring him on the spot.

Combination interview

Small firms often combine the screening and selection interviews. The resulting combination tends to be long and arduous. It not only tests your match to the hiring requirements, but also measures your stamina and motivation for the job.

From the very first exchange, pull out all the stops in selling your top qualities and displaying a pleasant personality, because you won't get a second chance.

Promotion interview

Moving up from the inside as an internal candidate often is easier than gaining access as an outside candidate. But it's not a sure thing.

Approach a promotion interview as though you were heading out to a new company. Research diligently, as I describe in Chapter 6, to be able to talk about industry trends and other big issues.

When you're the only insider wrangling for the job, use your knowledge of the company's policies, plans, and culture to emphasize that you alone can hit the floor running — which no outsider can actually do. Then identify several current company problems you could deal with right off the bat.

Be cautious about suggesting solutions to company problems caused by the hiring authority. When in doubt, don't.

Should you emphasize your 20 years of loyal service with a show-and-tell of your successes at a time when your company is handing off generational control from boomers to Xers? Although it may seem counterintuitive to boomers, if that's you, tread carefully. The familiar "tried-and-proven" strategy won't have legs during a time when new captains are determined to justify taking the wheel by steering in different directions.

A youth-oriented management doesn't care about the glories of Ancient Rome or Ancient You — what they care about is whether you can do the work ahead — now and tomorrow.

So while you include the accomplishments of the past ten years (no more than that), reframe the discussion to focus on work samples and skills that highlight your ability to do the new job. Give examples of your flexible personality. Identify times when you welcomed new tasks and responsibilities. Help them see you as the way forward, not as star-spangled yesteryear.

Recruiter courtesy interview

A *retained recruiter* gets paid whether or not the recruiter matches a candidate to a position. These professionals typically run the other way to avoid job seekers who come unbidden to their offices. (Time is money.) But you may know a client or friend of a retained recruiter who can get you through the door with a courtesy interview.

Unless the retained recruiter giving you a courtesy interview is recruiting for a position that's perfect for you — which is very unlikely — focus on providing the recruiter with information that may qualify you for a future search. Follow these practices:

- ✔ Always give the recruiter a current resume.
- ✔ Get straight to the point; don't take more than 20 minutes of the recruiter's time.
- ✔ Explain your experience, accomplishments, and skills.
- ✔ If the recruiter asks whether you know someone qualified for a specific position for which the recruiter is trying to collect candidates, rack your brain to be accommodating if you know someone who fills the bill. The recruiter may remember your favor for future searches more appropriate for you.
- ✔ Thank the recruiter for time invested in you.

Don't play the role of a coy, amateur job seeker. The retained recruiter is in no business for games. You wouldn't ask for a courtesy interview if you didn't need a job. Your conciseness and ability to communicate efficiently count. Review your resume and get to the point.

Recruiter general screening interview

Contingency recruiters, unlike retained recruiters, get paid only when they match up a candidate with a position. The more people they see, the larger their candidate pool from which to fill employers' job orders. Getting an interview with a contingency recruiter or employment agency consultant is easier than with a retained recruiter.

Brainteaser job interview

If you were to eliminate one of the 50 United States, leaving only 49 states, which one would it be and why?

That's a question Microsoft interviewers like to ask, says John Kador, business writing consultant (www.jkador.com) and author of a smart book on logic-driven riddles and oxygen-sucking puzzles that job interviewers may spring on you without warning.

Brainteasers ("Why are manhole covers round?" or "How would you test a salt shaker?") ordinarily are reserved for very bright candidates as a challenge to see who can rise and shine in professional and managerial positions in today's hypercompetitive work environment.

When you suspect that you're heading into interview combat, find guidance in Kador's book, *How to Ace the Brain Teaser Interview* (McGraw-Hill).

So what's the best answer if you're smacked upside the head with that Microsoft state-elimination haymaker? "Well, it's *not* the state of Washington," Kador says with a grin. (Microsoft is headquartered in Redmond, Wash.)

But you still can't waste a contingency recruiter's time. Hand over your resume and give your best performance to show a broad selection of work experiences. You're trying to make the contingency recruiter remember you for a variety of future job openings.

Take care to rate high scores in the following qualities:

- ✔ Competence in skills and knowledge
- ✔ Enthusiasm and motivated interest in work
- ✔ Experience (some job history)
- ✔ Good communication
- ✔ Leadership and initiative
- ✔ Personality/likeability

Recruiter search interview

A recruiter may contact you about a specific job opening. Chances are that you've done or are doing a job similar to the one the recruiter's client wants to fill, and that's why the recruiter called you. So you already know the basics of your industry, even though at first you may not know the identity of the client.

The recruiter is prepared for the (de facto screening) interview on first contact; you're not. Level the playing field by saying you were walking out the door for an important appointment and schedule the interview for the following day.

Recruiters — whether third-party or internal — can't hire you, but you've got to pass their muster before you see their client hiring authorities.

To impress a recruiter in a search interview:

✔ Show that you have definite career goals and indicate how this position fits those goals.

✔ Ask probing, thoughtful questions about the company and position, showing you've done your homework.

When you want to make the initial recruiter contact, use the web to research recruiting firms that specialize in your industry or occupation.

✔ The gold standard is *Kennedy's Directory of Executive Recruiters* (with purchase of a print copy, you're entitled to a free online version): www. kennedyinfo.com.

✔ A good free resource is *Oya's Directory of Recruiters* at www.i-recruit. com/oya. You can search by keyword or browse the listings by specialty or location.

✔ Find many other directories of recruiting firms, both free and for a fee, on The Riley Guide (www.rileyguide.com/recruiters.html).

Second interview

Being called back is a good sign: You're a few steps closer to being offered the job you want.

To come out first in the second interview, be sure you understand the dynamics at play. (Actually, the second interview may turn out to be a series of interviews, but the purpose is typically the same in all of them.)

I count three kinds of second interviews and suggest tips to come out ahead in each one:

✔ **The yours-to-lose selection interview:** The decision is virtually made in your favor. But the hiring manager is confirming it with endorsements and buy-in consensus from the team. Your qualifications aren't in question, but your fit (how you fit in with the company culture) is being probed. Relax a little — these are your new colleagues. Keep your answers pleasant, straightforward, and brief but not terse.

Why offers don't follow interviews

When you've been through three, four, five, six, or more interviews for the job that ultimately went to another person, suspect any of the following reasons:

✔ Your image doesn't reflect the role you seek to play. (See Chapter 9.)

✔ Your references are failing to meet your expectations of high praise. (See Chapter 12.)

✔ You're asking for a bigger share of the box office than your performance supports. (See Chapter 8.)

✔ Someone on the "panel of judges" voted you off the show, and you may never know who the sneak is.

✔ The interviewing flurry was a dodge to cover up the real script — the job was always going to go to a friend or relative.

✔ OMG, another candidate really was more perfect than you in the role that slipped from your grasp.

✔ **The finalists' selection interview:** The decision has narrowed to two or three finalists. Keep selling your qualifications. Allude to cultural fit with subtle comments suggesting that you're one of them. ("I agree that we must build adequate electrical power into the infrastructure.") Ask intelligent questions, such as depth of support for stated missions and professional development opportunities.

✔ **The do-over screening interview:** Management still wonders whether you're underqualified and overpriced and wants to make another pass at you, perhaps with different screeners. Expect questions all over again about your job history, skills, salary history or requirements, resume gaps, and the kind of person you are. (You're reliable, honest, team-oriented, and, overall, have laudable values.)

If you're working with a recruiter, ask the recruiter for tips and where you are in the selection process. If not, ask the same question of the interviewer who has shown you the greatest interest.

Mastering Interviews by Interviewer

The most common interview style you'll encounter is the one in which a solo interviewer meets and questions you. Another possibility is that you meet face to face with several pairs of measuring eyes — all at once. Still another format shuffles you from one interview to another to another, all with the same company. In the upcoming sections, I sketch the possibilities.

One-to-one interview

You and the employer meet, usually at the employer's office, and discuss the job and your relevant skills and other qualifications that relate to it. You find suggestions on how to take victory laps in the one-to-one interview format throughout this book.

Group interview

The plot thickens. Also called a panel, board, team, collective, or committee interview, this style puts you center stage before a comparatively huge crowd — perhaps 5 to 12 questioners. Usually they are people from the department where you would work, or they may come from various departments throughout the organization.

You wouldn't be at this expensive meeting (think of all the salaries for the group's time) if you hadn't already been screened to be sure your qualifications are acceptable. These people are gathered to see whether they like you and whether you'll fit into their operation. Greet each person, handing out a fresh copy of your resume. Appear confident. Make a quick seating chart to help you remember names.

Before you answer a first question, smile, thank everyone for inviting you to meet with them, and then begin your answer, which will probably be "You asked me to tell you about myself . . .."

Should you try to identify the leader and direct most of your remarks to that person? Not necessarily. The boss may be the quiet observer in the corner. Play it safe — maintain eye contact with all committee members. When your curtain goes up, play to a full house!

Group interviews highlight your interpersonal skills, leadership, and ability to think on your feet and deal with issues in a stressful setting. The purpose of a group interview is not only to hear what you say, but to see what behaviors and skills you display within a group.

When the interview is over, thank the group as though you just finished a speech.

> *Thank you for having me here today. I enjoyed being with you. This interview confirmed my research indicating that this company is a good place to work. I'll look forward to hearing from you and, hopefully, joining you.*

Ask questions. Periodically summarize important points to keep the group focused. Use a notebook to record several simultaneous questions, explaining that you don't want to omit responding to anyone's important concern.

Serial interview

A serial interview also involves a group of people, but not all at once. You are handed off from person to person. You typically are passed from screener to line manager to top manager — and perhaps a half-dozen people in between in the drawn-out process of the serial interview. You strengthen your chances each time you are passed onward.

Use your screening (plain vanilla personality) interview behavior with all interviewers you meet except those with whom you would work. Then go into your selection (full personality) mode.

When the initial interviewer says that you're being passed on to the second interviewer, try to find out a little about the second interviewer. Ask a question like "Does number two feel the same way about customer service as you do?" You'll get information you need to establish common ground with your next interviewer. Continue the advance-tip technique all the way to the finish line.

When you're interviewed by one person after another, consistency counts. Don't tell a rainbow of stories about the same black-and-white topics. When interview team members later compare notes, they should be discussing the same person.

Mastering Interviews by Technique

One of the funniest movie reviews ever was for the 1960s film *Chitty Chitty, Bang Bang.*

The entire review read: "It went bang bang and it was chitty!"

The film's director, who here shall remain nameless, couldn't have been happy about that review. No happier than a job interviewer bearing responsibility for the hiring of a candidate who disappoints.

A film director calls the shots on a movie set, placing actors and cameras to best advantage.

Similarly, a job interviewer sets the technique and tone of the interview, whether it is behavior based, tightly or loosely controlled, intentionally stressful, or loaded with brain-crunching puzzles.

Behavior-based interview

Behavior-based interviewing relies on storytelling — examples of what you've done that support your claims. Premised on the belief that the past predicts the future, behavior-based interviewing techniques are used to ask candidates how they have handled specific situations — what kinds of behaviors they used to solve problems.

The presumption is that if you were a good problem solver in the past, you'll be a good problem solver in the future. Behavior-based interviewing emphasizes "What did you do when?" instead of "What would you do if?"

Interview questions are designed to draw out clues to a candidate's workplace DNA. All candidates are asked virtually the same questions. The tip-off that you've just been handed a behavior-based question, which should be answered with a demonstrated skill or trait, is when the question begins with such words as these:

- ✔ Tell me about a time when —
- ✔ Give me an example of your skills in —
- ✔ Describe a time when you —
- ✔ Why did you —

A few fleshed-out examples illustrate the behavior-based technique more fully:

Think back to a time when you were on the verge of making a huge sale, and the customer balked at the last minute, promised to get back to you, but didn't. What action did you take?

Remember a time when you improved inventory turns; how big of an improvement did you make?

Tell me about an on-the-job disaster that you turned around, making lemonade from lemons.

Describe the types of risks you have allowed your direct reports to take.

Can you give me an example of when you were able to implement a vision for your organization?

Why did you decide to major in sociology at San Marcos State University instead of at a small private college?

Companies using behavior-based interviewing first must identify the behaviors important to the job. If leadership, for instance, is one of the valued behaviors, several questions asking for stories of demonstrated leadership will be asked:

Tell me about the last time you had to take charge of a project but were lacking in clear direction. How did you carry forward the project?

Because the behavioral style of interviewing attempts to measure predictable behavior rather than pure paid work experience, it can help level the playing field for rookies competing against seasoned candidates.

In mining your past for anecdotes, you can draw from virtually any part of your past behavior — education, school projects, paid work experience, volunteer work, activities, hobbies, family life.

As you sift through your memories, be on the lookout for a theme, the motif that runs through your choices of education, jobs, and activities. Put at least half a dozen anecdotes that illustrate your theme in your mental pocket and pull them out when you need them. Examples of themes are

- ✔ Displaying leadership
- ✔ Solving problems
- ✔ Negotiating
- ✔ Showing initiative
- ✔ Overcoming adversity
- ✔ Succeeding
- ✔ Dealing with stress
- ✔ Sacrificing to achieve an important work goal
- ✔ Dealing with someone who disagrees with you
- ✔ Displaying commitment
- ✔ Demonstrating work ethic
- ✔ Staying task orientated
- ✔ Practicing communication skills

Here are several more suggestions to tap-dance your way through behavior-based questions:

- ✔ Tell a story with a beginning, a middle, and an end using the PAR technique — problem, action, result.

Here's an example: *Problem:* An e-commerce company was operating at a substantial loss. *Action:* I outsourced technical support and added seven new product lines. *Result:* We cut our expenses by 8 percent, increased our revenues by 14 percent, and had our first profitable year, with expectations of higher profits next year.

✔ Rookies: Don't simply cite the subject of your classes — "I couldn't solve my accounting problem, so I asked my professor." No! Look back at your student class projects, previous work experience, and extracurricular activities. Reach into real life for your success stories.

✔ Try not to sound as though you memorized every syllable and inflection, or like a machine with all the answers. Admitting that your example was a complex problem and that you experimented until you found its best solution humanizes you.

Realize that the interviewer is more interested in the process than in the details of your success stories. What was the reasoning behind your actions? Why did you behave the way you did? What skills did you use?

Behavior-based interviewing, which arrived nearly 50 years ago, is popular today because employers are trying to snatch clues from history to project the future. The underlying rationale is that people tend to play the same roles in life over and over.

Theatrical insiders call this tendency "typecasting." In explaining a shift away from action films, film star Bruce Willis quipped, "I've saved the world so many times, they've given me an 800 number."

Directive interview

The *directive interview* is one in which the interviewer maintains complete control and walks you through the discussion to uncover what the interviewer wants to know.

The *structured interview* is directive because the interviewer works from a written list of questions asked of all candidates and writes down your answers.

The argument in favor of structured interviews is that they promote fairness, uncover superior candidates, and eliminate the cloning effect (in which an interviewer essentially hires candidates in his own image — or one who the interviewer thinks will "fit in" merely because of shared values).

In structured interviews, the interviewer may throw out a *critical incident* and ask you to respond. A critical incident is a specific problem or challenge that was successfully handled by employees of the company. Like a quiz show, the host (the interviewer) has the "answer sheet" — the actual behavior that solved the problem or met the challenge.

Some critical incidents can be anticipated by researching industry trends and inferred by reading company press releases online.

Whether you are in an unwritten directive interview or a scripted structured interview, expect interviewers to ask both closed- and open-ended questions.

A *closed-end question* can be answered with *yes* or *no:*

> *Did you find my office easily?*

An open-ended question usually asks *how* or *why:*

> *How do you like this industry?*

This interviewer has an agenda and is intent on seeing that it's followed. Being too assertive in changing the topic is a mistake. The only safe way you can introduce one of your skills is to ask a question:

> *Would you like to hear about my experience in quality assessment?*

Nondirective interview

A *nondirective interview* rewards you for leading the discussion. It's often an approach of line managers who don't know much about professional interviewing.

Questions tend to be broad and general so that you can elaborate and tell all kinds of terrific stories about yourself. A few questions may reveal key areas of the employer's needs. These questions may sound at first as though they're critical incidents, but in this loose-limbed interview, the interviewer probably doesn't assume that he or she knows the answers. Examples of non-directive interview questions include the following:

> *We had a problem employee last quarter who revealed information about our marketing strategies to a competitor — how would you handle this situation?*

> *You understand some of the difficulties this department faces — how would you approach these in your first four months?*

> *Tell me about your goals in the next five years and how this position fits in with them.*

> *Your resume shows you have a degree in Spanish and another in computer science — how do you plan to use both of these in this position?*

Carry agenda cards or a small notebook with a list of your qualifications and a list of questions about the company. When you have to carry the ball, working from notes can be a lifesaver if you have a leaky memory.

If all your preparation fails you, fall back on "I wish I had the answer. What's your viewpoint on this?"

Stress interview

Recognizing the hazing that goes on in a stress interview is important; recognize it for what it is — either it's a genuine test of your ability to do the job, or you're being punk'd by a certified jerk.

Whichever it is, don't take the horrors of a stress interview personally. Keep your cool and play the game if you want the job. Don't sweat. Don't cry. Your most reliable tactic is to speak with calm, unflagging confidence. You may have to practice remaining poised in the face of an interviewer's intimidation tactics.

Suppose that you're in sales. Asking you to sell the interviewer something — like the office chair — is fairly common. But having you face blinding sunlight while sitting in a chair with one short leg is, at best, immature.

Stress interviews often consist of

- Hour-long waits before the interview
- Long, uncomfortable silences
- Challenges of your beliefs
- A brusque interviewer or multiple curt interviewers
- Deliberate misinterpretation of your comments and outright insults

Typical questions run along these lines:

Why weren't you working for so long?

Why eight jobs in ten years?

Your resume shows that you were with your last company for a number of years without promotion and a virtually flat salary; why is that?

Can you describe a situation when your work was criticized or you disliked your boss?

Storytelling your way to a job

Prepare for all your interviews — not just behavior-based interviews — by recalling anecdotes from your past experience that back up your claims of skills and other qualifications. Work on these stories as though you're going to present them in a speech before hundreds of people. Make them fun, interesting — even exciting! Few of us are natural-born storytellers, but do your best to tell a good story.

Experts claim the way to breeze through behavior-based interviews is to prepare, rehearse, and deliver one- to two-minute stories about your skills, experience, and accomplishments that relate directly to the job. Your commitment to meeting their interests shows as you recognize their goals and pay your respects in full with relevant stories.

Would you like to have my job?

What would you do if violence erupted in your workplace?

A famous admiral, now dead, used to nail the furniture to the floor and ask the applicant to pull up a chair. If an interviewer crosses your personal line of reasonable business behavior, stand up with dignity, thank the interviewer for the time, and run like hell for the emergency exit.

Mastering Interviews at Remote Locations

A filming location is a place where some or all of a film or television series is produced, instead of using sets built on a studio backlit or soundstage.

Going on location isn't always a cushy assignment. Some years ago, while filming in a Philippines jungle, the movie's production chief warned star actor Michael Caine to beware of a poisonous serpent called the 1-2-3 snake.

Asking about the odd name, Caine was told it was because, once bitten, after taking 1-2-3 steps, you're dead! Worse luck, the snake looked like a twig. The saving grace was that the film's native guides could smell the snake. Unsurprisingly, each morning Caine and the crew checked to be sure the guides hadn't caught colds.

While not every interview takes place across a desk at the company's home base, presumably you won't have to worry about snakes as you head out for an interview over a meal, in a campus interviewing room, at a job fair, or even at home where the whole family is inspected.

Mealtime interview

Just when you thought you'd been through all the interviewing hoops and assumed that landing the job was a done deal, you get a luncheon invitation from a higher-up in the company, perhaps your potential boss. Why?

Robin Jay, author of *The Art of the Business Lunch: Building Relationships Between 12 and 2* (Career Press), identifies the following reasons:

- ✔ To judge you on your social skills and manners
- ✔ To find out additional information about you that an employer may not legally be able to ask
- ✔ To get to know you better
- ✔ To compare your social behavior to that of other candidates

As an account executive, Jay ate her way through 3,000 business lunches. (No, she's not fat.) She says that sharing a meal with someone reveals her personality faster and more effectively than all the office interviews in the world. "Many a job has been won or lost at the table," Jay observes.

So while a mealtime interview may seem more relaxed and social, stay as alert as you would in any other location. Mealtime interviewers are watching you with big eyes.

To avoid spilling precious job opportunities, mind your manners:

- ✔ Don't order entrees so hard to eat that you spend the entire interview lost in your plate with long pasta or saucy, messy, or bony food.
- ✔ Don't order alcohol unless you're at dinner — even then, have only one drink. White wine is a good choice.
- ✔ Don't order the most expensive or the most inexpensive thing on the menu.
- ✔ Don't smoke (companies are obsessed with employee health costs).
- ✔ Don't complain about anything — the food, the service, or the restaurant.
- ✔ Don't over-order or leave too much food on your plate.

To look classy in a mealtime interview, be sure to

- ✔ Order something that's easy to eat (like a club or veggie sandwich).
- ✔ Chew with your mouth closed, speak with your mouth empty.
- ✔ Order something similar to what the interviewer orders or ask the interviewer to suggest something.
- ✔ Show your appreciation for the treat — once hired, you may find yourself brown-bagging your lunch.

Practice a technique known as *mirroring* — what the boss or the interviewer does, you do. Take the interviewer's lead in where to rest arms on the table, which fork to hold, and how fast to shovel in the food. Subconsciously, you're establishing similarities, making the interviewer like you (See the sidebar "Bravo moves for all interviewing styles," later in this chapter.)

Always be polite to the food server, even if the service or food is so bad you make a mental note never to set foot in the place again. Treating the server with disrespect is worse than spilling spaghetti sauce all over the interviewer's new suit.

No matter how much or how little the tab, the interviewer always pays, so don't reach for the bill when it comes, even if it's placed closer to you. Let it sit there unclaimed, unloved. Remember, this could be a test of your confidence or of your knowledge of protocol.

On-campus interview

Some employers recruit on campuses by setting up interviews through your college's career center. These are screening interviews conducted by company recruiters. (Check out the earlier section in this chapter titled "Screening interview," and also see Chapter 2.)

Job market to college seniors: Snag the interviews you want by learning and using the system. Sign up for resume and job interviewing workshops, make friends with the career center counselors, ask for job leads.

When you don't get interview slots you want, check back for last-minute cancellations or additions to the interview schedules.

Job fair interview

Job fairs are brief but significant encounters in which you hand over documents — either your resume or a summary sheet of your qualifications (carry both types of documents). Your objective is to land an interview, not get a job offer on the spot at the fair. At best, you'll get a screening interview at the event site.

Try to preregister for the job fair, get a list of participating employers, and research those you plan to visit. Your edge is to be better prepared than the competition.

Fair lines are long, so accept the likelihood that you'll be standing in many of them. Make use of your time by writing up notes from one recruiter while standing in line to meet another.

Everyone tries to arrive early, so think about arriving at halftime when the first flood has subsided. Dress professionally, whatever that means in your career field.

Work up a branding brief (see Chapter 16) with at least one strong memorable point to say to recruiters. Here's an example: *I am in the top 10 percent of my environmental engineering class.* If there's no immediate feedback inviting you for an interview, hand over your summary sheet and ask, "Do you have positions appropriate for my background?" If the answer is positive, your next question is "I'd like to take the next step — can we set up an interview?" If you don't get a positive response, continue with "Can we talk on the phone next week?"

Whether or not you're able to schedule an interview on the spot, when you leave, hand over your resume. Think of your job fair interaction with recruiters as a major star's cameo performance in a film: Move in, make a high-profile impression through dress and preparedness, and move on to the next prospect.

What's Playing on the Interview Scene?

You may not know in advance the type of interview you'll encounter, but at least you won't be caught off guard if you take seriously the message in the next chapter showing you how to research your way to a smooth performance followed by bouquets of greenbacks.

Bravo moves for all interviewing styles

No matter what style of interview you're doing, some factors are all-purpose job winners.

✔ **Make them like you.** No matter how scientific the interviewing style, the quality of likeability is a powerful influence in deciding who gets the job. And it's human nature to like people who like us, and who are like us in common interests and outlooks.

Show your similarities to the interviewer and company culture. You need not be clones of each other, but do find areas of mutual interest: preferences in movies, methods of doing work, or favorite company

products, for instance. When you successfully intimate that you and the decision-making interviewer share similar worldviews, values, or approaches to work, you create affinity that leads to job offers, as this true story shows:

After trying for months, Julia Benz (not her real name) finally won an interview with a major Los Angeles company, and she was taking no chances on botching the interview. As a part of her preparation, Benz went to the office the evening before her appointment.

(continued)

(continued)

She had merely intended to peek inside to see what the building was like, but just as she looked in, a janitor cleaning the floor noticed her and asked if she needed help.

Benz told the truth. She said, "I wanted to get a feel for the place where I'm having an important interview tomorrow." Probably against company policy, the janitor invited Benz into the interviewer's office and pointed out several meticulously detailed models of old ships mounted on a high shelf. The interviewer was clearly an avid collector. Later that night, Benz read up on old ships.

You know what happens next: When Benz met the interviewer, she pointed at one of the models and remarked, "Say, isn't that a Hudson sloop?" The affinity was instant. Benz got the job.

✔ **Listen well to interviewers' questions, statements, and feelings.** People like to be listened to more than they like to listen. Show your likeability by summarizing, rephrasing, and playing back what interviewers say instead of concentrating just on what you have to say.

✔ **Don't drip honey by overdoing compliments or small talk.** Take cues from the interviewer's office mementos just long enough to break the ice. Most interviewers will be turned off by such transparent plays for empty approval. Get to the point — the job.

✔ **Pause thoughtfully.** Show that you think as you talk. It's okay to pause in thoughtfulness during an in-person interview, where interviewers can tell you're contemplating and thinking things through before answering. *Exception:* Don't take a thinking pause in a telephone or videoconferencing interview, where any pause is dead airtime.

✔ **Take notes.** Have a small notebook handy and use it when the interviewer is talking, especially after you've asked a question or the interviewer has put special emphasis on a subject. Taking notes not only shows that you're paying attention, but also flatters the interviewer. If you prefer to use a laptop or tablet to take notes, ask first: "May I make a few notes as we talk? I don't want to forget any of your key points."

Part II
Backstage Researching and Rehearsing

The 5th Wave   By Rich Tennant

GRICHTENNANT

"Oh great! The one part of the interview process I didn't practice for!"

In this part . . .

Anyone who tells you to be yourself in an interview is missing the point entirely. The self you present in a job interview is your best self, your fully prepared and ready for your close-up self. This part shows you how to step into that role.

I show you how to find out what you need to know about a job and company before you step into the interview room as well as how to rehearse so you're ready to market yourself powerfully. I tell you how to dress the part and how to handle salary talk.

Chapter 6

Research Is Your Ticket Inside

A cademy Award winners Natalie Portman and Nicholas Cage understand that research breeds advantage.

When Portman prepared for her ballerina role in *Black Swan,* she studied and practiced ballet many hours every day for months. To authenticate his role in *Bringing Out the Dead,* Nicolas Cage, playing a paramedic, rode along with real paramedics to a real drive-by shooting of a young boy.

You may not want to go as far as practicing ballet or comforting a suffering gunshot victim. But figuratively speaking, I hope you won't tie your hands behind your back and put a blindfold around your eyes by failing to gather the data that can change your life.

Investigate Like a Quiz-Show Winner

Even if you'd rather scrub morgue floors than do quiz-show-quality research on organizations and their people, suck it up and dig right in — or hire some-one to handle the research ditch-digging for you. Consider the rewards:

✔ You'll have solid facts demonstrating harmony between your qualifica-tions and the job's requirements.

✔ You'll grab data suggesting you're a good fit with an employer's organi-zational culture.

✔ You'll own ammo for brilliant answers when asked, "What do you know about our company?"

✔ You'll gain the foundation to absorb new facts during the interview.

✔ Your preparedness will show you're a headliner, not a bit player.

Here's What Online Search Tells Us

Building a treasury of free and useful information on most public — and some private — companies is as fast and easy as following directions to "click here."

In just an hour or two, you can feast your eyes on these resources:

- ✔ Annual reports
- ✔ Financial data
- ✔ News releases
- ✔ Information about products and services
- ✔ Industry trends
- ✔ Competitor information

You may be able to find out about

- ✔ Employee views on a company
- ✔ Pending mergers and acquisitions
- ✔ Pending layoffs
- ✔ Shifts in management personnel
- ✔ Corporate culture
- ✔ Wall Street's outlook for the company

Take a pass when you discover a company teetering on a legal edge or dumping employees despite its past promises. But when you discover no impending corporate collapse or toxic bosses running the show, and you want the job, research is a tiebreaker in a tight race with another candidate.

Asking Questions about Potential Employers

Use the following questions as a checklist to gather all the information you need. (Additionally, see Chapter 11.) You probably won't be able to use information on all the factors that follow, and you may think of others as important for your specific search.

Here's the rule on how much research to do: The more responsible the job — or the more competitive the race — the greater amount of research you must do to pull ahead.

Size and growth patterns

The size of a company and the scope of its operations say a great deal about the company's ambitions and opportunities for advancement. Try to answer the following questions:

- ✔ What is the company's industry?
- ✔ Has the company expanded globally?
- ✔ Is it expanding or downsizing?
- ✔ What are its divisions and subsidiaries?
- ✔ How many employees does it have?
- ✔ How many clients does it serve?
- ✔ How many locations does it have?
- ✔ Does it have foreign satellites?

Direction and planning

Answers to questions about the company's plans may be difficult to find outside of the company's website, its annual report, newspaper business pages, business magazines, or the industry's trade publications. The following information is worth pursuing, as it lets you know some of the hot issues to address or avoid:

- ✔ What are the company's current priorities?
- ✔ What is its mission?
- ✔ What long-term contracts has it established?
- ✔ What are its prospects?
- ✔ What are its problems?
- ✔ Is it initiating any new products or projects?

Products or services

You don't want to go into a job interview without at least knowing what products or services are the bedrock of the company's business. Find answers to these questions about any company you pursue:

✔ What services or products does the company provide?

✔ What are its areas of expertise?

✔ How does it innovate in the industry — by maintaining cutting-edge products, cutting costs, or what?

Competitive profile

How the company is positioned within its industry and how hard competitors are nipping at its heels are measures of the company's long-term health and the relative stability of your prospective job there. Get to the bottom of these issues by asking some questions:

✔ Who are the company's competitors?

✔ What are the company's current projects?

✔ What setbacks has it experienced?

✔ What are its greatest accomplishments?

✔ Is the company in a growing industry?

✔ Will technology dim its future?

✔ Does it operate with updated technology?

✔ Cheaper labor: Does it move jobs to another country?

Culture and reputation

How fast is the pace? Frantic? Laid-back? Formal? Informal? Aggressive? Answers to the following questions give you clues about a company's culture:

✔ Does the company run lean on staffing?

✔ What's the picture on mergers and acquisitions?

✔ What's its reputation?

✔ What types of employees does it hire?

✔ What's the buzz on its managers?

✔ How does it treat employees?

✔ Does it push out older workers?

Company financials

Collecting current and accurate information about financials is a long chase, but it's better to learn a company's shaky financial picture before you're hired than after you're laid off. Dig for the following nuggets:

- ✔ What are the company's sales?
- ✔ What are its earnings?
- ✔ What are its assets?
- ✔ How stable is its financial base?
- ✔ Is its profit trend up or down?
- ✔ How much of its earnings go to pay employees?
- ✔ Is it privately or publicly owned?
- ✔ Is it a subsidiary or a division of a big company?
- ✔ How deep in debt is the company?

Ready, Aim, Fact-Find

As you begin to scope out and scoop up information for your job search, what curtains must you part?

Privately owned companies are harder to track than publicly owned companies. Local and regional companies are harder to check out than national companies. And discovering the details on a corporation's subsidiaries or divisions is more challenging than finding out about the corporation as a whole.

Ferreting out the financial and personnel scoop on small and medium-size companies — where the great majority of jobs are found — is a still greater challenge. And unpeeling the onion on start-ups is a major sleuthing gig.

Here are basic questions paired with concise answers to speed you on your way.

 Where can I find free guides and tutorials to research companies?

 The Riley Guide's *How to Research Employers* offers a collection of useful resources. Find it at `www.rileyguide.com/employer.html`.

Jobstar Central is a California library-sponsored website with organized research leads. The leads are useful almost anywhere in the United States. Find it at `http://jobstar.org/hidden/coinfo.php`.

View recruitment videos with eyes wide open

Companies are rushing to add videos picturing employees to their repertoires of recruiting tools. They often present these recruiting videos as a kind of day-in-the-life of a typical employee at ABC company. They can be very helpful when you watch for clues reflecting the people the company prefers to hire.

The videos are supposed to offer potential employees a glimpse of a company's work environment and culture. For example, a video may show employees seated in a cubicle farm. If you're an open-space type of person, you'll want to ask about the work-space assignment policy during your interview.

The workforce age mix is another inference you can draw from recruitment videos, according to Mark Mehler, a principal at CareerXroads, a recruiting technology consulting firm in Kendall Park, N.J. "Are all the people shown younger than 40? Or does a mix of age groups offer a hint that experienced professionals are encouraged to apply?" Mehler asks.

The videos offer insights on how to dress for your interview and the kind of work wardrobe you'd need in the related job. When everyone in the video is dressed in casual attire and your grooming hallmark is a business suit — or vice versa — you're probably in the wrong theater.

In an abundance of caution, you may want to watch a company's recruiting video twice. And when you see one that reminds you of an infomercial, put on your critical-thinking cap.

Remember that happy talkers are chosen to appear on the company's silver screen instead of grousers who tell ugly little secrets. When you see employees shown merely talking about their jobs rather than doing their jobs at their workstations, ask yourself why.

In fact, some of those smiling faces appearing in recruitment videos may belong to human relations professionals, says Todd Raphael, editorial chief at ERE Media (www.ere.net), the leading publisher of recruiting news. Raphael notes that a video may use an unfamiliar job title rather than a familiar version. A "sourcing manager" is actually a recruiter. "You want to hear from a person doing the job you want, not a company spokesperson," he advises.

Where can I find a variety of free information about companies?

Here's a sampling of available research that's not too hard to prospect.

- Company websites are the best place to begin. Run a Google search on the company name. Find Google at www.google.com.

- EDGAR is a government database that provides public access to corporate information. It allows you to quickly research a company's financial information and operations by reviewing documents filed on Forms 10-K and 10-Q with the Securities Exchange Commission. Find it at www.sec.gov/edgar.shtml.

- The Public Register Online (www.annualreportservice.com) is the largest free directory of online annual reports available on the web.

- Yahoo! Finance (http://finance.yahoo.com) publishes a wide variety of business information you may deem useful.

- Large public and college libraries with business and reference departments inventory a number of resources priced for institutions but free for your use. (College and university libraries typically restrict subscription database access to students, alumni, and faculty.) For example, Plunkett Research Online is a terrific resource for easy-to-understand analysis of trends, challenges, and opportunities in the most important industry sectors, from health care to InfoTech, from banking to energy.

- The social network LinkedIn (`www.linkedin.com`) allows you to find people who work at a company you're researching and ask them about it.

Q **Where do employees and others post what they really think about a company?**

A Employee review websites where past and current employees post comments about their experiences working for an organization are coming under new scrutiny. Readers speculate about what's changing the mix of reviews — negative reviews of companies as employers seem to be disappearing, leaving only positive reviews standing. Judge for yourself by browsing for "employee review websites."

Q **How can I find out about smaller companies that aren't in the databases?**

A Jack Plunkett, who heads Plunkett Research Ltd. (`www.plunkett`
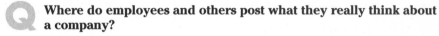
`research.com`), a leading provider of business and industry information, says that most private companies will not divulge financial information to employees or to job seekers. "However, a few very entrepreneurial firms call themselves 'open companies,' meaning that they let all employees know about financial results each month," Plunkett explains.

What about a company that's not "open"? Plunkett advises that you politely ask such questions as, *What's the source of the company's backing? Venture capital? Partners? Family-owned? Angel investors? Is the company profitable?* When the company is funded by venture capital or angel investors, the business research expert warns job seekers to beware of potential financial instability.

Here are further ways to get the goods when information isn't readily available:

- Search local business newspapers published by American City Business Journals. Find them at `www.bizjournals.com`.

- Company websites won't tell you about financial stability, but you may get clues to the company's customers and suppliers. Call and say you're doing a credit check (which is true) on the company you're investigating.

- Competitors often have a fair idea of a company's financials. Perhaps you can find someone who knows someone who knows someone.

- When you really want reassurance, go to Hoover's, Inc. (www. hoovers.com), and use its links to order a credit report on the employer. These reports, compiled by D&B or a credit bureau, aren't cheap — find out the cost before ordering. The reports can help you determine whether the company is paying its bills on time or has other problems that warn you away from accepting a job offer.

- Suppose you're dealing with a mini company, such as one with a half-dozen employees. You can't find a shred of information written anywhere about the company. After the job offer, you may ask to speak privately with one or two employees "to get a sense of the company culture." Once alone, you can try to find out what, if anything, the employer doesn't want you to know. If you're replacing someone, ask to be put in touch with your predecessor.

- Notice the furnishings as you interview. Are you looking at cement blocks and boards for bookcases? The bare minimum in decor may be a clue to a serious operating capital problem.

 How can I check out a start-up company?

 When historical data on a company doesn't exist, you can ask questions of the interviewer: *How much capital is on hand? How fast is it being spent? Is additional funding in place?*

Additionally, if you can snare a copy of the company's business plan, review it for probability of success with an accountant, investment banker, or SCORE consultant (a volunteer, free to you, of the U.S. Small Business Administration).

You also can make an informed guess about the competence of the principals of the firm by checking out the track record of the management team and financial backers. Try the free service of ZoomInfo, a people search engine. Find it at www.zoominfo.com.

Also check out the principles on LinkedIn (www.linkedin.com).

Library copies of *Standard & Poor's Industry Surveys* and *Plunkett's Industry Almanacs* are other good places to poke around.

Start-ups, hit with a massive credit crunch in recent years, are hiring about a third fewer people than usual these days. But don't count them out as places to get in on the ground floor and do very well for yourself in later years.

While no new venture is Oscar-certain, you're wise to avoid taking a part in a real-life production of *Frankenstein Meets Godzilla.*

Extra! Extra! Print resources to the rescue!

When you need to pull out all the stops in preparing for a job you really, really want, turn to print publications. Study back-issue indexes and archives to major newspapers to see what journalists were and are reporting about a prospective employer. Many libraries have back issues of *The Wall Street Journal, The New York Times, Financial Times,* and other important newspapers on microfilm. Try *BusinessWeek* and *Forbes* magazines, as well as industry-specific trade journals and newsletters.

Preparation Rocks!

As you approach important job interviews, your research is the first step toward changing your life for the better.

That's because employers consider company research a reflection of your interest and enthusiasm, intelligence, and commitment. Research shows that you're thorough, competent, and revved up to work. Every employer likes these profit-building or cost-saving traits.

And not so incidentally, finding out what you need to know about a company may encourage you to look elsewhere.

Chapter 7

Your Close-Up: Personality Tests

In This Chapter

▶ Understanding why personality tests matter

▶ Uncovering surprising facts about personality tests

▶ Doing your best with proven test tips

*T*he online world offers all kinds of unscientific ways for you to plumb your depth — from your taste in music to your choice in colors. But flip that coin to the employment world, and personality testing becomes a serious assessment tool that helps decide who gets hired and who gets promoted.

This chapter is a serious close-up on genuine, nonfake, Real Deal assessments that have become rites of passage in today's workplace.

Wendell Williams, PhD, Managing Director of ScientificSelection.com, is one of the world's leading employment-assessment authorities. Dr. Williams is my guide through the psychometric minefield of employment testing.

Personality Testing Means Business

In a nutshell, employers are trying to anticipate why you do what you do at work. That's the reason you may be required to take a *personality test* before being granted an interview or offered a job.

An *integrity test* may or may not be part of the personality assessment. Here's what each measures:

✔ Employment personality tests measure choice, preference, values, behavior, decisions, attitudes, and job-related interests.

✔ Integrity tests rate honesty, responsibility, and reliability for the job.

Test development expert Dr. Williams throws more light on the overall reason personality tests have become a favored business-assessment tool:

"Employers administer personality and integrity tests because they try to avoid making a bad hire, which means they want to know as much about a potential employee as possible."

How many companies require job candidates to take personality tests? Estimates are all over the place, currently topping out at 40 percent. Despite sketchy data, the personality-discovery star is rising. Don't be surprised if you face an online employment personality test in your not-too-distant future.

What You May Not Know about Personality Tests

To borrow from an anonymous saying, "If you can stay calm, while all around you is chaos in the pressure of a pre-employment personality test, then you probably haven't completely understood the seriousness of the situation." Personality tests, love 'em or loathe 'em, guard the gateways to your future.

A rundown of six important things to understand about your future encounters with personality tests follows.

Asking questions before the test

Although you can't blow off a request to sit for an employment test and get hired, you can ask a few questions to spread a small safety net under your candidacy. Try these feelers:

- ✔ I read about a rash of lawsuits over hyperintrusive personality tests that originally were developed to spot mental illness, such as The Minnesota Multiphasic Personality Inventory and its knock-offs. Can you tell me the name of the test I'll be taking, whether the test provider has been involved in any legal challenges of the test, and, if so, what was the outcome?

- ✔ What kind of test(s) are you asking me to take? Personality, integrity, performance, or other? What is the title of the test?

- ✔ Have you done a formal validity study to determine whether the test actually predicts job performance?

- ✔ Can I get any feedback regarding test results? How about areas I didn't do well in? At least I'll know what areas need improvement.

- ✔ Will I still be considered for the job if I don't do well on the test?

Expect to hear "no" more often than "yes" to these questions, but any one of them is worth a try. If the interviewer is dismissive, at least you'll know the kind of company you're dealing with — if you think they're tough now, wait until you're hired and the honeymoon is over.

Anyone can write a personality test, but is it validated?

Would you be surprised to learn that literally anyone can author a personality test? It's true, and virtually anyone does, from creative homemaker and college psych major, to advertising writer and company hiring manager. From their fertile minds come questions such as these:

- ✔ Do you prefer riding in a car to riding a motorcycle?
- ✔ Can a white drummer kick with a black band?
- ✔ Do you sometimes get bored, or do you always find life interesting?

Yes, anyone can write the questions, add up the answers, and declare statements about what they mean. The problem is that, without basing the items on a strong theory of performance — and doing validation research to compare test scores to job performance — the statements are virtually meaningless.

To prove valuable, psychometric tests must be *statistically validated. Valid* means the test works. Validation studies involve giving the test to hundreds of people and statistically comparing their scores to job performance. You need testing on enough people over enough time to give users confidence that the tests actually predict what the test-makers claim — that they work as advertised.

"Once a company knows what it wants to measure and has chosen a legitimate hiring test, the company studies its own employees to prove test scores are associated with job performance, turnover, training, or other essentials of a successful organization before judging the test to be validated," Dr. Williams explains.

That's why psychometrically trained professionals are assigned to identify the kinds of psychological traits that lead to the selection of an achieving, profitable workforce. Statistically supportable personality tests typically are written by experienced professionals who take courses in statistics and test design and hold doctorates in some aspect of applied psychology.

Personality test scores are self-reports. They represent how someone wants to be seen by the world. Scores on personality tests have almost no relationship to actual skills.

Finding out what a test measures

If you can discover the title of the personality test you'll be taking, you may be able to identify the traits measured by the test. In pursuing a test chase, look for test reviews published by the Buros Institute of Mental Measurements at the University of Nebraska–Lincoln, a gateway for serious and validated testing information.

Be sure to read the FAQs on the Buros website (`www.unl.edu/buros`) to learn about

- Locating tests in Buros's *Mental Measurements Yearbook,* a regularly updated reference containing test reviews. It's available to read free in many large public and university libraries.
- Accessing *Tests in Print, a* bibliography of commercially available tests in the English language.
- Using *Test Reviews Online,* a service that provides access to the same test reviews that appear in the Mental Measurement Yearbook series. You can download each test for a modest fee.

Most popular general traits

When you have no inclination or time to do a test chase, don't give up — Dr. Williams has your back. The widely quoted industrial psychologist reports university research showing that only about three general personality traits are associated with job performance:

- Conscientiousness about the job
- Ability to get along with people
- Non-neurotic

Of the Big Five personality traits (which may go by different names, depending on whom you talk to), Dr. Williams says these three traits are most commonly associated with good job performance:

- Conscientiousness
- Extroversion
- Neuroticism (low)

Expressed another way, good workers care about their work, get along with others, and are emotionally stable.

Who's most likely to use tests

High-level executives in any industry rarely are asked to undergo a personality test. Government agencies typically use their own tests and assessments.

Nonmanufacturing businesses tend to use personality tests more than do manufacturing industries. Examples of nonmanufacturing businesses include retailers, banks, utilities, insurance companies, staffing agencies, and communications corporations. Integrity tests are prevalent in jobs involving money, public safety, or merchandise — especially in entry-level positions.

Your civil rights in testing

When gauging job candidates, using personality tests that weren't specifically designed for hiring has led to lawsuits. Usually employers have been on the losing end because the tests were ruled invalid, invasive, or discriminatory.

You have the following rights when it comes to testing:

✔ You have a right not to be subjected to wanton invasion of privacy with intrusions into non-job-related areas such as your sex life, religious beliefs, and political views.

✔ You have a right to expect compliance with the Americans with Disabilities Act, which prohibits requiring medical examinations before you get a job offer.

✔ You have a right not to be subjected to a test that has a "disparate impact" on a protected class of people, such as certain racial or ethnic groups.

If you think your rights may have been violated by a personality or integrity test, research the topic online (browse for "personality test civil rights") or consult an employment lawyer.

Peeking into privacy issues

"Personality tests need to be handled like confidential medical records," observes Anne Hart, senior author of *Employment Personality Tests Decoded* (Career Press).

"Find out whether test results are given to your health insurance company along with medical information. Psychological testing, like medical exams, should not be stored in open-ended databases in your employer's human resources department," Hart adds.

What if you're not hired — how long will your records be kept at the employer's office and/or at the vendor testing company? I asked a legal expert in pre-employment testing about that issue.

"Testing companies should be willing to discuss their records and security procedures with candidates," noted eminent employment attorney Joseph Schmitt at the Halleland Lewis Nilan & Johnson firm in Minneapolis. "Reputable testing firms won't be offended if you ask about confidentiality, and should be able to detail their security procedures upon request."

But Schmitt explains that the tests legally can't be destroyed overnight: "Candidates should be aware that their records will be retained for a minimum of one year (two years in California) under federal and state regulations regarding retention of hiring records. You may wish to ask when records are destroyed, and for a confirmation that your records are deleted after the records retention period has expired."

You certainly don't want your test results whizzing around the Internet. Underscoring the serious need to protect test score privacy, reports of irreparable damage to someone's reputation surface too often. The reports are caused by accidental or malicious posting of another person's personal information online. Even if your records are online for just minutes, they can be copied and distributed around the world for employers to read. You can never be 100% certain that an online image has been killed off.

Making the Grade on Job Tests

Conventional wisdom advises that you get a good night's sleep, be truthful in all your answers, and relax and enjoy a personality test that the interviewer says is standard operating procedure.

About the kicked-back mindset, at least, conventional wisdom is wrong. Instead, consider the flower vendor who sells her basket of posies by arranging the freshest pieces on the top. If you want cash for your flowers, learn how to display your best blooms.

In the following sections, I give you tips for displaying your best blooms (traits) in a personality test, tips that I gathered from the four corners of the testing industry.

Visualize yourself fitting in

Based on your research of the company, imagine the ideal candidate. How would that paragon of virtue think? When you hit a wall with a weird question, your fallback position is to try to answer as the ideal candidate/perfect employee.

Obviously, answering as the ideal candidate/perfect employee isn't easy. You need to guess what the paragon is like. (*Hint:* Review video clips featuring employees on the company website.) How much and what kind of personality characteristics are you being compared to?

When in doubt, position yourself as a person of moderation in the mainstream of contemporary thought. Test administrators tend to grade unconventional beliefs as potential trouble.

Company managers prefer to hire people like themselves. Although similarly minded employees don't always do better, a personality kinship gives managers a warm, fuzzy feeling by knowing that everyone looks and talks alike — at least in spirit.

Watch for combination tests

Many tests are combinations of several types of test questions. Even if the first ten questions ask about your personality traits, stay alert for questions about your aptitudes (such as potential for leadership or creativity) or abilities, or your integrity (such as lying). These questions may require greater concentration to answer in ways that will help you.

Beware of absolutes

Watch out for absolutes like *always, ever,* and *never.* For example, saying you never took more than your share of things in your life may paint you as goody-two-shoes who can't be trusted. For most questions, answer in the middle of the range. But answer integrity questions with full agreement that honesty is the best policy.

Choose answers suggesting positive traits

Try to select answers that put you in the most positive light. Examples of favored characteristics include

- ✔ Achievement oriented
- ✔ Agreeable
- ✔ Assertive
- ✔ Conscientious
- ✔ Dependable
- ✔ Emotionally stable

- Good communicator
- Imaginative
- Intellectually curious
- Open to new experiences
- Optimistic
- Responsible
- Sociable
- Tolerant
- Trustworthy

Avoid answers suggesting negative traits

Stay away from answers that show you in a less-than-stellar light. Examples of negative characteristics to avoid implying include

- Acceptance of fraud, as in filing a fraudulent worker's compensation claim
- Dishonesty
- Disregard for rules
- Emotional dysfunction
- Illegal drug use
- Inability to function under stressful conditions
- Lack of self-worth
- No opposition to stirring up legal trouble
- Poor impulse control
- Predisposition for negative interpersonal relationships
- Prejudice
- Propensity for interpersonal conflicts
- Rigidity
- Tendency to be tense or suspicious
- Tendency toward time theft (sick leave abuse, tardiness)
- Thievery

Be alert to replayed questions

Some tests ask virtually the same question on page one, page three, and page ten. The test is trying to catch inconsistencies — figuring you forgot a lie you told 30 questions ago. If possible, read through the test before you start. Cosistency counts.

Anticipate integrity test questions

Integrity questioning may be part of a personality test or a separate test.

A lie scale measures the position of a test answer on a gamut from lie to truth. The scale functions as a kind of lie detector by looking for unexpected answers or unusual response patterns.

But even if you're as truthful as Honest Abe, people under pressure of testing sometimes give questionable answers. For example, if you're asked to estimate the percentage of workers who steal from their employers, make a low guess. A high guess may be interpreted to mean you think employee theft is common and, therefore, acceptable.

Special tips for salespeople

The sales representative who maintains long-term relationships selling ongoing telecom services to a company has a different kind of job than does a sales representative who sells an automobile to a customer in a one-time transaction. Personality tests for salespeople differ as well. Even so, any test administered for the sales industry probably measures such core characteristics as the following:

- Achievement orientation — a drive for learning new abilities and impatiently accomplishing goals

- Empathy — the capacity to identify or sympathize with another individual's feelings

- High energy — the force to stay with a challenge until you meet it

- Intellect — qualities showing culture and imagination

- Positive resilience — the ability to not take sales failure personally, but also to bounce back for the next sales call

- Self-control — a feeling of being in personal control of your destiny

- Self-efficacy — the belief that you can meet your expectations if you try hard enough

- Self-monitoring — the tendency to use social cues (not only your personal convictions) about what is expected

Can you game the tests?

In *The Perfect Score,* a 2004 film comedy, six teenagers conspire to break into a college SAT testing center to steal the answers. But real-life attempts to snag the right answers is no comedy.

Many retailers require that applicants score well on a personality test before investing time and money interviewing them, which is why a number of aspirants try to beat the system by bagging the right answers before testing.

A detailed 2009 article in *The Wall Street Journal* created a hornet's nest of reaction in the recruiting industry. It suggested that efforts to screen out unqualified or poor job-fit candidates during these difficult times have created such a competitive environment that job seekers have turned to cheating on work attitude and personality tests

(browse online for "Test for Dwindling Retail Jobs Spawns a Culture of Cheating").

How does the cheating happen? The *WSJ* storyline reported that some job seekers attempt to acquire test-taking savvy by applying to several retailers known to use the same test. Others use surrogate test takers. Still others seek out online answer keys (browse for "Answers to the Unicru personality test").

Reactions to the idea of gaming the tests is a case of where you stand depending upon where you sit. Test producers insist that gaming can't be done, that it's dishonest, and that it's a mistake leading to a job you won't like. But apparently their rationale isn't stopping desperate job seekers from trying anything to gain an interview.

Most integrity questions are fashioned for entry-level or midlevel workers who have access to merchandise or trade secrets, or for financial workers who handle money.

Take practice personality tests

Ready yourself for employment personality tests by working through a few practice questions and tests. Review free practice tests on www.outofservice.com and other websites. Find the others by browsing online for "employment personality tests."

Free online tests are for educational purposes only and are not intended to be the Real Deal. Genuine employment personality tests and their answer keys are kept under lock and key.

Sample Personality Questions

Questions on all types of tests may require uncomfortable yes/no answers. (Following the questions, I interpret their meaning in parentheses.) Here are some examples:

✔ *Do you believe that children or spouses are far more important than anything?*

(Will your family life interfere with your job?)

✔ *Do you exercise regularly?*

(Are you likely to be a high risk for health insurance?)

✔ *I would like to be a florist.*

(Are your interests suited to this field?)

✔ *I still maintain close contact with friends from high school.*

(Do you get along with people for long periods of time?)

✔ *I have thought of trying to get even with someone who hurt me.*

(Are you vindictive, or can you put hurts behind you?)

Some questions require specific answers rather than *yes* or *no:*

✔ *How often do you make your bed?*

(Do you clean up after yourself? Are you obsessive about it?)

✔ *On average, how often during the week do you go to parties?*

(Will you frequently come to work hung over?)

✔ *Describe how you see work.*

(Do you see work as mandatory or as a way to obtain rewards?)

Concerned That You Didn't Do Well?

The stark truth is that you can't really do much about a test score when you mess up. Busy employers are focused on finding the right people to hire, not on helping those who are among the unchosen.

"Do-overs are rare," explains Dr. Williams. "Regardless of what you say or do, most hiring managers have a die-hard perception of their favorite personality profiles. If you don't fit their molds, you seldom get a second chance. In the final analysis, testing is a roll of the dice for the unwary and quicksand for the uneducated."

Keep On Keeping On

When you've taken a personality test but you weren't invited to an interview, soldier on to your next opportunity. The way to win employment is to keep applying for more jobs.

And remember the words of our old friend Anonymous: "If at first you do succeed, try to hide your astonishment."

Chapter 8

Showing You the Money

. . . .

In This Chapter

▶ Recognizing sales pitches for you to accept less cash

▶ Finding out what the position is worth

▶ Banishing premature money talk

▶ Avoiding tipping your hand in a negotiation

▶ Gracefully addressing your less-than-stellar salary history

▶ Scripting the best deals for your negotiation

. . . .

*I*magine this uncomfortable scenario: After accepting and starting a new job, you discover that you're paid 20 percent under market and that, instead of climbing what an enthusiastic recruiter called a stairway to the stars, you're on a road to nowhere.

Fiascos like this can happen when you fall hook, line, and sinker for a recruitment pitch that deflects a position's cheapo cash compensation. The pitch distracts you by spotlighting nonmonetary aspects of the position — growth opportunity, the latest technology, fabulous coworkers, super company — you name it.

Although this chapter shows you how to deal with undermarket offers in general, there are a few justifiable exceptions when you will and should seriously consider making cash secondary to opportunity or lifestyle in a job you accept. A few examples:

✔ You're a new graduate or career changer with scant experience, and you need good breaks and helping hands in a nourishing environment.

✔ You're taking a lower rung on a ladder that positions you to compete for a higher rung.

✔ You're a parent who needs home time with the kids.

Special concerns aside, most of the time thee and me are zeroed in on the legal tender we want to earn for the rent of our brains and labor, to maximize cold cash and monetary-based employee benefits. We begin our pursuit for fair compensation through salary negotiations with recruiters.

Recruiters are employers' personal shoppers, tasked with going into the marketplace and bringing back the best-qualified candidates for the thriftiest prices. In this chapter, I list the types of recruiters you're likely to encounter, the siren songs they may sing to snag the best bargains, and the ways you can get the best employment deal for yourself.

Decoding Recruiters and Their Talking Points

Recruiters are sales professionals, not your new best friends. This is true when

✔ The recruiter (also known as a headhunter) is an external recruiter (a third-party recruiter or independent recruiter).

✔ An external recruiter is employed as a retained recruiter on an ongoing basis and is paid a set fee — much like a retained lawyer or accountant.

✔ An external recruiter is employed on a transaction basis as a contingency recruiter and is paid only when a submitted candidate is hired.

✔ The recruiter is an internal recruiter (that is, a company recruiter), who is staffed in a company's human resources department and paid a salary.

All recruiters are engaged by employers to find people for jobs — not jobs for people. And they do it by being superb sales professionals.

Recruiters who deem you qualified for a position pass you up to a hiring decision maker, often the individual to whom you would report.

How can you tell when you're being recruited with a song-and-dance to divert your attention from a chintzy salary? Look out for yourself by discovering the insider secrets straight ahead.

Tactics meant to sell low offers

When a company gives a recruiter a limited compensation budget to offer candidates, the recruiter's job and livelihood depend upon convincing you, a qualified candidate, to take the "downpay" job offer by pointing out collateral benefits the job may or may not truly offer.

It's a tough sell — so tough that employment consultants write industry articles for recruiters advising them on how to increase their offer acceptance rate, when, in the words of one prominent consultant, "your company pays crummy wages."

The consultants' suggestions include the following sales techniques and talking points:

- ✔ Offer "exploding bonuses" that shrink in amount the longer you take to consider the offer. (Don't give candidates too long to think about accepting a job that pays under market.)

- ✔ For a management job, invite comradeship with the company CEO, who calls asking you to accept the offer, commenting, "You and I can build this company together." In a variation, a potential coworker calls, urging you, "Join the team — it's great." (This, too, refocuses your attention from legal tender.)

- ✔ Make a great "higher-calling" offer. This tactic includes such rewards as a title, a telecommuting opportunity, training options, a socially responsible and environmentally friendly employer, the chance to work with new technology, and the opportunity to make a difference in people's lives rather than "just make money."

- ✔ Reframe the discussion by speaking less of cash compensation and benefits and more of job stretch and growth opportunity.

  Job stretch describes an environment in which you show what you can do on a larger stage — heftier operating budget, bigger challenges, and supervision of more employees. In baseball, a job-stretch move is from the minors to the majors.

  Growth opportunity is the lure of future raises, promotions, and company growth. In entertainment, a growth opportunity move could be from stunt double to featured player.

In a funny kind of arithmetic, a recruiter may speak the language of "an overall increase of 30 percent" if you take the offered position. Here's a typical breakdown of what the recruiter may really mean by that 30-percent figure: perhaps 15 percent for stretch in the job, plus likely long-term growth of 10 percent and 5 percent for a cash compensation boost over your last job. Do the arithmetic. And do due diligence before you buy that reasoning.

You're not yet finished with the give-and-take of sophisticated salary negotiation. The recruiter has plenty of arguments in reserve, as the next section reveals.

Recruiter comebacks when you stick up for yourself

When you're hot on the track of treasure and refuse to budge from your "show me the money" stance ("If this is such a great job opportunity, I need greater money."), experienced recruiters may balk. They, who practically live in the salary negotiation space that you infrequently visit, are famous for classic comebacks. Here are five golden oldies with suggestions for countering their rejoinders.

✔ *Don't make the mistake of overvaluing compensation and undervaluing opportunity.* (I appreciate your calling that important point to my attention, and I'll bear it in mind.)

✔ *If I succeed in getting the cash compensation increased, the company will probably want me to produce other candidates with more experience.* (I hope not. But you have a fiduciary responsibility to your client to produce the best candidate for a fair price — and I'm that person, hands down.)

✔ *We're looking at other candidates who don't share the level of expectations you express. Why should we consider raising the bar so high in your case?* (I have the same level of performance expectations for the work I produce. I'm sure the other candidates know what they're worth better than I do. Are you looking for an outstanding or a mediocre hire? If it's talent you want, you should choose me because of my proven record in ___.)

✔ *Prove your ability. Do a great job and you could get a sizeable raise next year.* (I appreciate that and I admire your line of thinking about rewarding performance, provided promises for the future build on a fair market rate going in. I've done a lot of salary research and believe that a starting salary of $___ would be attractive to me because my performance with previous employers has been exceptional. Do you think your client can confirm your progressive thinking about a future raise based on a starting salary of $___ and include that promise in the offer letter?)

✔ *If I can get the cash increased, will you sign an iron-clad guarantee to take the position with no further haggling?* (Yes, I am very interested in this position, but we need to clarify figures. How much of a cash increase and what benefits are included?)

The lesson: To avoid walking away wishing you'd come up with a better answer to recruiter comebacks than you did, plan your responses ahead.

New thinking for new times

Perhaps the hour has come for a rethinking of conventional wisdom extolling job seekers to take the long view. The 21st-century rate of company upheavals, mergers, downsizings, and other job-busters may mean that you won't be around long enough to fully benefit from job stretch and growth opportunity.

Whether you choose to take the money and run or to put your faith in blue-sky projections of a rosy future, invest the necessary time learning the ropes of salary negotiation, to avoid being snookered on future offers.

A first step toward being shown the money is discovering what the market will pay someone with your qualifications. The next section, "Discovering Market Pay Rates," shows you how to find out.

Discovering Market Pay Rates

Knowing your market value — the going rate for people in your industry with skills and a job description similar to yours — is the centerpiece for negotiating the compensation you deserve.

Finding salary information online

Discovering the market rate for the kind of work you do has never been easier than it is today. Among popular websites offering free salary survey information to job seekers are Salary.com (www.salary.com) and Payscale (www.payscale.com).

Salary.com also offers a modestly priced custom report for your specific situation. Why would you want to pay for something you can get for free?

Another very useful free resource is the job search engine Indeed.com (www.indeed.com), which reports actual salary ranges currently posted on job boards.

Generalized averages produced by online salary calculators aren't always spot-on for specific companies and jobs.

Be certain to benchmark the job you're applying for by *job content* — not just by job title. The same job title can mean different things to different people in different companies.

Handling salary boxes in online applications

Recently I was asked for a practical way to handle the *salary requirement* and *salary history* (two different things) questions when either or both are embedded as required fields in an online application. B.I. (before Internet), you could write "Negotiable" for salary expectation, to keep from under- or overpricing yourself. But most online applications won't accept "Negotiable" (or "Open" or "Will discuss in an interview") for expected salary as a viable answer, so that tactic is out history's window. What now?

Jack Chapman (www.salarynegotiations.com) rides to the rescue. Salary consultant and workshop leader, Chapman is the author of the best-selling guide *Negotiating Your Salary: How to Make $1,000 a Minute* (Mount Vernon Press, 2011), my favorite book in the genre. Here's what Chapman told me about working those windows:

> *Your self-interest is best served by putting whatever number in the salary-requirement box that you think won't get you screened out. The employer is essentially asking, "Can we afford you?" Since you won't require anything other than a competitive salary, your answer, by putting in a competitive number, is "Yes, you can afford me."*

> *This strategy works nicely when the box is titled "Salary Requirements" or "Expected Salary," but requires an additional step if it is labeled "Current Salary." Once you're in the interview, you'll need to explain that you interpreted "Current Salary" to mean "Current Salary Requirements," and if they want a "Salary History," you'll be glad to provide it later as needed.*

Background on the bucks

WorldatWork (www.worldatwork.org), an international association of human resource practitioners, is a recognized authority on compensation matters. Here's a selected glossary of WorldatWork terminology:

Cash Compensation

Pay provided by an employer to an employee for services rendered (time, effort, and skill). Compensation comprises four core elements:

✔ **Fixed pay:** Also known as "base pay," fixed pay is nondiscretionary compensation that doesn't vary according to performance or results achieved.

✔ **Variable pay:** Also known as "pay at risk," variable pay changes directly with the level of performance or results achieved. It's a one-time payment that must be re-established and re-earned each performance period.

✔ **Short-term incentive pay:** A form of variable pay, short-term incentive pay is designed to focus and reward performance over a period of one year or less.

✔ **Long-term incentive pay:** A form of variable pay, long-term incentive pay is designed to focus and reward performance over a period longer than one year. Typical forms include stock options, restricted stock, performance shares, performance units, and cash.

Benefits

Programs an employer uses to supplement the cash compensation that employees receive. Some are legally mandated, such as social security and workers' compensation. Others are awarded at the discretion of the employer, such as health and life insurance, vacations, holidays, personal days, tuition assistance, automobiles, and professional group and club memberships.

Who wins, who loses on a lowball offer

When you're working with a contingency recruiter who encourages you to take less than the going rate for a job, the recruiter may have your best interests at heart. Or the recruiter may just want to close the job order quickly.

A contingency recruiter's fee is based on your first-year earnings. Follow this admittedly over-simplified example: Say the recruiter is to be paid 25 percent of the job's first-year salary. If the job's market rate is $100,000, the recruiter

would earn a $25,000 fee. But when the job's budget figure is under market — say, only $90,000 — the recruiter takes a hit of $2,500, compared to your loss of $10,000.

From the contingency recruiter's viewpoint, most of a loaf is better than none. And the recruiter hopes for future assignments from the employer that can more than compensate for losing relatively few dollars on a single transaction.

Negotiating in the Moment

After all your salary prep, the time has arrived to reap your rewards: You're in the interview room, and the back-and-forth begins.

But just when the interview is starting to fly, *bam!* — the interviewer lets go with a dangerous question that can severely clip your wings: *How much money are you looking for?* Should you name your price right then and there? Not if you can help it.

A salary request that's too low devalues your abilities; a salary request that's too high looks like you're too big for the company budget. Both bids leave you out of luck. Be aware that some employers have already budgeted for the position, and the first offer is their best offer. They ask what you want merely to confirm that the money's enough to interest you in the job.

Your compensation should be based on the value of the job someone wants to pay you to do, not on the value of the job someone has paid you to do in the past.

Giving and taking at the right times

Sure, you have a pretty good idea going in about the remuneration you're shooting for, but you may discover wildcards while you're in the interview. You knew, for instance, that the job requires travel, and you figured maybe

25 percent of your time would be spent on the road, but now the interviewer reveals the true travel requirement — 75 percent. Would that revelation cause you to rethink the money or reevaluate whether you should accept the job at any salary?

Moreover, if you have to talk salary too early in the interviewing process, a decision maker may not yet be sufficiently smitten with you to make the company's best offer.

In the previous edition of this book, I posed a key question for salary negotiation: What is the single best thing you can do to receive a higher pay offer when you're interviewing for a job? My answer:

Delay discussing salary until you're offered (or nearly offered) a specific position.

Until you have the offer, the employer holds all the weight. Once you have the offer, the scales shift. You have something the employer wants, and you become equals negotiating a business proposition. From outsider, you have become poised to become the newest insider — a good place to be.

Learning to deflect salary questions until the timing shifts to your advantage can greatly influence the amount of money that you take from the bargaining table.

But although the advice to sit tight until the timing is right is still on the mark, doing so is easier said than done these days, says salary negotiation pro Jack Chapman. He explains:

In the l980s, it was easy to postpone the salary talk. That has changed over the years. Employers are more demanding or inquisitive or something. Yet the principle is the same — postpone when and if you can.

But when you're pressured to talk money sooner rather than later, Chapman warns that digging in your heels and flat-out refusing to comply is a mistake. By being hard-nosed, you set up a power struggle that you can't win. You'll be seen as obstinate and hard to work with. A power struggle can cost you the job.

Nor should you move to the other extreme, in which you meekly cave in, tell all, and let it go at that. Just as a dogmatic refusal earns you a label of being too strong, a roll-over-and-scratch-my-belly response may make you seem too weak.

Moreover, when you're too low or too high for the company's budget, you hand the employer's interviewing screener information to judge you by your price, not by your whole package of qualifications. Even in the final interview round, premature dollars talk may lead a decision maker to see you as too expensive without your being given an opportunity to justify your worth and negotiate.

Sometimes you can just ask

To make certain your salary research is on target, network in professional groups. At association meetings, speak to people in a position to hire you. Work the conversation around to asking a question: "What can someone with my skill set expect to earn in your organization?"

Fortunately, there's a better way to connect when you're giving away your bargaining leverage too soon: Get a quid pro quo. I think of this kind of fair exchange as Chapman's rule:

> *When you comply with an early request for your salary numbers, get markers in return. Something for something.*

What markers do you want as IOUs for your upfront compliance? You want agreement that your early money talk won't screen you out of further interview opportunities. And you want agreement that your salary discussion will focus on the market value of the position and not on your salary history.

To side-step the negative consequences of early revelation as much as possible, you want fair consideration. Here are Chapman's illustrations of what you can say to get fair consideration in three interviewing situations (Find out about the differences between screening and selection interviews in Chapter 5.):

 ✔ **Phone screening:** *Before I give you all that information, can I ask a question? (Yes.) I don't know who you'll hire, but from what I've seen so far, you should definitely at least interview me. If I'm forthright about all my compensation factors, can I be assured of an interview?*

 ✔ **Interview screening:** *Before I give you all that information, can I ask a question? (Yes.) I don't know who you'll hire, but from what I've seen so far, I would definitely like to participate in the second round of interviews. If I'm forthright about all my compensation factors, can I be assured of that?*

 ✔ **Selection interviewing:** *Before I give you all that information, can I ask a question? (Yes.) I'm a little concerned that we could lose a perfectly good match over salary expectations. And I'm confident that you'll pay a competitive salary — which is all I need. Can you first give me your rough range, your ballpark compensation, and I'll be candid and tell you how that compares?*

If you're too high or too low, Chapman's approach gives you the opportunity to address the discrepancy in the interview process instead of having the employer decide behind closed doors with no input from you.

Understanding why salary questions come early

Some interviewers know exactly what they're doing by front-loading the salary question; others may just be feeling their way through the process. The salary question comes up quickly when the interviewer

> ✔ Is trying to instantly determine your professional level, or is slyly probing to see whether you'll be happy with the low side of an offer.

> ✔ Wants to test the market. The interviewer may not even have an idea of the position's market value and is shopping candidates to simplify budgeting.

> ✔ Is open to paying whatever is necessary to get the right person and just wants to know what he's in for.

Whatever the interviewer's motivation for prying a salary disclosure from you, without a job offer, salary disclosures put too much power in the employer's hands. That point was confirmed to me by an HR executive (who, understandably, wishes to remain anonymous): "While I may request salary histories from others, I never comply with that demand when I'm in the job market. Why not? I know a guillotine when I see one — I design them."

So what should you do when the salary question comes at you too soon? What can you gracefully say to hold off a precipitate discussion? The following section, "Stalling Money Talk with Smart Replies" gives you a number of script lines to use in response to premature questions about your salary expectations. They're followed by lines useful in sidestepping a salary history so low that interviewers will wonder why — if you're such a standout candidate — you've been so grossly underpaid in the past.

Tell recruiters your salary history

Should you ever disclose your salary history or salary expectations before a job offer? Yes. Tell all when you're asked by third-party employment specialists — chiefly, executive recruiters and employment consultants who find people for jobs.

These professionals are specialists at their work and are paid for their time, on either a retained or contingency basis. They get paid to find good talent, and so they won't let salary deter them from presenting you when your skills are a match for a job opening. Recruiters are far too busy with the matchmaking task to waste time with you if you make their work difficult. Time is money.

Stalling Money Talk with Smart Replies

Don't let a frog clog your throat when an interviewer presses for the salary discussion before you've established your value. Instead, answer along the following lines:

I'm sure that money won't be a problem after I'm able to show you how my qualifications can work to your advantage because they closely match your requirements.

My salary requirements are open to discussion. Your company has a reputation of being fair with employees, and I trust you would do the same in my case. I don't think salary will be a problem if I'm the right person for the job.

I'm aware of the general range for my kind of work, but I'd feel better talking about pay once we've established what specific performance goals the job calls for.

I'd be kidding if I said money isn't important to me — sure, it is! But the job itself and the work environment are also very important to me. I wonder if we can hold the pay issue for a bit?

I'm a great believer in matching pay with performance, so I can't speak with any certainty about the kind of money I'm looking for until I know more about what you need.

Money is not my only priority; I'd really like to discuss my contributions to the company first — if that's okay with you.

I can't answer that question until I know more about this job.

The amount of my starting compensation is not as much of an issue to me as how satisfying my filling the position will be for both of us. Can we talk more about what the position entails?

Before we get into the compensation issue, can you tell me more about the kind of skills and the type of individual you're looking for to help you reach your goals? What do you expect the person you hire to accomplish within the first three months?

All I need is fair market value for the job's demands, which I'm sure you'll pay, so is it okay if we talk about the details of the job first?

As far as I can tell, the position seems like a perfect fit for me — tit for tat on your requirements and my qualifications. So as long as you pay in the industry ballpark, I'm sure that we won't have a problem coming up with a figure we're both happy with.

Before we can come to an agreement, I need to know more about your strategy for compensation, as well as confirm my understanding of the results you're looking for. Can we hold that question for a bit?

Since pay includes so many possibilities for compensation, I'd like to first know more about your compensation plan overall and how it relates to the position.

I'm sure that you have a fair salary structure, and if I'm the best candidate for the position, we can work something out that we'll all like.

I'm not used to talking money before a job offer; are you making me an offer?

My requirement is market within the area — shouldn't be a problem. Can we put that off to the side until we decide if there's any need to go further down the money road?

I will consider any reasonable offer. Should we talk about it after we've wrapped up the details of the job, and I've been able to show you what I bring to your company?

I'm paid roughly the market value of a (occupational title) with (number of years') experience and the ability to (manage, or do something special). If you're competitive with the market, there won't be a problem with salary.

Downplaying a Low Salary History

You know that disclosing an undermarket salary history can jeopardize your negotiating power. Try these scripts to lessen the impact of having worked for too little money:

I'm uncertain how my salary history will help you, because salaries are affected by geography, benefits packages, and company priorities. Maybe I'm wrong, but it seems to me that the going market value for the position will be more useful. According to my research, that's a range of $X to $Y.

A biting-the-bullet answer: *My salary history won't bring us to any conclusive figures. I've been working under market value, and that's one more reason I want to make a change. This job seems perfect for me. I wonder whether we could price the position on the basis of its worth to you?*

I don't feel comfortable limiting the discussion to my salary history because a large portion of my compensation has been in variable and indirect pay. I've received bonuses regularly based on my performance. What I think you're really asking is how I plan to do the job you need done — can we talk about that?

If we discuss my salary history, can I say up front that I view this position as a new challenge that will require higher performance than my last? I'd like to think I'm worth more to you than to previous employers.

To get the best return on your negotiation when you've been working for less than market value, repeat after me: *Focus on my worth, not on my past. Focus on my worth, not on my past. Focus on my worth, not on my past.* Get it? Got it? Good!

Considering More Factors That Affect Job Pay

In addition to the timing of the offer, the size of the company influences how high the interviewer will bid for you. Although large companies typically pay more, small companies without formal pay structures are easier to negotiate with than corporate titans.

But even at huge companies where pay scales are cut and dried, your potential boss may have the latitude to cut you a better deal. In fact, some interviewers see your negotiation attempts at improving your compensation as a desirable trait — yet another indicator that they've made the right choice. Their reasoning: *If you can look after your own best interests, you can look after ours.*

Other factors identified by negotiation authority Jack Chapman that influence the size of pay offers include the following:

- ✔ **Supply and demand:** In employee-driven markets, salary offers tend to rise; in employer-driven markets, salary offers don't rise and may even fall.

- ✔ **Special skills:** Skills in short supply may merit premium pay.

- ✔ **Urgency:** A company losing revenue because a job goes unfilled may offer higher pay.

- ✔ **Recruiting fatigue:** A company weary of failure in filling a position may ease salary limits.

- ✔ **Salary compression:** Concern that paying you a higher wage may lead to revolt by current employees can cause a company to stick rigidly to a certain salary.

Getting Your Worth's Money

Oh, happy day. Your interviewer looks you straight in the eye and says, "We'd like you to join our team; I'm offering you a job, but before we go any further, we should talk about how much you'd like to be paid." The moment of truth has arrived. You've got the offer. No more dodging the money issue.

To nab the best offers, follow the guidelines in the sections that follow.

Find a home in the range

The market rate that big companies typically pay for a job is often stated in a range with a minimum, midpoint, and maximum salary. Smaller companies may not operate on such a formal spectrum.

Negotiating doctrine has long insisted that he who goes first in a price negotiation loses. To follow classic counsel, when you're offered (or virtually offered) a job and are asked to name your price, bounce the ball back into the interviewer's court: *Can I ask you to take the lead on this question — can you tell me your range for this position?* (If you did your homework, you already know the range. You're merely asking for confirmation.)

Most often the interviewer who doesn't mind tossing the first figure on the table will respond with a straightforward answer. But anecdotes abound in recruiting circles about interviewers who try to save the company a few dollars by purposely misrepresenting the midpoint to be the maximum salary. For example, suppose you're applying for a job that through research you've learned is budgeted at between $50,000 and $60,000. To your surprise, the interviewer claims that $55,000 is the maximum wage. And you know it's really the midpoint. Hmmm.

Polite probing is one way to respond: *I'm not sure I heard you correctly, or perhaps my research is wrong. Did you say that $55,000 (midpoint figure) is the high end of the range for this position? I thought it was $60,000, which fits in my range.*

But when the interviewer bounces the ball right back into your court and you have to go first or look like a sock puppet, express your salary requirements in a range based on the going rate for the job: *I'd be expecting salary in the range of ($58,000 to $65,000). I think that's a range we can work with, don't you?*

Citing a range is good because it gives you haggling room and shows that you're economically aware.

Not sure where you realistically should land in the range? Match your request to your experience level. The following guidelines show you how:

- Don't ask for bottom of the range unless you're a rookie. Even then, if you've worked while in school, ask for a two-striped corporal's pay rather than a one-striped private's. You're positioning yourself as a top rookie candidate.

- A conservative school of thought recommends that experienced people ask for a pay point just above midrange — not only to show that you're above average, but also that you understand the need to leave room for raises.

- Highly qualified candidates head toward the top of the company's projected range where they belong.

Plot your salary history carefully

Bear in mind that salary is a cash figure; total compensation includes benefits and such variable pay as potential annual bonuses, stock options, and expected merit raises. Example: *Last year I earned $42,000 to $45,000 compensation, based on a salary of $30,000.* (Review the sidebar titled "Background on the bucks," earlier in this chapter.)

When your salary history ranks you at the top or above the range of market value, you can afford to discuss that history verbatim.

When your history is less impressive, be less specific. State your figures in wide ranges so that you're more likely to stay in the game for positions for which you're qualified. Include figures slightly above and below the market value to cover all your bases. Usually this approach requires bundling your income figures for multiple years: *For the past three years, I have earned total annual compensation ranging from $95,000 to $125,000 for my work in this field.*

Some job seekers feel they should inflate their salary histories. That's a risky idea — the odds of discovery are stacked in the employer's favor.

Instead of misrepresenting your history to try to improve your lot in salary negotiations, try the following:

- Show compensation modules. List base pay and variable pay in one figure; give another figure for benefits; then add the figures together for the total compensation package.

- At executive levels, list compensation items line by line.

You may be asked to back up your salary claims. Decide in advance what you will do if your interviewer asks you for tax forms or pay stubs. The request isn't illegal, but you should anticipate whether you will comply.

Some job seekers adamantly refuse to supply a salary history and give a middle-finger salute to requests for one. They look at their pay records as a supreme privacy issue and may feel that they're grossly underpaid or wouldn't be looking for another job. As one job seeker anonymously commented online: "I don't want to work for a company that demands to know my salary. I want to work for a company that wants me and will do whatever it takes to get me." I applaud that sentiment but know that a dogged flat refusal is unlikely to produce the most invitations to audition.

Stonewalled? Try to upgrade the job

When you've established what the position entails and you're told you've received the best offer and that the job isn't worth more, try to make the position more important in the scheme of things.

- ✔ Point out that the job requires more than the standard duties suggested by the job title — that the job's content fits into a job description that merits a higher pay bracket. Clarify how you plan to minimize company costs through your performance. Explain how you'll pay for yourself. By using this tactic, you more firmly establish your worth to the company and justify your performance-based reason for asking a higher price.

- ✔ Beef up the job. I once became one of the highest-paid managers in an organization by combining two positions and creating a new job title. An employer may be interested in considering a "two-for-one" who is paid a "one-and-a-half" salary.

Even if you don't succeed in your upgrade move, you'll have put your new boss on notice that you're ready to see the money.

Use dramatic silence

What should you do when the interviewer offers you a salary on a lower level of the salary range for the position? Two words: Keep quiet!

As the interviewer finishes the offer and waits for your reply, let the interviewer wait for enough time to notice your silence. Everyone has trouble outwaiting 30 seconds of silence. Look at the floor. Keep your face glum.

Finding web-based negotiation help

Continue learning all you can about the ins and outs of getting employers to show you the money. Here are three suggestions:

✔ Jack Chapman's website, Salary Negotiations (www.salary negotiations.com).

✔ Jack Chapman's Webinar Schedule on Lucrative Careers Inc. (www.lucrativecareersinc.com).

Click "Special Workshops of the Month" and choose from a list of excellent free hour-long webinars, including a don't-miss presentation on salary negotiations."

✔ Online salary calculators noted earlier in this chapter under the headline "Finding salary information online" provide a number of responsible how-to articles.

These moments of nonverbal communication show your dissatisfaction with the offer, without a word to incriminate you as overly hungry for money. The interviewer may feel compelled by this uncomfortable silence to improve the offer — or at least open a dialogue in which you can campaign for other kinds of rewards.

Don't try this technique on video interviews; see Chapter 3 to find out how to handle these unique interview situations.

Turn to words of last resort

When it seems as though the right numbers just aren't on your radar, you have little to lose by trying a straightforward response:

> *It pains me to say this. While I'm very attracted to what we've been discussing, the figure you named is just not an incentive for me to join your group. The good news is that we're both interested, so let's keep talking. What do you think?*

No flexibility? Make creative suggestions

In negotiating with a small company, you're less likely to encounter fixed pay policies, permitting you to get creative about your compensation package. If a small company can't afford you on a cash basis, what else do you want?

How's your imagination?

In the iconic movie *Star Wars,* do you remember the part where Han Solo (Harrison Ford) asks Luke Skywalker (Mark Hamill) how much the reward would be to rescue rich Princess Leia (Carrie Fisher)? Luke tells him it would be more wealth than he could imagine. Han's knockout answer: "I don't know, I can imagine quite a bit!"

You have a wide range of options for sweetening an offer. Ask for some combination of the following:

- Additional paid vacations
- A company car
- Dental plan
- An early salary review
- An expense account
- Extra-generous mileage reimbursement
- Parking privileges
- Recreational or daycare facilities
- Stock options
- Tuition reimbursement

If you're negotiating for a job that pays below $30,000 and you know the company's salary cap can't be raised right now, try to get a shorter work week or flexible work hours, and take a second job to keep a roof over your head. If your spouse can cover you with health benefits, maybe you can trade health insurance for cash.

Using the Magic of Market Value

You researched the fair market value of your work before negotiating a price. Slip those exact words into the discussion whenever you can — *fair* and *market value* are terms that people like. Remember, too, that you can always come down on your price — but coming up is almost impossible after you name a low figure.

Most of us want to get the most we can in return for the parts of our lives that we sell. Negotiating pay with skill and savvy can mean that you gain hundreds of thousands of extra dollars throughout your career.

Chapter 9

Costuming Yourself for a Starring Role

The clothes on your back are the tip-off to the line of work you're in. Any observer over the age of 5 knows that Lady Gaga is an entertainer, not a firefighter or a police officer.

Sports team members wear their own color-coded costumes, physicians favor white coats, priests don clerical clothing. Bankers dress to impress in hand-tailored dress suits, and hazmat technicians dress to survive in chemical coveralls.

When you want to launch your career — or take it up a notch, or pull it back from the edge — you need the right "costume" for your job interviews. You want your clothes, accessories, and grooming to make a smash-hit first impression because first impressions strongly impact the entire interview.

This chapter details how to impress the hiring squad by selecting interviewing attire that boosts your confidence. When you look good, you feel great — and you act better.

You Are What You Wear

"Send a message through your clothing and be aware of the details," is solid advice from international business dress expert Barbara Pachter, who lectures, consults, and writes on the topic.

So what are the wrong messages to send? Pachter (www.pachter.com) cuts to the chase, naming eight succinct knock-out punches you don't want your costume to deliver at job interviews:

- ✔ **Wearing clothes that are too big:** You'll look like a little kid in your big brother or sister's clothing! Your clothing needs to fit.

- ✔ **Wearing skirts that are too short:** A short skirt draws attention to legs. Is that where you want people to look?

- ✔ **Showing cleavage:** Sexy isn't a corporate look. Low-cut tops that expose cleavage draw attention to this body part and are not appropriate in the office.

- ✔ **Wearing short socks:** Socks that fall down expose skin and hairy legs when men sit or cross their legs.

- ✔ **Using color to draw attention to your clothing:** Do you want to be remembered for what you said or what you wore? A man wearing bright green slacks, which are not typical corporate clothing, would probably be labeled as "the man in green pants."

- ✔ **Wearing clothing with inappropriate messaging or design:** A candidate wearing a shirt with small teddy bears won't get the job — his interviewers will just be talking about his shirt.

- ✔ **Forgetting about your shoes:** People notice shoes. Your shoes must be clean, polished, and in good condition.

- ✔ **Ignoring your grooming:** Your clothes need to be clean and pressed. No safety pins for buttons. No holes. No frays. No chipped nail polish. No nose hairs. They become distractions that lead to no job offer.

Starting Well to End Well

You set the stage for the *halo effect* when you make your appearance appropriate for the job you seek. That is, when the interviewer likes you right away, the interviewer may assume that if you excel in one area (your image), you excel in others. Some potential employers make a subconscious hiring decision within seconds of meeting a candidate and spend the rest of the interview validating their initial impression. With these stakes in mind, be sure your appearance is a real curtain raiser.

Minding the Three Commandments of Style

By choosing appropriate costuming for the job, you signal employers that you respect their company's culture and that you care enough to expend the effort to make the right impression.

Begin your mastery of interviewing impressions with these three key principals of costuming yourself in the right team uniform.

Dress to fit the job and the job's culture

Social DNA draws people to others who are like them. When extending a warm welcome to a newcomer, you pay compliments that communicate the message "You're one of us."

Companies and organizations are made of people working as a group to accomplish common goals. An anthropologist may think of such a group as a kind of workplace tribe.

When your choice of clothing or your grooming keeps you from looking as though you're a member of the tribe, you create an image of an outsider, perhaps causing the interviewer to perceive you as "not one of us." You must make the effort to look as though you absolutely belong on the company's tribal land.

How can you find out about the company's dress code and grooming conventions? You have several options:

- ✔ Visit the company's website and search for videos of employees. *Pay attention to how employees dress at the level of position you seek — clerk, manager, or executive.*

- ✔ Check for beards, mustaches, and long, loose hair. Notice whether the men are wearing sport jackets or suits, or simply shirts with or without a tie. Observe whether the women are in pants or skirts.

- ✔ Call the human resources office and ask about the company's dress code.

- ✔ Use your personal network — or an online social network — to find an employee whom you can quiz.

- ✔ Loiter near the workplace and observe employees coming and going.

Correctly interpreting the company dress code is the Number One Commandment to follow in dressing for job interviews.

Think of interviewing attire as a costume

As I emphasize repeatedly in this chapter, interview attire is a work-related costume. With a few exceptions, which I touch on later in this chapter under "Selecting creative fashion," the job interview is not an outlet for flaming self-expression.

(A rookie job seeker once debated this point with me, insisting on her right to wear whatever she chose to wear to an interview: "My personal style and how I look is my business," she petulantly insisted. "True," I agreed, "and the person an interviewer chooses to hire is the interviewer's business.")

When you're not sure whether your interview wardrobe borders on bizarre or is more appropriate for after-hours wear, apply this litmus test:

> *Would my favorite film director cast me as a person portraying XYZ employee if I auditioned for the part wearing this get-up?*

By wearing an interview-appropriate costume, you're not selling out your authentic self; you're moving on. And if fortune and preparation smile, you're moving on to a better place: making the short list of candidates and then being hired.

"Look the part, and the part plays itself"

The old theater adage in the headline is the Number Three Commandment in constructing your interview image, says Jack D. Stewart of Abilene, Texas.

A retired recruiter, Stewart once accepted a recruiting search for an industrial sales rep. The job order came from a new client. Stewart's firm began referring quality candidates, recommending to the candidates that they dress conservatively for their interviews, meaning business suits, well-pressed shirts, and silk ties.

Six interviews with different individuals brought the same puzzling response from the new client: "Each candidate was basically qualified, but not what we're looking for."

Stewart's firm had a policy of reevaluating a client's assignment when six candidates were referred and none received a job offer. A recruiter was sent to the client's offices to uncover the problem.

Imagine the recruiter's astonishment when he entered an office filled with people dressed in very casual slacks and sport shirts sans ties. "Well," the recruiter thought, "these must be the foot soldiers. What does the captain wear?" The recruiter found out soon enough when the sales manager arrived to greet him in a pair of black work shoes topped by white socks.

"From that day forward," Stewart explains, "we dressed down our candidates for their interviews with that client — but we couldn't bring ourselves to tell them to wear white socks. Finally, one of our referrals was hired. The experience is a good reminder for job interviewees: *When in Rome, wear a toga.*"

Changing with the Times: Dress Codes

Is the following statement true or false? "You can never be overdressed. Even if they say to wear business casual, it's appropriate for you to be in a suit and tie."

If you guessed "true," you probably guessed wrong.

A new wind is blowing into American workplaces defining what constitutes acceptable clothing to wear on the job. And to a certain extent, the lightening up on dress codes has spilled over into job interviewing.

First, a little background: I can't remember a time when virtually every job interviewing expert hasn't hammered home the basic tenet that dressing conservatively is the safest route. Period.

That advice often retains validity, but here's the thing: For many people, the notion of what dressing conservatively means has changed. Traditional suit-and-tie wisdom is no longer universally and automatically correct. *Conservative,* in many cases, now means carefully selected business casual apparel.

Surveys spotlight more casual wardrobe

A handful of studies over the past decade confirm that workplace dress codes have become more liberal than they were back in the starchier 20th-century days:

✔ A 2011 survey on behalf of CareerBuilder (2,500 U.S. hiring managers and 3,900 U.S. workers) found that employers are becoming more relaxed about dress codes. Fifteen percent reported they are right now changing to a more casual dress code.

✔ A 2006 tally of employers conducted by the National Association of Colleges and Employers revealed that companies seem to be considerably more relaxed about appearance these days. Just 12 percent said that a male job candidate wearing an earring would be a negative, and only 28 percent said they'd frown at weird hair color (like blue, green, or violet).

✔ A 2003 survey by Business Research Lab, a research and management consulting firm, noted that about half of respondents said the dress code where they work had changed in the previous two years; by three to one, they said the code had become more casual.

✔ A 2001 poll by the Society for Human Resource Management reported that 87 percent of U.S. companies allow some form of casual dress in the workplace.

The casual and laid-back dressing trend working its way across the country has moved beyond workers who work alone or in creative groups.

Even public-meeting sales professionals have jumped on the casual fashion runway — but not all. Many, such as those in medical, pharmaceutical, and financial investments sales, continue to wear a suit.

Body art is drawing new fans

While some companies continue to drop the curtain on job seekers with tattoos and body piercings, the practice is now so common that employers would be severely limiting their candidate pool if they rejected everyone with a tat or a nose ring.

A 2010 Pew Research Center report on Millennials aged 18 to 29 reveals that 38 percent have ink. Tattooed Gen Xers aged 30 to 45 came in at a close 32 percent. Across all generations. The Food and Drug Administration estimates that as many as 45 million Americans have at least one tattoo.

As for bling, nearly one in four Millennials has a piercing somewhere other than the earlobe. (Your guess on its location is as good as mine.)

An even more surprising 2006 statistic reported by the National Association of Colleges and Employers notes that two-thirds of employers surveyed said body piercing would not strongly influence a hiring decision.

Workplace authority John A. Challenger agrees that overall attitudes about body art have changed: "Employers' anti-tattoo stance probably softened considerably during the labor shortage of the late 1990s," says Challenger, chief executive officer of global outplacement firm Challenger, Gray & Christmas.

Should you dress 10 percent above your level?

When you go job interviewing, the classic advice is, "Dress one step up from what you'd typically wear to work in that position." Other lines you may hear are "Dress 10 percent better than you ordinarily would" or "Dress for the position you'd like to have one day, so you'll be seen as promotable."

My take on upscaling for interview days is to "Dress the best you're ever going to look in the job you're competing for."

He adds, "With everyone from soccer moms to MIT computer science graduates sporting tattoos, preconceptions about tattooed individuals are no longer valid. More importantly, companies have a vested interest in hiring the most qualified candidates."

Challenger says that we may never see visible tattoos on bankers, lawyers, accountants, or the clergy, but career fields such as advertising, marketing, sales, and technology are more accepting of new fashion and lifestyle trends.

When your research of a company's dress code is still thumbs down on tattoos and body piercings, cover up the ink and remove the bling — or pass on the interview. Maybe it's not the place for you.

Oh pantyhose, oh pantyhose, wherefore art thou pantyhose?

If you think the issue of tats and bling on the interview stage is a touchy subject, reflect on the issue of bare-legged ladies.

Opinions on both sides of the generational divide could start a new rumble in a Shakespearean tale of feuding noble families. Regardless of the weather or locale, younger women say that wearing pantyhose is silly, while their elders huff that not wearing pantyhose is tacky.

Professional presence guru Barbara Pachter makes two excellent points for women on how to handle the dilemma:

✔ When you wear pants or a pantsuit, your legs are not exposed, and the issue of whether to wear hose becomes moot.

✔ When your legs have blemishes, scars, or varicose veins (think ugly), pantyhose diminishes their unattractive appearance.

Advance dress code research before an interview gives you a leg up on the pantyhose predicament.

Selecting from the Basic Types of Interview Wardrobes

Both women and men should expect every nuance of their appearance to be noted and interpreted at a job interview. As Mark Twain supposedly said, "Clothes make the man. Naked people have little or no influence on society."

When you're getting ready for the big days, choose your attire from these four basic fashion categories:

- ✔ **Conservative:** Examples of conservative dressing environments include banks, law offices, accounting firms, and management offices — especially in big corporations.

- ✔ **Business casual:** Business-casual environments and career fields include information technology, sales, government agencies, education, retail, real estate, engineering, small companies, and Internet firms. (*Smart casual* — a term sometimes interchangeably used with *business casual* — means a loosely defined but pulled-together informal look for both men and women.)

- ✔ **Casual:** Plain casual environments are those such as construction, trucking, maintenance, repair, landscaping, and other jobs where work clothes may end the day stained and sweaty.

- ✔ **Creative fashion:** Clothing worn in career fields such as entertainment, fashion, graphic design, interior design, popular music, and other arts.

A discussion of each category follows.

Remaining conservative

Conservative dressing means no surprises. Your look is traditional or restrained in style. You avoid showiness. You aren't flamboyant. Conservative dressing means you not only wear the established team uniform, but you wear it well, from the tip of your white collar to the closed toe of your dark shoes.

About that fragrance

Perfumes and after-shave scents should be minimal or missing. A number of people are allergic; others may be reminded by the fragrance of someone they didn't enjoy knowing.

For *women,* a conservative checklist includes the following:

- ✔ **Suit:** Wear a two-piece suit or a simple dress with a jacket. Good colors are navy blue, gray, dark green, dark red, burgundy, and black. Make sure your skirt length is a bit below the knee or not shorter than just above the knee.

  In a dark color, a pantsuit is a tasteful choice. Accessorize it with a simple shell and silk scarf. *Caveat:* If your research shows you're interviewing with a super-traditionalist, stick to skirts.

- ✔ **Shirt:** A white, off-white, or neutral-colored blouse is a safe choice.

- ✔ **Shoes:** Closed-toe pumps with low heels or midheels (2½ to 3½ inches) suggest that you're work-minded.

- ✔ **Accessories:** Briefcases look more serious than purses, but a handsome leather purse is fine. Avoid distracting jewelry or watches.

- ✔ **Makeup:** Moderate makeup for daytime wear is appropriate. No looking like a Pamela Anderson stunt double.

- ✔ **Hair:** Simply styled hair looks contemporary; observe styles on TV anchors, for whom maintaining a professional image is essential.

For *men,* the following conservative checklist applies:

- ✔ **Suit:** Power-suit colors are navy or charcoal gray. (Black on men is seen as somber.) Tans and medium-tone colors work well if your research shows they're included in the company's color chart for team uniforms. Suits should be well tailored.

- ✔ **Shirt:** White is the first choice for shirts; blue is second. In either case, wear only long sleeves.

- ✔ **Tie:** Dark or low-key (blue, black, navy, blue, or gray) or power-red colors bring to mind executives. Geometric patterns are okay, but only if they're minimal. Be sure your necktie knot is neat and centered on your neck; the bottom of the tie should just reach your belt. Skip the bowtie.

- ✔ **Shoes:** Wear lace-up shoes in the same color as your belt. Wear black shoes if your suit is gray or navy; wear dark brown shoes for tans or medium-tone colors — in both cases, choose polished and clean shoes that are in good condition, of course. Rubber-soled shoes are a bad match for a professional suit and tie, as are alligator shoes or sandals.

- ✔ **Socks:** Wear dark socks in midcalf length so no skin shows when you sit down.

- ✔ **Accessories:** Limit jewelry to a wristwatch and, if you wear them, cufflinks.

Online wardrobe mistresses and masters

Fashion-focused websites are the perfect media to track the latest fashion scene (what's hot and what's not seems to change every 15 minutes). For starters, try these sites:

✔ Fashion.About.com (www.fashion.about.com): A guide to women's fashion, including fashion trends

✔ MensFashion.About.com (www.mensfashion.about.com): A men's

fashion and grooming guide for today and tomorrow

✔ Ask Andy About Clothes (www.askandyaboutclothes.com): A popular and comprehensive site devoted to men's wear that includes a feature enabling you to ask questions of an expert

Cruising business casual

An increasing number of recruiters say that a business suit is too formal for an interview at their company. (Remember the true story earlier in this chapter with the punch line "When in Rome, wear a toga"?)

The interpretation of *business casual* varies too widely for universally accepted rules, but mainstream opinion nixes casual clothing you'd wear to a picnic or a ballgame, such as sweat suits, spandex, shorts, T-shirts with slogans or commercial logos, bare midriffs, halter tops, and tank tops.

For *women,* a business casual checklist includes the following:

✔ **Clothing:** Guidelines here are looser than for conservative dress. Sticking with the following points is a safe bet:

- A casual jacket or blazer with well-pressed trousers or a skirt is a top option.

- A jacketed tailored dress is a fine choice.

- Tailored knit sweaters and sweater sets are appropriate.

- A skirt that's knee length, or longer paired with a blouse works well for support jobs.

- Avoid pastel overload (pink, baby blue); those colors work great for a nursery but not for your professional outfit.

- Provocative clothing (see-through tops, uncovered cleavage, second-skin pants, shimmering fabric, super-short skirts) isn't your best look for offers at the top of the salary scale.

✔ **Shoes:** Shoes should look businesslike and be dark colored — no strappy shoes, sandals, or mile-high stilettos.

✔ **Makeup:** Avoid wearing heavy makeup — on you or on your collar line.

✔ **Accessories:** Leave flashy or distracting jewelry — dangly ding-a-ling earrings, clunky bracelets, giant spiky rings that bruise fingers when shaking hands — at home in your jewelry box. And avoid chipped nail polish, if you wear it.

For *men,* a business casual checklist includes the following:

✔ **Clothing:** Don a sport jacket or blazer, especially navy blue, black, or gray, with color-coordinated long trousers or pressed khakis. Shirts should have collars, be long sleeved, and stay tucked into pants; button-down shirts are good but not mandatory.

✔ **Shoes:** Choose dress shoes and a matching belt; loafers are acceptable.

✔ **Socks:** Wear dark socks that are midcalf length.

✔ **Ties:** Choose simple (not too busy) ties for job interviews, unless you know from your research that a tie isn't part of the uniform where you're interviewing.

✔ **Accessories:** Limit jewelry to a conservative wristwatch.

Any interviewee, male or female, is better off steering clear of the following:

✔ Dark-tinted glasses, and sunglasses atop your head or hanging in front of your collar

✔ Electronic devices (even on vibrate mode — the buzzing sound is annoying)

✔ Joke watches or fad watches

Nail polish gone wild

Should you sport any nail color other than the classic reds and pinks at a job interview? How about blue, green, orange, purple, or turquoise nail polish? So many women apply wild nail colors that this color celebration once thought to be a passing fad has moved into mainstream acceptance. Good idea? Bad idea? Career coaches' opinions vary.

The "No" answer: Stick with conservative colors, in case the hiring decider is a fuddy-duddy who hates trying new things or who considers the unconventional end of the color palette to be in vulgar taste.

The "Yes" answer: Ditch the sparkles and yard-long nails, but don't leave wild colors to tweens, teens, and twenty-somethings. Become an early adopter because it suggests that you lean forward to stay up with the times — a good strategy for the more mature set.

Don't let them smell you first

Grooming has a strong influence on hiring decisions. Who hasn't nearly passed out after smelling someone's salami breath? Who hasn't been revolted by rank body odor? Who hasn't been turned off by spinach flecks on teeth?

A recent National Association of Colleges and Employers survey reports a rejection of candidates who don't pass the sniff test. In fact, 73 percent of respondents stated they don't want slovenly, smelly, or dirt-ridden employees working anywhere on the premises.

Translation: Shower. Brush. Comb. Clean is as clean smells.

This advice is so important that it bears repeating: Advance research is the only way to be on sure footing. You're gambling if you assume that you know what business casual means in your interview setting — or even whether you should dress in business casual. When in doubt, scout it out.

Working in casual wear

True casual work attire is suitable for hands-on working men and women. Often a company uniform is required when you're on the job, but when you're in job interview mode, the main point to remember is to look neat and clean, with no holes or tears in your clothing. Colors and style don't matter as much as they do in conservative and business casual interview dressing, but your overall appearance does.

Here's a short checklist for both men and women:

- ✔ **Clothing:** Shirts or knit tops and well-pressed pants are appropriate. Avoid wrinkled or soiled clothing, and don't wear T-shirts with writing on them.

- ✔ **Shoes:** Polished leather shoes or rubber-soled athletic shoes are fine. Just don't embarrass yourself by waltzing in wearing grungy sneakers.

- ✔ **Grooming:** Make 100-percent sure your hair and fingernails are neat and clean.

Selecting creative fashion

Most job seekers interview in attire suggesting that they're serious and centered in a business culture. But if you work in a creative environment, take fashion risks and go for artistry, design consciousness, innovation, trendiness, new styles, and, yes, even whimsy.

You're probably way ahead of me and already follow high- and low-fashion statements online and in magazines like *Vogue* and *Marie Claire, GQ* and *Details.* You know what they say about fashion: in one year and out the other. So I don't attempt to compile a checklist for either sex, because in a fashion-forward office, everything would be outdated by the time the fifth edition of this book is published.

In offices where employees are encouraged to show originality, a reasonably creative look (not too far over the top) beats out conservative dress, and maybe business casual as well. It all depends on the company culture as seen through the hiring boss's eyes.

Guessing at Tomorrow's Styles

As this chapter fades to black, I share a few forecasts gleaned from America's fashion observers:

- ✔ The era of the traditional suit is nearing an end.
- ✔ Business casual is becoming the new traditional dress in the workplace.
- ✔ Americans are moving toward a standard where there's virtually no difference between what you wear during work and what you wear after hours.

These predictions hint at a developing new paradigm in how you costume yourself for a job interview and what you wear to work after you get the job.

No worse for wear

When you've no budget to burn but need quality-looking interview wardrobe items, why not treasure-hunt in resale shops? When you've no budget at all, seek free donated workplace clothing, which is available to help economically disadvantaged women acquire and keep jobs. Dress for Success (www.dressfor success.org) is a worldwide nonprofit organization with chapters in many American cities.

The Women's Alliance (www.thewomens alliance.org) is another national organization whose members provide professional clothing and other services to low-income women seeking employment.

Men seeking free gently used work clothing can check for local "clothes closets," usually church sponsored, by inquiring at public job service offices.

Chapter 10

Beat Stage Fright with the R-Word: Rehearse

. . . .

In This Chapter

▶ Staring down your jitters

▶ Kicking stress with video rehearsal

▶ Making body language walk your talk

. . . .

*Y*ou're nervous. You have a mouthful of "ah" and "um" cotton. You're a bundle of nerves, from shaking knees and clammy palms to racing pulse beats and tummy butterflies as you make your appearance on an interview stage.

What you have is a galloping case of stage fright. Sound familiar? As the late great American newscaster Walter Cronkite remarked, "It's natural to have butterflies. The secret is to get them to fly in formation."

Refocusing Attitude Can Calm Nerves

You're not alone in your nervousness. Most people — including me — start out with a case of the shakes when interviewing or making a speech. When I began giving speeches, I could feel my throat drying up as panic fried my memory banks. I knew I had to go out and orate to promote my media careers column, but doing so was not my idea of fun.

Then one day things changed. I was in Florida addressing a group of career counselors when a teacher with whom I shared a podium watched me shake my way through my remarks. The teacher, herself an accomplished speaker, took me aside after the program and delivered one of the best pieces of advice I've ever been given. The teacher explained that nervousness is caused by the fear of looking ridiculous to others. She said:

When you are nervous, you are focusing on yourself. Try to focus on how you are helping other people by sharing with them the knowledge you've acquired.

You've been privileged to gather information not many people have. Think about serving others, not about yourself when you're on stage.

Her simple words of wisdom were an epiphany, a wakeup call. Thanks, Teach, for putting my nervousness into perspective.

How can *you* use that perspective? By realizing that preparing for a job interview is not unlike preparing for a speech or theatrical performance.

Three steps to fright-free interviewing

Aim for a flawless performance by following three basic steps in your interview plan.

1. **Memorize your basic message.**

   Get your skills and competencies, accomplishments, and other qualifications down pat. Rehearse until you're comfortable answering questions and you've practiced your basic presentation techniques. Rehearse until you know your self-marketing material cold.

2. **Personalize each self-marketing interview pitch.**

   Research each potential employer to customize your basic presentation for each job. Learn how to research each interviewing company in Chapter 6.

3. **Spotlight your audience.**

   Focus on how your talents can benefit your audience. Don't worry about how imperfect you may appear. Making your audience the center of attention goes a long way toward writing "The End" to your nervousness.

More techniques to stop stressing out

When stars of the theater walk on stage, they claim the stage from wing to wing, backdrop to footlights. With confidence and charisma, they win the audience's undivided interest. In a phrase, stars have stage presence. They are comfortable on stage.

Rehearsing out loud

Practice speaking aloud the messages you plan to deliver at your job interview — such as a listing of your five top skills, how you will answer questions (Chapters 16–22), and how you will ask questions (Chapter 11).

Why not just silently read your message statements over and over? Coaching experts say *rehearsing* information helps fix content in your mind. Rehearsing your statements at least five times makes them yours.

Yes, that's a lot of repetition, but remember this: Rehearsing five times beats the time frame of a famous orator in ancient Greece. A dude named Demosthenes worked to improve his elocution by talking with pebbles in his mouth and reciting verses while running along the seashore over the roar of the waves. Supposedly Demosthenes also went into a cave to learn oratory skills.

Not having a watch, a calendar, or a smartphone (and unable to use a sundial in a cave), Demosthenes shaved off the hair on half of his head and didn't come out until it grew back three months later. When he finally came out, listeners gladly lent him their ears because he had turned himself into the man with the golden tonsils.

Career coaches offer a variety of suggestions to get your butterflies flying like Air Force Blue Angels, ranging from relaxation techniques to visualization exercises. Here's a list of ideas that may be just what you need:

- ✔ **Deep breaths are an instant stress reliever.** Take a deep breath, breathing from your toes all the way through your body, and then slowly exhale. Repeat twice more, for three deep breaths in all.

- ✔ **Clench your fists.** Hold for three to five seconds. Release. Releasing your hands relaxes your shoulders and jaw. Repeat three times.

- ✔ **Push away anxiety.** Go into a nearby restroom and lean into a wall like a suspect being frisked in a cop show. Push hard, as though you want to push the wall down. Grunt as you push. Speech coaches say that when you push a wall and grunt, you contract certain muscles, which, in turn, reduces anxiety. Don't let anyone see you do this exercise, though — an observer may think you're loony tunes.

- ✔ **Visualize the outcome you want.** Top athletes often use visualization techniques to calm jitters, improve concentration, and boost athletic performance. They picture in their mind opponents' actions and strategy, and then picture them countering the maneuver.

    A golfer may run a movie in his head of where he wants the ball to go before he takes a swing. For an interview, you can visualize meeting the interviewer, answering and asking questions, closing the interview well (see Chapter 13), or even being offered the job on the spot (see Chapter 14).

> ✔ **Combine relaxation with visualization.** Visualize a quiet, beautiful scene, such as a green valley filled with wildflowers or a soothing garden with a waterfall. Inhale and think, "I am." Exhale and think, "Calm." Breathe at least 12 times. Next, recall a successful interview experience.

Before an interview, free your mind of personal worries — like paying the mortgage or picking up your kid after school. When your personal concerns can't be handled immediately — and most can't — write them down and promise yourself that you'll deal with them after your job interview.

Practicing with a Video Recorder

Discover yourself through an employer's eyes. With a friend feeding you expected questions, practice your answers using a video-recording device.

Video-recording devices range from computer-connected video cams with microphones and smartphones with recording software, to camcorders that both record and play back, to full-blown theater systems. (Review Chapter 3, in which I describe best practices for video interviewing.)

You don't have to rush out and buy some gee-whiz new technology. Use whatever device is available to you that will record and play back an hour-long picture and audio. Your performance is the message, not the system you use to make it happen.

Recording a practice session enables you to see how — with image improvement and mannerism modification — you can look alert, competent, and confident. You can refine actions that turn on hiring action and eliminate those that turn off hiring action. As I discuss next, body language has long been overlooked as a tool in the hiring calculus, but it's now beginning to be recognized as a critical component. Rehearse nonverbal as well as spoken messages, and keep an eye out for the following image-detracting actions:

> ✔ Leg swinging
>
> ✔ Foot tapping
>
> ✔ Rocking from side to side
>
> ✔ Fiddling with your hair
>
> ✔ Waving around nervous hands
>
> ✔ Leaning back
>
> ✔ Crossing your arms
>
> ✔ Bowing your head frequently
>
> ✔ Darting your eyes

✔ Blinking slowly (comes across as disinterest or slow thinking)

✔ Touching your mouth constantly

✔ Forgetting to smile

Use the following techniques to put your readiest foot forward:

✔ Look interested when you're seated by leaning slightly forward with the small of your back against the chair.

✔ Look the interviewer squarely in the nose, and you appear to be making eye contact. You look open and honest. More earnest honesty is communicated by upturned, open palms.

✔ Pause and think before answering a question to seem thoughtful and unflappable.

✔ Refer to your notes, and you're seen as one who covers all the bases. Just don't make the mistake of holding on to your notes like they're a life preserver.

✔ If you find your voice sounds tight and creaky on tape, try warming up before an interview or your next practice run: Sing in the shower or in your car on the way to the interview. La la la la. . . . Maybe you shouldn't sing on the bus.

Unlock the Power of Body Language

Carol Kinsey Goman is one of the business world's foremost authorities on body language. An executive coach, popular author, and keynote speaker, Dr. Goman explains a phenomenon that you probably haven't thought much about.

In a job interview, two conversations are going on at the same time.

The second conversion, the nonverbal one, can seriously support or disastrously weaken your spoken words.

Fascinated, on behalf of job seekers everywhere, I interviewed Dr. Goman. Here are my questions, followed by Dr. Goman's answers:

How quickly does body language impact your interview?

Immediately! Starting with the first steps you take inside the interviewing room, interviewers make judgments about you within seconds. The precise number of seconds is debated by social psychologists and interviewing professionals — it's complicated.

Learn your best moves in living color

Reinforce your new understanding of communicating nonverbally through gestures and movements by viewing the five-star videos on body language expert Dr. Goman's website, www.nonverbaladvantage.com. They're short and they're free.

But most researchers and first-impression observers agree that initially sizing you up requires mere seconds. In that wisp of time, decisions are made about your credibility, trustworthiness, warmth, empathy, confidence, and competence.

While you can't stop people from making snap decisions — the human brain is hardwired in this way — you *can* understand how to make those decisions work in your favor.

What can you say in seconds, other than "Hello"?

Obviously, you won't impress anyone by what you say in time measured by seconds. Instead, it's all about what you *don't* say. It's all about your body language.

But if you fail to score during the first impressionable seconds, can't you recover your chances later in the interview?

A poor first impression is hard to overcome, no matter how solid your credentials or impressive your resume.

So how can you do well in an interview from the get-go?

Here are powerful ways you can make a favorable first impression.

- ✔ **Command your attitude.** People pick up your attitude instantly. Think about the situation. Make a conscious choice about the attitude you want to communicate. Attitudes that attract people are friendly, cheerful, receptive, patient, approachable, welcoming, helpful, and curious. Attitudes that deter people are angry, impatient, bored, arrogant, fearful, disheartened, and distrustful.

- ✔ **Stand tall.** Your body language is a reflection of your emotions, but it also influences your emotions. Start projecting confidence and credibility by standing up straight, pulling your shoulders back, and holding your head high. Just by assuming this physical position, you will begin to feel surer of yourself.

✔ **Smile.** A smile is an invitation, a sign of welcome. It says, "I'm friendly and approachable." Smiling influences how other people respond.

The human brain prefers happy faces, recognizing them more quickly than those with negative expressions. Research shows that when you smile at someone, the smile activates that person's reward center. It's a natural response for the other person to smile back at you.

✔ **Make eye contact.** Looking at someone's eyes transmits energy and indicates interest and openness. A simple way to improve your eye contact in those first few seconds is to look into the interviewer's eyes long enough to notice what color they are. With this one simple technique, you will dramatically increase your likeability factor.

If you feel uncomfortable looking into an interviewer's eyes too long, look the interviewer squarely in the nose, and you appear to be making eye contact. You communicate openness and honesty.

Caveat: Although good eye contact is excellent body language, don't try for a laser lock on the interviewer. Imagine two cats in a staring contest — in the Animal Kingdom, nobody moves until somebody swats. Break the tension by periodically looking away.

✔ **Raise your eyebrows.** Open your eyes slightly more than normal to simulate the "eyebrow flash" that is the universal signal of recognition and acknowledgment.

✔ **Lean in slightly.** Leaning forward with the small of your back against the chair shows you're engaged and interested. We naturally lean toward people and things we like or agree with. But be respectful of the other person's space.

✔ **Shake hands.** This is the quickest way to establish rapport. It's also the most effective. Research confirms that it takes an average of three hours of continuous interaction to develop the same level of rapport that you can get with a single handshake.

But make sure you keep your body squared off to the other person, facing the person fully. Use a firm — but not bone-crushing — grip with palm-to-palm contact. And hold the other person's hand a few fractions of a second longer than you are naturally inclined to do. This action conveys additional sincerity and quite literally "holds" the other person's attention while you exchange greetings.

What are some of the top flops in body language?

Avoid signs that indicate nervousness, submission, or weakness.

✔ **Projecting agitation:** Try not to fidget or change positions frequently. Don't bounce your legs, lock your ankles, or rock from side to side. Don't dart your eyes, blink in slow motion, or blink abnormally fast. Never wave your arms with hands over your head to make a point because it implies that you're out of control.

✔ **Looking disinterested:** Overcome any tendency to cross your arms, which suggests disagreement or disbelief, especially when leaning back. Avoid continually bowing your head, as though you are saying, "I have no idea of the right answer" or "Poor me."

✔ **Seeming unsure:** Standing with your feet close together can make you seem timid. (Widen your stance, relax your knees, and center your weight in your lower body, to look more "solid" and sure of yourself.) Avoid hanging on to your laptop, purse, or briefcase as though it was toddler Linus's security blanket in the Charlie Brown comics.

✔ **Appearing tired:** Slumping in the chair is a really bad idea. "Slacker" is the first thing that comes to mind if you're a member of the Gen Y generation, and "old timer" arises if you're a boomer.

✔ **Suggesting arrogance:** A nonverbal signal of confidence is holding your head up. But if you tilt your head back even slightly, the signal changes to one of looking down your nose at the interviewer or job being discussed. Snooty.

Stage Directions for All Players

As you rehearse your interviewing presentation, aim for the A-list of candidates by heeding the following hints:

✔ Practice focusing your discussion on the employer's needs. Show that you understand those needs, that you possess the specific skills to handle the job, and that you are in sync with the company culture.

✔ Don't discuss previous employment rejections — you come off as a constant audition reject.

✔ Develop and practice justifiably proud statements of your accomplishments — that is, those that directly relate to the job you want.

✔ Practice descriptions of your leadership qualities and initiative, and remember to express them *in context* of what you accomplished. (Did you lead 10 people, 100 people, or 1,000 people? What was the result? Has anyone in the company accomplished the same thing?)

✔ It's okay to admit a misstep. If pressed, you can fess up to a goof you've made in your career (when was it — 3:48 p.m. on June 14, 2012?). But rehearse satisfying explanations of how you learned from your one mistake — or two or three. And try not to laugh while you're admitting that you're human.

✔ Don't practice long monologues — be fair: Split air time with your interviewer.

Different strokes for different folks

Interviewing coaches say winning role-related voice and head tilts vary as much as appropriate dress codes for Oscar performances. Examples:

When applying for a service job: You'll seem more personable by slightly tilting up your chin and letting your voice rise by a hair at the end of each key sentence.

When applying for a management job: You'll come across as more boss-like by using a steady calm and confident voice as you keep your chin level.

Anticipating Interview Trapdoors

No matter how well you're doing as you sail through an interview, certain things can throw you off balance when you're not forewarned. Rehearse in your mind how you would handle the situations in the upcoming sections.

Disruptions

As you rehearse, keep in mind that not everything that happens during the interview is related to you. Your meeting may be interrupted by a ringing phone, the interviewer's coworkers, or even the interviewer's emergency needs. Add the factor of interview interference to your mock drills.

Because the show must go on, find language to politely overlook these interruptions with patient concentration. Practice keeping a tab on what you're discussing between disruptions, in case the interviewer doesn't.

Silent treatment

Interviewers sometimes use silence strategically. Moments of silence are intended to get candidates to answer questions more fully — and even to get them to blurt out harmful information they had no intention of revealing.

Instead of concentrating on your discomfort during these silences, recognize the technique. Either wait out the silence until the interviewer speaks or fill it with a well-chosen question (see Chapter 11) that you have tucked up your sleeve. Don't bite on the silent treatment ploy, panic, and spill information that doesn't advance your cause. Don't run your mouth for no reason.

Turning the tables, you can use your own silence strategy to encourage the interviewer to elaborate or to show that you're carefully considering issues under discussion.

Take One . . . Take Two . . . Take Three . . .

Practice your scenes until they feel right, until they feel spontaneous. Rehearsing gives you the power to become a confident communicator with the gift of presence. No more nervousness, no more zoning out. No more undercutting body language. Your butterflies fly in formation.

Tell me why I care

"So what?" "Who cares?" "What good does your past accomplishment do me?" This kind of question may be unspoken, but it's lying in ambush deep in every employer's mind. Each time you mention a previous job duty or accomplishment, pretend the employer is really thinking,

"What does this all mean for my benefit? Will it make money? Save money? Grow my company's market reach? What? Tell me why I care." Rehearse telling me why I care and make the sale!

Chapter 11

Looking Good with Questions You Ask

In This Chapter

▶ Asking work questions before the offer

▶ Asking personal questions after the offer

▶ Drawing out hidden objections

▶ Treading lightly around delicate questions

▶ Finishing with the right question

So you just finished answering a seemingly endless line of questions about your work history and your education, and you're pretty confident that you held your own. Now the interviewer turns to you and asks, "Do you have any questions?" This question is your cue to ask how much money you're gonna make at this outfit anyway, right? Wrong!

The types of questions you ask and when you ask them are the least understood parts of the interview. Your questions offer major chances for garnering curtain calls or being booed off the stage. Sort your question opportunities into two categories:

✔ **Questions that sell you:** These questions help you get an offer; they're a way to sell without selling.

✔ **Questions that address your personal agenda:** These questions about pay, benefits, and other self-interest items need to be asked only after you receive an offer — or at least a heavy hint of an offer.

Asking Selling Questions before the Offer

For all jobs, asking about anything other than work issues before a hiring offer comes your way is a serious strategic error. The interviewer, particularly a hiring manager who resents the time "diverted" from typical duties to an interview, is totally uninterested in your needs at this point.

What's important to the interviewer is solving the hiring problem. *First we decide, then we deal* — that's the thinking.

To talk about your needs before an offer turns the interviewer's mind to negative thoughts: All you want is money, insurance, and a nice vacation on the company. You're not interested in doing the job.

As an Applause candidate, you're not going to make that mistake. Keep your focus on the employer's needs and how you can meet them. Sell yourself by asking questions that are

- ✔ Work focused
- ✔ Task focused
- ✔ Function focused

Ask about the position's duties and challenges. Ask what outcomes you're expected to produce. Ask how the position fits into the department, and the department into the company. Ask about typical assignments. Here are examples of work-related questions:

- ✔ What would be my first project if I were hired for this position?
- ✔ What would my key responsibilities be?
- ✔ Who (and how many) would I supervise? To whom would I report?
- ✔ Would I be working as a member of a team?
- ✔ What percentage of time would I spend communicating with customers, coworkers, and managers?
- ✔ Would on-the-job training be required for a new product?
- ✔ Can you describe a typical day?
- ✔ If I produced double my quota, would you double my base pay?
- ✔ Was the last person in this job promoted? What's the potential for promotion?
- ✔ How would you describe the atmosphere here? Formal and traditional? Energetically informal?
- ✔ Where is the company headed? Merger? Growth?
- ✔ What type of training would I receive?

✔ What resources would I have to do the job?

✔ How much would I travel, if any?

✔ (If a contract job) Do you anticipate extensive overtime to finish the project on schedule?

✔ Where does this position fit into the company's organizational structure?

✔ What results would you expect from my efforts and on what timetable? What improvements need to be made on how the job has been done until now?

How much time should you invest in asking selling questions? Five to ten minutes is not too much. Gregory J. Walling, a top executive recruiter based in Alexandria, Virginia, says he's never heard an employer complain about a candidate being too interested in work.

Don't ask questions about information you can glean from research. Portraying yourself as an A-list candidate and then asking "lazy questions" dims your star power.

Asking Self-Interest Questions after the Offer

When you have the offer, you're ready to make the switch from giving to receiving information. I discuss negotiating salary and benefits in Chapter 8, but you'll also want to know about information like leave time, overtime, flextime, frequency of performance reviews, and (if it's a contract job) how long the job will last.

Although asking personal agenda questions in advance of an offer is unwise, after the offer, scoop up details of interest, such as these examples:

✔ Is my future relocation a possibility?

✔ Is my employee parking included in the offer?

✔ Does management delegate decision making to others, or does it micromanage and require that I get approval of even the tiniest details?

✔ Where would I work in the building? Can I take a quick look at the location?

✔ Is the schedule fixed (such as 9 a.m. to 5 p.m.) or flexible (my choice of hours)?

✔ Would I have an exempt (from overtime pay) or nonexempt position?

Ask with confidence

Be aware of how you phrase questions. Ask "what would" questions that presume you'll be offered the job ("What would my key responsibilities be?" not "What are the job's key responsibilities?").

Presumption phrasing shows self-confidence and subtly encourages the interviewer to visualize you in the position.

Drawing Out Hidden Objections

The questions you ask have one more mission: They're a good way to smoke out hidden concerns or objections that may keep you from finishing first in the competition.

Reasons that employers hang back with unspoken anxieties often relate to legal vulnerability (see Chapter 22 on inappropriate questions), or the interviewer may simply be uncomfortable asking about them.

Whatever the reason, silent concerns are hurdles standing in the way of your getting the job. Before the interview is over, you need to find a way to address any thorny issues and overcome them.

Good salespeople call techniques that do this "drawing out objections." Once you know the issues that — under the surface — are chilling your chances, try calling them out.

One of the best questions I've ever heard to jar loose unspoken doubts was passed on by legendry recruiting authority and author John Lucht (www. ritesite.com). When the interview is about four-fifths complete, Lucht suggests you ask this question:

What do you think would be the biggest challenge for someone with my background coming into this position?

Here's your golden opportunity to bury any concerns on the spot or in your thank-you letter. (If you can't collect your thoughts quickly enough, at least you'll have a clue for your next interview once you know what may be holding back employers from choosing you.)

Another tactic to control a problem lurking below the surface is to introduce it head-on and tell the employer what you want known about the situation. Here's an example of easing an interviewer's hidden concerns by bringing up a legally risky topic:

In your place, I'd probably be wondering how my children are cared for during the day. I may be concerned that I'd miss work should they become ill. Let me explain my very reliable childcare arrangements to you. . . .

After hidden objections see daylight, you have a chance to shoo away elephants in the room that are standing between you and a job offer.

Asking Certain Questions Very Carefully

Handle questions to potential employers about their own performance with great tact — especially when a Millennium-generation candidate asks them of a Boomer-generation boss. Proceed with caution into territory like the following:

✔ How would you describe your management style?

✔ Do your employees admire you as a boss?

Although you need as much information as possible to make good job choices, asking a potential boss these kinds of questions in the wrong tone of voice may make you seem way too audacious. Moreover, direct questions about personal characteristics and values tend to elicit pure topspin.

PRATFALL

Critics pan showoffs

I noticed in subsection 3.a of the government defense contractor's manual I.2.A, concerning future plans, that you squared the round table, using your supercomputer's component play box, and found that your sandbox is 95 percent superior to the market's. Does this mean you plan to circle an outer galaxy and return to Earth on Greenwich Mean Time?

Huh? Research is essential, but guard against flaunting your newly found knowledge with questions that would have given Einstein a little headache. Interviewers interpret these questions as a transparent bid to look smart.

But, you ask, shouldn't you look "smart" at an interview? Yes. Just don't cross the fine line that exists between being well researched and fully prepared for an interview, and trying to be *a nouveau omniscient.* (Don't you love that term? I looked it up. It means newly informed know-it-all.)

Showing off is a quality that causes otherwise charming, bright, gregarious, and attractive people to be turned down. It's just not a likable trait. If you don't have a good handle on what is and what isn't showing off, maybe a friend can help you work on that distinction.

Instead, ask questions designed to draw out companywide anecdotal answers:

✔ How did the company handle a recent downsizing?

✔ How did managers react to someone who took a stand on principle?

✔ Who are the company's heroes?

This approach encourages conversation that can be very informative. Questions are tools. Use them wisely

Ending Suspense by Asking the Right Question

Page ahead to Chapter 12, and you see a lineup of fundamental questions to ask at the end of each interview. Want another option for immediate feedback? When your meeting has sailed smoothly along and you want to know your odds right now but you don't want to appear overconfident or too anxious, ask the right question:

Should I assume you'd like me to continue in the interviewing process?

[yes] *What would the next step be?*

[no] *I'm sorry to hear that. Can you tell me why I won't be in the running?* (If you can overcome the objections, give it a try; if not, thank the interviewer for the time spent with you and move on.)

When you don't hear the *yes* word, at least you won't be holding your breath to know whether this particular work opportunity is a lost cause. If the *no* word sparks a serious state of doldrums, break out an effective mood elevator — hot fudge sundae? funny movie? upbeat music?

Chapter 12

Closing the Show

. . . .

. . . .

Curtain call time! You sense that it's almost the moment to go. The interview seems to be winding down. In most instances, a job offer doesn't come at this point.

How can you be sure the interview is almost over? Watch for these nonverbal clues: The interviewer may begin shuffling papers, glancing at a wall clock or watch, stretching silences, and perhaps standing up. Then you hear words that confirm your hunch:

✔ *Thanks for coming in. We'll be interviewing more candidates through the next week or so. After that, I'll probably get back to you about a second interview.*

✔ *Thanks for talking with me. I think your qualifications make you a definite candidate for this position. When I'm done with all the initial interviews, I'll get back to you.*

✔ *All your input has been really helpful. Now that I know everything I need to know about you, do you have any questions about the company or the position?* (Careful — ask only job-related questions — you don't have the offer; see Chapter 11.)

In this chapter, I cue your best exit lines and remind you to exhibit friendly confidence, no matter how the interviewer behaves.

Making a Strategic Exit

Do yourself a favor by never leaving a job interview empty-handed. Rather than quietly fading into history, memorize these four important points.

- Immerse your departure in *interactive selling*. Sales professionals use this term to mean a great deal of back and forth, give and take, and questions and answers. You're alive!

- Reprise your qualifications and the benefits you bring to the job. You're a great match and a wonderful fit, and you'll be quickly productive.

- Find out what happens next in the hiring process. Mysteries are for crime show viewers.

- Prop open the door for your follow-up. Without paving the way, you may seem desperate when you call back to see what's up.

Your parting sales pitch

Haven't you sold yourself enough during this ShowStopper interview? Yes and no. People — including interviewers — often forget what they hear. Start your close with another chorus of your five best skills. (See Chapter 16 for answers to the question, "Why should I hire you?") Then ask

Do you see any gaps between my qualifications and the requirements for the job?

Based on what we've discussed today, do you have any concerns about my ability to do well in this job? Any reservations about hiring me?

You're looking for gaps and hidden objections so that you can make them seem insignificant. But if the gaps aren't wide and the objections not lethal to your candidacy, attempt to overcome stated shortcomings. You can make this attempt based on what you found out in your earlier research. Here's an effective formula you can use to *engage the interviewer:*

1. **Sell your qualifications (skills and other requirements for the job).**

2. **Ask for objections.**

3. **Listen carefully.**

4. **Overcome objections.**

5. **Restate your qualifications (using different words).**

After you restate your qualifications, you may find the time is ripe to reaffirm your interest in the job and subtly lead toward an offer. Here's one example to illustrate how such a scenario might play out:

I hope I've answered your concerns on the X issue. Do you have further questions or issues about my background, qualifications, or anything else at this point? This job and I sound like a terrific match.

Depending upon the interviewer's response, make your move.

I hope you agree that this position has my name on it. As I understand, your position requires X, and I can deliver X; your position requires Y, and I can deliver Y; your position requires Z, and I can deliver Z.

So there seems to be a good match here! Don't you think so?

I'm really glad I had the chance to talk with you. I know that with what I learned at Violet Tech when I established its Internet website, I can set up an excellent website for you, too.

Leaving the door open

How can you prop the door open for a follow-up? You seek the interviewer's permission to call back; with permission, you won't seem intrusive. Use these statements as models to gain the permission:

What's the next step in the hiring process, and when do you expect to make a decision? (You're trying to get a sense of the timetable.)

I'm quite enthusiastic about this position. When and how do we take the next step?

May I call if I have further questions? Or would you prefer that I e-mail or text you?

I know you're not done reviewing candidates; when can I reach you to check up on the progress of your search?

I understand you'll call me back after you've seen every candidate for this position; would you mind if I call you for an update or if I have more questions?

I appreciate the time you spent with me; I know you're going to be really busy recruiting, so when can I call you?

I look forward to that second interview you mentioned — can I call you later to schedule it after my work hours so I don't have to throw off my current employer's schedule?

You say I'm the leading candidate for this position. Terrific! That's great to hear — when shall we talk again?

In the final moments, be certain to express thanks to the interviewer for the time spent with you. Say it with a smile, eye-to-nose, and a firm but gentle handshake: *This position looks like a terrific opportunity and a great fit for me — I look forward to hearing from you.* Then leave. Don't linger.

As soon as you're alone at a place where you can make notes, write a summary of the meeting. Concentrate especially on material for your follow-up moves, described later in this chapter.

How Hard Should You Sell?

How hard you should sell and how eager you should be depends on such things as age, critical experience, and the level of the job you're seeking. No behavior is perfect for every candidate and every situation.

When you're in a sales field, are just starting out, lack experience in a job's requirements, or aren't obviously superior to your competition, don't hold back on selling your advantages or showing your enthusiasm.

When you have relevant experience and offer in-demand skills or are being considered for a senior-level job, allow yourself to be wooed a bit. You don't want to be seen as jumping at every opportunity. It's the old story: The more anxious you seem, the less money you're offered.

When the gap between your qualifications and the job's requirements is the size of the Grand Canyon, accept the fact that the job will go to someone else. Suppose, for instance, that the position requires five years' experience, including two years of supervisory experience. You thought you could talk your way through the gap with your three years of total experience and no years of supervisory experience. Fat chance!

When you just don't have the chops for the position, salvage your time and effort by acknowledging that although you may not be ideal for this particular position, interviewing for it has caused you to admire the company and its people. You'd appreciate being contacted if a better match comes along.

Recruiters follow up for you

You don't have to follow up with the employer when you were introduced to the company by a third-party recruiter — the recruiter follows up for you, negotiating the offer or accepting the turndown. You can get a report card from your recruiter fairly quickly.

Follow Up or Fall Behind

What takes place after the first selection interview — when candidates are ranked — decides who has the inside track on winning the job.

Your follow-up may be the tiebreaker that gives you the win over other promising candidates. And even if the employer already planned to offer you the job, your follow-up creates goodwill that kick-starts your success when you join the company.

Follow up vigorously. It's your caring that counts.

Your basic tools are

- ✔ Print letters
- ✔ E-mails and other media
- ✔ Telephone calls
- ✔ References

Letters

How much do *post-interview* thank-you letters really impact hiring decisions? It depends on the letter.

When your letter is canned, flat, routine, boring, and of the "Dear Aunt Martha, Thanks for the graduation gift" model, interviewers may yawn and toss it.

But when your letter is a persuasive self-marketing communication masquerading as a thank-you letter (see Figure 12-1), interviewers are likely to pay attention to you as a thoughtful and conscientious top contender.

[Date]

Mr. A.J. Cortes, Vice President
21st Century Developments
[Address]

Dear Mr. Cortes:

Thank you for the opportunity to interview for a subcontractor coordinator position. I would very much like to be on the respected 21st Century Developments team. I'm appreciative of your genuine interest in acquainting me with your staff and company goals. In summary, here's a review of what I offer as a potential colleague:

I have delivered on building working relationships with key vendors:

- Beginning 11 years ago [date], when I became a subcontractor coordinator, I have consistently achieved high-quality results by keeping abreast of the quality of materials used by various companies. Among my favorite suppliers, you may recognize the following names: Namath Re-bar, Drywall By-the-Mile, and Lionel Fixtures.
- Two years ago, [date] I eliminated one whole clerical position by implementing a new software package to manage daily progress reports from subs, making the work competition intelligence faster and cheaper.

I have delivered on facilitating the control of subcontractor costs:

- I have carefully monitored signs of cost run-ups, strategizing with project managers on cost control. On the previous three projects alone, my notifications saved my employer $X dollars, an amount equal to 13 percent of the total cost.

I have delivered on first-class scheduling strategies:

- Because I have solid competencies, skills and experience in construction requirements, I have been able to reverse errors made by my predecessors at several organizations where I have been employed. For example, at Bogart Industries, I was able to turn around a looming fiasco due to improper scheduling of subs (more than $2 million) and bring the project in nearly on time. Bogart's CEO said that my extreme scheduling turnaround kept the company from losing the project to creditors.

High standards have always been central in my work. Now, as an accomplished professional, I feel ready to join such a demanding company as yours. Thanks again for the interview. I look forward to speaking with you soon.

Sincerely,

Max Hong

[*Contact information*]

Figure 12-1:
Use a thank-you letter (also known as self-marketing communication) as a tool to boost your chances of being hired.

In constructing a thanks/marketing letter that actually does you some good, use the same powerful concepts you would employ for a targeted resume that directly matches your qualifications with the job's requirements (Read my book *Resumes For Dummies,* 6th Edition; John Wiley & Sons.)

Prime-time pointers for letters

Get started with the following content capsules for your thanks/marketing letter aimed at converting your candidacy into a job offer.

- ✔ Express appreciation for the interviewer's time and for giving you a fresh update on the organization's immediate direction.

- ✔ Remind the interviewer of what specifically you can do for a company, not what a company can do for you. As you did in closing your interview, draw verbal links between a company's immediate needs and your qualifications: "You want X, I offer X; you want Y, I offer Y; you want Z, I offer Z."

- ✔ Repeat your experience in handling concerns that were discussed during the interview. Write very brief paragraphs about how you solved problems of interest to the company.

- ✔ Tie up loose ends by adding information to a question you didn't handle well during the interview.

- ✔ Overcome objections the interviewer expressed about offering you the job. For example, if the job has an international component and the interviewer was concerned that you've never worked in Europe or Asia, explain that you've worked productively in other cultures, notably the Caribbean and in Mexico.

- ✔ Reaffirm your interest in the position and respect for the company.

Looks, timing, delivery, and frequency

Content isn't the only factor to consider when preparing a follow-up letter. The following considerations can cause it to be read or rejected.

- ✔ For an important job, a letter (suitable for printing) is impressive and memorable. Write a thank-you letter for the interview within 24 hours to strengthen the good impression you made in person. Deliver it via e-mail, drop it off at the company's front desk, send it by courier, or mail it at a post office.

- ✔ In most instances, the letter will be effective when limited to one page with five to seven short paragraphs. But a killer letter can run two, even three pages, if it is flush with white space, easy to read, and written for a professional-level position.

- ✔ Some very savvy people swear by handwritten notes. But here's my take: Even when your penmanship is good, a note doesn't readily lend itself to heavy-duty service as a marketing tool.

- ✔ When an employer leaves you stranded — waiting for a hiring decision — try to think of new facts to add in a second or even third letter.

- ✔ After the third letter, switch to sending a note with a relevant news clipping or even an appropriate cartoon. The interviewer will know what's going on, but at least you're keeping your name where it can be seen. Remember the truth of the adage, "Out of sight, out of mind."

Figure 12-1 shows you a sample letter to impress interviewers.

E-mail

In this digital age, an e-mail follow-up is fine for most jobs. Consider these observations on communicating after an interview by e-mail:

- ✔ E-mail is more conversational and easier for a quick reply. On the other hand, it's also easier to say *no* in an e-mail message than on the telephone.

- ✔ Use e-mail if that's the way you sent your resume and especially if the employer requested electronic communication in a job ad.

- ✔ Use e-mail when you're dealing with a high-tech firm; the firm's hiring authority probably doesn't remember what paper is and may think voicemail is a bother.

Don't make blanket assumptions about whether spam filters will prevent your message from reaching the interviewer. Instead, ask the interviewer or a receptionist in advance about the best way to send an e-mail message.

The content for a thank-you e-mail need not differ much, if at all, from that of a paper thank-you letter (see Figure 12-1). You can write a couple of lines in your e-mail referring to your attached letter:

> *I was impressed with the warmth and efficiency of your offices, as I explain in my attached letter.*

Or you can enclose the letter's content within the body of your e-mail if plain text is satisfactory.

Other digital media

Newer media tools — chiefly the casual communication of *texting, instant messaging,* and *social networking* — have jumped in to the job search, mostly driven by younger generations. Reports so far suggest an age-based cultural divide on short-form messages. What about employer acceptance of thank-you messages after an interview?

Hiring professionals are frowning at such quickie and lax communication — everything from sending an SMS message to a recruiter after an interview in texting lingo, to adding the interviewer as a friend on Facebook. They consider such throw-away thanks disrespectful.

Another new idea — creating a 30-second *video e-mail* to send interview thanks to a hiring professional — doesn't have a track record yet. But I can see how it could be a fresh tool to stand out from the crowd. Using search terms such as "video e-mail," "vid mail," video messaging," and "vmail," browse for services that provide this option; add the year of your inquiry to your search.

Telephone calls

Once upon a time, all that job seekers had to worry about when calling about potential employment was getting past gatekeepers. They solved that problem in various ways, by adopting a pleasant and honest manner and making an ally of the assistant by revealing the refreshing truth about why they're calling, as one example.

Some job seekers battled back by trying to reach the interviewer before 8:30 a.m. or after 5:30 p.m., when the assistant wasn't likely to be on deck and the interviewer alone would pick up the phone.

Those were the good old days. Now voicemail has joined gatekeepers in throwing 800-lb. roadblocks in front of job seekers who try to follow up on interviews.

The big voicemail question for job seekers is whether to leave a message on voicemail. Opinions vary, but, as a practical matter, you may have to leave a message if you don't connect after the first few calls. All your calls won't be returned, but your chances improve when you say something interesting in a 30-second sound bite:

This is _____. I'm calling about the (job title or department) opening. After reflecting on some of the issues you mentioned during our meeting, I thought of a solution for one problem you might like to know. My number is _____.

Opening the conversation

Here's a sprinkling of conversation starters:

- ✔ *Is this a good time to talk?*
- ✔ *I think you'll be interested to know _____.*
- ✔ *I understand you're still reviewing many applications, but. . . .*
- ✔ *I forgot to go into the key details of (something mentioned during the interview) that may be important to you.*
- ✔ *While listening to you, I neglected to mention my experience in (function). It was too important for me to leave out, since the position calls for substantial background in that area.*
- ✔ *I was impressed with your _____.*
- ✔ *I appreciate your emphasis on _____.*

Keeping the conversational ball rolling

Try these approaches to maintain the conversation:

- ✔ Remind the interviewer of why you're so special and what makes you unique (exceptional work in a specific situation, innovating).

  Let me review what I'm offering you that's special.

- ✔ Establish a common denominator — a work or business philosophy.

  It seems like we both approach work in the (name of) industry from the same angle.

- ✔ Note a shared interest that benefits the employer.

  I found a new website that may interest you — it's XYZ. It reports on the news items we discussed. . . . Would you like the URL?

Reminding your references

References can make all the difference. Spend adequate time choosing and preparing the people who give you glowing testimonials. What they say about you is more convincing than what you say about yourself.

Call your references and fill them in on your interview:

I had an interview today with (person, company). We talked about the position, and it sounds like a perfect match for me. They wanted (give a list of key requirements), and that's just what I can supply.

For instance, I have all this experience (match five key requirements with five of your qualifications) from when I worked with (name of company).

Would you like me to fax you those points I just mentioned? . . . I was so happy about the interview I just wanted to thank you once more for all your help and support. I couldn't have done it without you.

Be stingy with references

"Don't give references to anyone unless they're ready to offer you a job you'll accept," advises John Lucht, author of the bible of executive job hunting, *Rites of Passage at $100,000 to $1 Million+: Your Insider's Lifetime Guide to Executive Job-Changing and Faster Career Progress in the 21st Century* (Viceroy Press).

Lucht says the first time references are contacted; they put on their best performance. He explains what happens next: "The second time, they're a bit more hurried and perfunctory. As that sequence lengthens, they'll become less enthusiastic and begin to wonder why, if you're as good as they originally thought, are you still repeatedly referenced and not hired?"

Pre-Employment Contracts Promise Protection for Everyone

Although your verbal job offer covers such specifics as the term of employment, duties, and compensation, what happens if disputes arise in the future and memories fade? It's your word against theirs. He said, she said. That's why getting your offer in writing is to your advantage. (Would you buy a house or an insurance plan without a written contract?)

A written pre-employment contract, or its little brother, the job offer letter, also benefits an employer because you, as an employee, agree to provide specific work benefits and make certain promises (for example, you promise not to reveal company secrets or steal company customers).

Legally, no iron-clad contract rules apply in every state, and each employment contract is different.

Fifty years ago, employment contracts were reserved for theatrical royalty and big-shot corporate executives. That's changing. Employment relationships are increasingly contract oriented for professional, managerial, technical, and administrative positions.

So when you're asked to sign a pre-employment contract, you know that the company considers you an investment it wants to protect. But what should you do when a contract's provisions include factors that you don't like and haven't verbally agreed to? Can you negotiate the boilerplate? In most cases, the answer is *yes* — to a degree. You have more leverage to negotiate a contract to get what you want in tight labor markets; you have less leverage in surplus labor markets when ten people are standing behind you ready to grab the job.

What do pre-employment agreements cover? Usually they regulate one or more of the following issues:

- ✔ The position being offered and accepted.
- ✔ The compensation that will be paid.
- ✔ Whether the job is for a specified length of time or at will. (You or the employer can call it quits at any time for any reason.)
- ✔ Specific benefits regarding paid leave time (like vacation and sick days) and whether such time accrues from year to year.
- ✔ Responsibilities of both parties concerning the work to be done.

Danger points for you to recognize and investigate fully before signing your acceptance include the following:

- ✔ Repayments of training cost or relocation expense that are required under certain conditions.
- ✔ Noncompete clauses that prevent you from working elsewhere in a given locale for a specified period of time.
- ✔ A statement that the terms of the agreement are subject to change in the future.
- ✔ A statement that you are to be bound by the terms of the company's employee handbook, which you may not yet have seen. (The handbook itself usually notes that it is subject to change at any time by the company.)
- ✔ Agreement to arbitration and other alternate dispute resolutions that come with a muzzle clause prohibiting you from discussing settlement details of disputes. Arbitration is a contentious issue with employees, who often feel that arbitrators (wishing to be hired again) may side with companies because they're more likely to be repeat customers. St. Louis

employment attorney Sheldon Weinhaus comments: "Companies keep track of previous awards. It is much harder for a worker to know the history of any arbitrator."

 If you're required to sign a pre-employment agreement that mandates arbitration, ask that language be inserted requiring that the arbitrator be chosen from a list maintained by the American Arbitration Association or another selection organization that operates with a code of ethics.

A *job offer letter* is the minimum promise protection you should have in any work opportunity requiring you to resign your current job or relocate out of your residence. A job offer letter is a condensed pre-employment contract outlining the basics of your employment. In small companies, a job offer letter may be written without a lawyer's help. Details and samples of offer letters are available on an About.com website, `http://jobsearchtech.about.com`; scroll past ads to Job Offer Letters.

Pre-employment agreements and job offer letters are generally legal and enforceable — but not always. If you can't afford to consult an employment lawyer before signing a pre-employment contract, bulk up your knowledge; run a Google search for "pre-employment contracts" and "employment contracts."

Last Chance to Back Out

Maybe you've decided to accept the offer. Before popping a champagne cork, make sure that you have the salary, benefits, and starting date in writing. Assurance that you correctly understand this information is critical when you're being asked to relocate or give up a job.

If you received the offer over the telephone, ask whether the company can mail you a job offer letter; if not, you write one, perhaps calling it a "letter of understanding."

Sometimes you decide the job isn't for you. Don't feel obligated to accept it merely because you've been dickering over your potential employment for weeks. If you ultimately decide to pass on it, send an amiable letter that reveals no details. Say that while you greatly appreciate the offer and the interviewer's time, you have made a difficult decision and that you have accepted a position with another employer (or that you have ultimately determined that you aren't a good fit with the company).

When the job offers the breakout role you've been searching for, throw a wrap party. Pop the champagne. Cheers all around!

When you get a job offer at the interview

With an offer is on the table, bring up your self-interest (vacation, benefits, lunch hours) requests for information. Whip out a note pad and say,

I'm excited and grateful for your interest. I'd like to clear up just a few issues. Can you tell me about — ?

Unless the circumstances are unusual, accepting or rejecting a job offer on the spot is not in your best interest. You're likely to think of something later that you forgot to negotiate. Improving an offer after you have accepted is difficult.

Your After-Interview Checklist

Experts in any field become experts because they've made more mistakes than the rest of us. After your interview, take a few minutes to rate your performance. The following checklist can help you curb bad habits and become an expert at job interviewing:

✔ Were you on time?

✔ Did you use storytelling, examples, results, and measurement of achievements to back up your claims and convince the questioner that you have the skills to do the job?

✔ Did you display high energy? Flexibility? Interest in learning new things?

✔ Did the opening of the interview go smoothly?

✔ Did you frequently make a strong connection between the job's requirements and your qualifications?

✔ Was your personal grooming immaculate? Were you dressed like company employees?

✔ Did you forget any important selling points? If so, did you put them in a follow-up e-mail, letter, or call-back?

✔ Did you smile? Did you make eye contact? Was your handshake good?

✔ Did you convey at least five major qualities the interviewer should remember about you?

✔ Did you make clear your understanding of the work involved in the job?

✔ Did you use enthusiasm and motivation to indicate that you're willing to do the job?

✔ Did you find some common ground to establish that you'll fit well into the company?

✔ Did you take the interviewer's clues to wrap it up?

✔ Did you find out the next step and leave the door open for your follow-up?

✔ After the interview, did you write down names and points discussed?

✔ What did you do or say that the interviewer obviously liked?

✔ Did you hijack the interview by grabbing control or speaking too much (more than half the time)?

✔ Would you have done something differently if you could redo the interview?

Onward and Upward

You've done it all — turned in a ShowStopper performance at your interview and followed up like a pro. Keep following up until you get another job or until you're told you aren't a good match for the position — or that while your qualifications were good, another candidate's are better.

Even then, write yet one more thank-you/self-marketing letter, expressing your hope that you may work together in the future. Sometimes the first choice declines the job offer, and the employer moves on to the next name — perhaps yours.

Please stay. We're not kidding.

Employers sometimes make counteroffers when a valued employee quits to take a better job. If you find yourself being wooed back, it's usually best to leave the counteroffer on the table, say thanks, and move on. Here's why:

✔ When substantial financial considerations aren't in the mix, most people leave a job because of a personality rift, blocked advancement, or boring work. A generous counteroffer doesn't fix any of these things.

✔ After you've announced a departure, count yourself out of the inner circle. You won't be trusted as before.

✔ Renewing your enthusiasm will be challenging: You already know why you want to find the exit. If your current employer wouldn't promote you or give you a decent raise before you put on your walking shoes, don't expect anything different when it's time to move up to your next career level.

✔ If a recruiter connected you with the new offer, and you say *yes* and then *no,* your credibility goes up in smoke — a negative that can come back to haunt you.

Feedback when you're not offered the part

Disappointed job seekers often ask interviewers for reasons why they weren't selected and for tips on how to do better in the future.

Don't waste your time: You almost never will be given the real reason. Employers have no legal or ethical obligation to explain why you weren't the one. Instead, they're likely to offer these kinds of useless rationales: "We didn't feel you were the best fit for this job" or "We chose another candidate who had more experience" or "Company policy won't allow me to comment."

Why won't interviewers share the truth? Here are some of the reasons:

✔ **Legal exposure:** Companies are extremely wary of lawsuits accusing them of discrimination. The less said, the less to be sued about.

✔ **Fast-paced world:** There's no profit in wasting prime hours on a dead end.

✔ **Discomfort factor:** Managers dislike giving negative feedback.

✔ **Scant information:** Human resources interviewers may not have enough details from hiring managers to give helpful answers, even if they were inclined to do so.

When you're not offered the part, review the After-Interview Checklist in this chapter. If you have the requisite qualifications and your performance doesn't need pumping up, the reason you didn't get an offer may have nothing to do with you. Square your shoulders for the next interview.

Part III
Actors' Studio: Casting Your Character

The 5th Wave   By Rich Tennant

PAWN BROKER

"Your resume won me over. Not many people can list looting and pillaging as a transferable skill."

In this part . . .

*B*eing typecast is a real danger in an interview situation. You're a recent graduate? *Bam* — you're inexperienced and ill-equipped for the responsibility of the position. You're 55 years old? Set in your ways and expensive to insure.

This part shows you ways to overcome preconceived notions about who you might be, whether you're looking to change careers or have a history of short-term work.

Chapter 13

Opening Acts for Younger Talent

*H*i there, new or recent college graduates! As a Millennial or Gen Y'er, you're in a huge generation that's movin' on up to run the workplace show in the foreseeable future.

Researchers tag you as a new breed of techno-savvy worker. They say that you're early adopters who are constantly hooked up to multiple devices in order to know who and what you need to know. You text, you tweet, you Facebook. You are connected to the world!

So What's the Problem?

But wait . . . although acknowledging the blessings of your magnificent digital sophistication, today's employers aren't ready to say all is well with your generation as workers, you self-indulgent young rascals, you.

They who still call the shots are highly critical of behavior like this:

✔ You show up for work with exposed midriffs that display a belly ring.

✔ They find you audaciously texting senior managers with requests about issues that should be handled with an immediate supervisor.

✔ They see you whipping out a smartphone and yukking it up on the company dime.

To further illustrate the problems employers report about younger workers, I offer this fictional but representative snippet of a job interview:

Management consulting firm interviewer: Would you like to know more about our company's quantitative analysis group?

Millennial professional: Who would I be working for? I am not interested if I can't choose my boss. Would I start as a senior analyst? What is the salary? How soon would I be eligible for a raise? When would I be considered for a promotion? Would I have to work past 5 p.m.? I need a vacation the first two weeks of every June because I have a timeshare in Costa Rica. And to be up front with you, I will need a half-day on Fridays because I have a cabin in the mountains and my friends count on me being there.

Admittedly, we're talking generational stereotypes here — certainly, no specific traits define an entire generation — but in job interviews, stereotypical criticism sometimes lurks but remains unspoken.

As a techno-savvy, well-educated person, you know you have to recognize a problem to fix it. In this chapter, I show you how to counter harmful youth-bashing stereotypes.

Now, on with the show. . . .

Beating a Bad Rap on Work Ethic

As a new or recent college graduate, your *ability* to do the work that a job requires isn't so much in question. The iffy factor is your *willingness* to do the work in a manner an employer prefers.

While the work-ethic gripe isn't singular to the younger crowd (Gen X members used to hear the same complaints when they were your age), it hits your generation the hardest. Here's what critics say about Millennials:

- ✔ You have an attitude toward work that looks like laziness-meets-impatience.

- ✔ You had to overachieve to get through the most competitive college admissions process in history, so you don't feel particularly inclined to pay your dues.

- ✔ You make up the most pampered generation in history; you were expected to spend your spare time making the varsity team, not working part-time in an internship.

✔ You're likely to look at a job interview in the way one 20-year-old candidate described it to a recruiter: "a two-way conversation where the company puts out what they want and expect from me, and I put out what I want and expect from the company."

✔ You're more demanding than previous generations and dismiss as hopelessly old-fashioned the traditional work ethic that people should work hard and do the best job possible.

✔ You can't think on your feet. You don't work well alone, maybe because you grew up on a steady stream of organized sports and other team activities. You're comfortable only when pursuing well-defined goals as part of a team and can't solve problems independently. (Mom, help!)

Today's rookies are too often stereotyped as refusing to pay their dues, slacking off, holding unrealistic expectations, being unwilling to work hard or long, and being limited in the ability to make independent decisions and solve problems. Nevertheless, if you don't meet the generalization head on, it can cause you to miss out on a job you want.

The positive performance you give during an interview dispelling the poor-work-ethic stereotyping can erase doubts about your willingness to do a job.

Tips for Millennials

Concentrating on the skills and accomplishments you provide and on what you bring to the employer — not what you want from the job — goes a long way toward wiping out unspoken concerns that chill job offers. Here are more tips for combating misperceptions:

✔ **Show perspective.** Every generation believes its is substantially different from those who have gone before and, therefore, deserves a pass to rewrite the rules. That's true only in the methods and technology used to make one's way in life.

As scholar and publisher of Impact Books, Dr. Ron Krannich (www.impactpublications.com) says, "Despite a trendy Generation Y designation, today's college graduates still must learn to connect with the right people who can hire them for good jobs, showing they can add value to the organizations they want to join."

✔ **Be confident.** But don't be a prancing pony in your interviewing persona, confusing attitude with confidence. Try to come across as able but eager to learn. Radiating arrogance that implies the workplace rules must bend to accommodate your preferences because you're young and techno savvy won't play well with older bosses who have the power to choose someone else.

✔ **Show respect.** Bring a notepad and take notes during the interview. This shows that you're interested and paying attention. Employers will reciprocate.

✔ **Test the waters.** Don't be shocked if an employer refuses to negotiate entry-level salaries. But after you've presented your value, do ask about the timing of performance reviews, as well as performance bonuses and how they're calculated. (See Chapter 8 for salary talk.)

✔ **Storytell.** Prepare detailed true examples of all your skills, with as many examples from off campus as from on campus. But stay away from personal stories that may work on Facebook but are more personal than interviewers want to know

✔ **Get insider secrets.** Interviewspy (www.interviewspy.com) is a tool created by Georgetown University students to help job seekers prepare for interviews. It is a user-driven site that provides candidates questions and information about many organizations, including Google, Bank of America, and Teach for America. The website solicits "spies" to post questions that they have been asked during interviews for jobs and internships, as well as information they think may be helpful for you.

Glassdoor (www.glassdoor.com) is another useful resource to get a jumpstart on learning about company interviews, reviews, and salaries from anonymous posts by employees.

Track down more resources to find out about interview questions by browsing for "employer review websites."

✔ **Be realistic.** Don't apologize for a lack of workplace experience beyond internships and student jobs. The employer already knows that you're starting out. Instead, explain how your experience at your summer job waiting tables helped you hone your customer-service skills. This is a golden oldie but is especially important to young graduates.

Scripts for Millennials

You find suggested scripts for answering a large number of interviewing questions elsewhere in this book, especially in Chapters 16 through 20. In addition, the following script examples suggest strategies for smacking down bad press aimed specifically at Gen Y candidates. Here goes:

✔ You should hire me because I'm the best person for this job. Not only am I a hard worker and a fast learner, but I bring a passion for excellence. I won't disappoint you. For example —.

✔ Yes, I'm an experienced team player. I've had opportunities in my internships, college, and athletics to maximize my skills as a team player. On a recent project, for example, —. But being on a team doesn't mean I can't lead a team. I was elected president of the Environmental Action Club at my college. I enjoy making well-reasoned, well-thought-out decisions. For instance, when I —.

✔ You asked how I handle conflict on a team. Basically, I try to make dispassionate judgments about what's best for the group and our goal, and then use good communication techniques to make my point. Let me tell you how I mediated a flap over —.

✔ I am excited to learn that your company encourages volunteering for service work. I believe that people who do not give back to their community make a misjudgment both personally and in their career development. Based on my volunteer stints in college, I find that service work adds another dimension to my understanding of what people really want and how to satisfy those longings. I hope you'll select me for this position, because we're on the same page here.

✔ You asked me where I would like to be in five years. I would like to become the best marketing representative you have in the company. At the same time, I'll be preparing to take on greater responsibilities. For example, I've enrolled in an advanced-level marketing course online to be ready for future challenges. I love creative challenges, and I'm comfortable making decisions.

✔ You asked how well I work with people who are considerably older than me. That's great. In my work with the Batiquitos Lagoon Foundation, which I've done for three years, all the volunteers have a mutual respect for each other. Obviously, I look to the older crowd for their experience, and I think they like what I bring in the way of my newer education and experience that maybe they don't have. So you could say it's a mutual admiration society.

✔ I have no problem working the hours you require. In fact, I would look forward to the opportunity to move around and see different areas of the company relatively early in my career, to get a better feel for what I can contribute down the line and where I want to go within the company. I'll work very hard to make a difference for this company and for the company's customers. I think my professors will back me up on that — would you like to see some of their letters of recommendation?

✔ Although I don't have formal work experience doing this exact kind of job, my education has given me considerable background in this area. With a combination of my educational background and my internship job experience, I know that I will be a productive new addition to your team, and I will go all out to make that happen.

✔ I know that many employers consider my generation, the Y generation, to be somewhat difficult to manage and inspire. The joke I've heard is, "You're in the Why generation — why aren't you more interested in your career prospects?" Mr. Clemons, that's not me. I've been focused on joining a team such as this one all during my senior year. And I've worked diligently to succeed at this goal, as I hope some of my earlier statements have conveyed. Do you think I'm the committed addition to your team whom you hope to hire?

Get ready for a competitive search

Although current prospects for new graduates are encouraging, employers receive many applications for each available starter-employee position. When you aren't snapped up by a campus recruiter, pull together a wish list of places you'd like to work and use online networking sites to connect with employees inside the prospective employer companies. Get more tips online from such Millennial-friendly websites as these:

- ✔ www.collegerecruiter.com
- ✔ www.collegegrad.com
- ✔ www.nacelink.com
- ✔ www.experience.com
- ✔ www.jobsearch.about.com
- ✔ www.monstertrak.com

Good Times and Your Future

The intergenerational shift in the workplace puts today's new and recent college graduates on the job market's red carpet. If that's you, enjoy your edge.

- ✔ Consider the flip-flop rhythm of the economy (remember Econ 101?). Cyclical recessions and hiring slowdowns force younger as well as older people to stalk jobs for months on end.

- ✔ As workforce ranks repopulate — until the year 2020 or so — with other Millennials who, like you, are techno savvy, you'll compete for jobs within your own age group.

- ✔ By far the biggest question mark for your future is how worldwide competition for the best jobs will impact Americans of all ages. Capital's chase for cheap labor across the planet has unleashed hundreds of millions of workers on global markets. A number of these competitors have a Bachelor's degree or an advanced degree.

As you gear up to begin your trip toward an award-winning work/life-balanced career, remember this one last tip: Some days you're the bug, some days you're the windshield.

Chapter 14

Selling Scripts for Career Switchers

. . . .

In This Chapter

▶ Career-changing without experience in a new field

▶ Bridging an experience gap with crossover skills

▶ Scripting persuasive answers to tough questions

. . . .

*P*eople change careers for many variations of two reasons: They leave their career, or their career leaves them. Either way, employment challenges are much the same when it comes to marketing yourself in places where you haven't been before.

Even when you think you can easily transition from one career field or industry to another (the manager-can-manage-anything syndrome), employers can be a hard sell when it comes to greenlighting career changers for a payroll. Except when they're filling entry-level jobs, hiring authorities have a frustrating habit of preferring candidates who, on someone else's payroll, have proven that they can do the work a job requires.

American poet Henry Wadsworth Longfellow's summary of the two views — yours and an employer's — leaps to mind:

> *We judge ourselves by what we feel capable of doing; others judge us by what we have done.*

When you're trying to swim in new ponds, you have to figure out ways to get past an employer's inner voice, the one that says you're a fish out of water.

Remembering Career Change Basics

How does that new cliché I just made up go? This isn't your father's interviewing market. Truer words were never spoken. Global trade is changing life for all of us. Technology is automating human processes. Computer modeling is trumping gut feeling. Teleconference marketing is replacing sales trips. Highly qualified candidates are being hired on temp contracts and cut loose when the project is over or the job is shipped offshore to cheaper-labor nations.

Keep your dreams alive as you assume the role of career changer in a new era, but be clear-eyed about the challenges you face when you set out to interview yourself into places where you're a stranger. Mull over the following points of practical straight talk about career changing:

- ✔ **Career change is not job change.** A career change involves a marked shift in jobs requiring new primary skills or knowledge, or a totally different work environment — or both. For example, when a manager in the telecom industry leaves one company for another managerial position in the same industry, he makes a job change; when he leaves the telecom industry to become a museum curator, he makes a career change to a different job and different industry.

- ✔ **Retraining may be unavoidable.** When you attempt to make a clear change to a different kind of job (for instance, engineer to sales rep) in the same industry, you may well be able to pitch your way into an employer's graces without investing in additional formal education or training. Your challenge is more difficult when you try to change both your job and your industry at the same time, but you may be able to pull it off without immediately spending additional time and money in school. However, you won't be able to get out of educational renewal to satisfy credibility and licensing requirements in such careers as law, public accounting, and nursing.

- ✔ **Employers worry most about risk.** Managers are concerned whether the crossover skills (which I tell you about in the upcoming section "Leveraging Crossover Skills for Change") you acquired in your former career will translate to your new career. When your skills don't convert and you can't do the work, the business suffers a negative impact and — if you're fired — a risk of being sued for wrongful discharge. Another worry is whether you'll suffer changer's remorse, quickly becoming dissatisfied and turning into a "bad hire." These risks drive employers to seek out directly applicable skills in proven performers.

✔ **Your competitors are new graduates.** When you're starting over, you compete with new graduates who are starting out. Expect to be paid entry-level money; an employer is unlikely to compensate you for your 15 years' experience in another field (unless you can show that your experience can save or earn money for the new employer). Even so, you have an ace up your sleeve: You bring *judgment, commitment, high motivation, proven good work habits,* and *real-world lessons.*

Eyeing the Best Career-Change Tips

When you want to give your best effort to prevent a career change, whether voluntary or involuntary, from going awry, pay attention to the following pointers.

✔ **Connect with others in your intended field.** When your change is voluntary, at least six months in advance of your leap, join a professional association of members in the career field or industry where you want to go. When your change is involuntary and you're suddenly left high and dry, scramble to assemble a skeleton personal network of people who can guide you into your intended field and beef it up as fast as you can. Make friends. Find out who's who and what's happening with professionals who can connect you with employment. Ask what you should read and what workshops you should attend. Ask if you can visit a professional's workplace as an observer.

✔ **Educate yourself.** Seek out short-term certificate programs and workshops offered during industry conferences, as well as those available locally. If you study online, get the scoop on pluses and pitfalls of distance learning. One starting spot: `www.geteducated.com`.

✔ **Bone up on the industry.** Even if you're a nonacademic type who always sneaked light rubbish reads or sports sections into your study halls, at this time in your life, you really can't afford to skip hard-core research on your proposed destination. (Check back to Chapter 6 for research leads.) Those greener pastures sometimes bleach out when something about the work isn't what a changer realistically expects or can do well. This probably happens as a result of skimpy research.

✔ **Talk the talk.** Learn the lingo of prospective new colleagues. You'll seem like one of them already — an insider, not an outsider.

✔ **Brace yourself for interview pitfalls.** When you find yourself trapped in a behavior-based interview setting (described in Chapter 5) and you're coming up short trying to answer a question about what you have done that's relevant to the new career, answer quickly. Then reframe your response, segueing from behavior-based interviewing (the past) to situational interviewing (the future): *That's a good question. And here's what I would do if we decide I'm the right person for this position. I would —.*

✔ **Make the experience connection.** The bridge you use to join the old with the new must be rational and reasonable. Your qualifications have to come from somewhere — skills you already possess, volunteer work, part-time jobs, training, hobbies, and so forth. Strive to present a believable relationship between your qualifications and the career you're targeting. The more convincing your bridge, the easier you make it for an employer to say, "Welcome, we want you."

✔ **Accentuate the positive.** Don't say you hope to change careers because there are no more jobs in your field. An exception may be when a condition is well known, such as real estate agents who got out during the recent downturn in home sales. Even then, add that you'd been thinking about making a change for a couple years and have decided to redesign your life for a better fit with your priorities and goals. As in any job search, you're moving toward a preferred future, not running away from a bad spot or a toxic boss.

✔ **Tell true stories.** Expect to be asked the same kinds of questions that new graduates often face, such as some version of "Why shouldn't we hire someone more experienced in this line of work?" When you work out your answers, remember to storytell — that is, to back up your claims of superior qualities with true examples of accomplishments. Otherwise, what you claim will likely be blown off as hot air. You must be believable.

✔ **Inventory your core skills and knowledge.** Sort through to see which will cross over to a different industry or career field. Push them to the front of your memory, where you can find and translate them as needed. The use of crossover skills is the topic of the next segment.

The leadership conundrum

When you're an entrepreneur who wants to come in out of the cold, tell stories about the skills and self-motivation that you developed being on your own. But be vigilant in countering any inference that, after being your own boss, you'd be hard to manage. Practice interviewing with a friendly "devil's advocate" who won't pull punches in evaluating your interviewing performance for dominance traits. Unless a company is interviewing for a chief officer, turn down the volume.

Leveraging Crossover Skills for Change

Midcareer, Roger (or so I'm calling our hero in this true story) woke up one morning asking himself, "Is this all there is?" Successful but unhappily employed, Roger wanted to find a new way to work, produce, self-actualize, earn a living, and be happy.

Pulling the plug on his job as a controller of a division of a big Midwestern corporation, Roger worked with an experienced career coach on self-analysis; a big part of the analysis focused on identifying Roger's crossover skills. Using judgment born of maturity, Roger realized that what he really wanted to do was work outdoors with boats. After leaving his land-locked state and moving to Florida, Roger's transferable skills, including boating and financial management, built his crossover bridge into a marina business that he liked so much he ended up buying it two years later.

Using crossover skills as a bridge from one career (or job) to another is your most important persuasion tool to gain acceptance in job interviews. So what exactly are crossover skills? In a nutshell, crossover skills (also called transferrable skills) are those you've gathered through jobs, classes, volunteer work, hobbies, sports, projects, parenting, or any other life experience that can be valuable in your new career.

Blogging, for example, is a crossover skill. Surprised? Don't be. Blogging is more than going online and telling the world about your day or what you think. For starters, blogging requires more than writing skills. As a blogger, you build a loyal readership and study visitor statistics to see what works and what doesn't. You meet self-announced deadlines for new material. You make intelligent responses to comments, including those that insult your own intelligence. As an extension of social networking, blogging can benefit many businesses (such as financial services) or causes (such as politics) that depend on large numbers of customers and supporters. Any entity seeking to establish or maintain a blog needs people who can make it work correctly.

A few better-known examples of crossover skills include the following:

- ✔ Decision making
- ✔ Oral and written communication
- ✔ Organization
- ✔ Problem solving
- ✔ Technological savvy

Crossovers are portable skills that you can use in many work settings. They go straight to the heart of an employer's question of "Can you do the job?" Considering the importance of been-there, done-that experience to the success of your career change, be ready to identify your crossover skills to an interviewer and to translate how they make you immediately productive.

There's a hitch. Even brilliant people have trouble correctly and comprehensively identifying their portable skills. Searching online for "crossover skills" or "transferable skills" is the cheapest and quickest way to get started on identifying yours. Additionally, look for books that contain multipage listings of portable skills, including my own *Cover Letters For Dummies,* 3rd Edition. When big, fat holes remain in your inventory of crossover skills, it's time to return to your college's career center for help or engage a career coach well versed in identifying skills and competencies.

Say What? Say This When You're in Change Mode

You aren't going to ring up a sale trying to explain why your previous experience as a restaurant manager qualifies you to manage a nuclear waste disposal company. But you are going to make headway with hiring decisions when you give convincing reasons why your lack of explicit prior experience doesn't matter. Study these sample answers and then add your own circumstances, interpretations, and phrases to the scripts that follow.

✔ To respond to hesitations about your career change:

This job is a good fit for what I've been interested in throughout my career — working with others to achieve an above-average outcome, enjoying the satisfaction of being technically competent, and having a serious interest in sports. For example, my work at Leader Public Relations taught me that a team needs bench strength. When the senior publicist left Leader unexpectedly, I was able to successfully step in and increase placements within six months by 20 percent. The persuasion skills I bring along with seven years of surfing ideally qualify me for this position as assistant manager of surf board production. Do you agree?

✔ To respond to concerns that your previous experience is irrelevant to the job you want:

I am a well-qualified candidate for this educational research position because cost control expertise required by the grant is more than met with my 15 years' experience as a manager with budget and supervisory responsibility.

✔ To respond to concerns that your previous position is irrelevant to the job you want:

Yes, I was a receptionist for 12 years, and it was great training to deal with all levels of individuals. Here's why I am so well matched to your brokerage department. Not only have I interacted with venture and equity capital managers and with retirement fund managers in a high-pressure environment, but I have taken a course in financial markets and stock, bonds, and other investments. With the world rushing forward, I think we need new thinking for new times, don't you? My people skills will help me to bring in the kinds of customers you've been losing to online traders. Do you see any reasons why I wouldn't be a great addition to your team?

✔ To demonstrate that you are changing directions with forethought and action:

As I matured and got to know myself better, I realized how I fit into Career X better than what I'd been doing, although my previous work has been fine preparation for what I plan to do with the rest of my life. I've been steadily drawn to Career X for several years, and getting ready for this transition, I did the following (attended school, researched and volunteered in the field, took a part-time job in the new industry). Since you didn't screen me out because of my prior experience, I assume you recognize my crossover skills.

I appreciate your valuable time invested in seeing me, so I have taken the initiative of working up a brief ledger sheet that shows you how I qualify for this position. May I come around the desk and walk you through it?

(A ledger sheet in this usage refers to a brief one-page sheet of paper with two columns. Title the left column "Job Requirements." Title the right column "My Qualifications." Show the matches item by item. You can do a ledger sheet for interviews on paper or on a laptop.)

✔ Waitress transitioning to wholesale sales rep:

Although I haven't yet specifically sold eyewear accessory products to retailers, I do have sales experience when you consider that, in my previous job, I was a de facto sales representative for the restaurant.

My upselling record consistently brought in high revenues each week. I've demonstrated that I pay close attention to detail, that I can multitask with precision and accuracy, and that I know how to build a loyal clientele of customers who rave about my service and attention to their requirements. (Smile.) While I'm certainly not the type of person who would lose her head if it weren't attached to her shoulder, I am the type of person who would lose her reading glasses if they weren't attached to lovely eyewear accessory chains such as the one around my neck.

I won't disappoint you. When can I start?

✔ To respond to reason you are interviewing:

As soon as I was sure I wanted to do work that makes a difference in people's lives, I researched this field and reached out to practitioners for informational interviews. I quickly learned that I had to have an associate degree for this work, but before I signed up at New School Community College, I researched the reputation of its program by checking with previous graduates and with the employers who hire them. I also went online to a social network and asked for comments on what people really thought about the program I was considering making sacrifices to attend. Everything I heard was good, so I attended and now have my degree. It was a great decision!

✔ To the issue of the cause of satisfaction in your last career and concern that you would experience changer's remorse:

> *I didn't see the results of all the hard work I put in. The structure was overly rigid and bureaucratic, and, frankly, I like to feel as though my contributions accomplish a positive outcome. And although I am pretty good with computers, I like to have a slice of my day working with people. I checked out your company with my network, and you get glowing reviews for rewarding outstanding performance, for giving employees breathing space to accomplish their assignments, for being able to observe the fruits of their labor, and for hiring great teams. Is that how you see this company? Are we made for each other?*

Steer Clear of Snap Judgments

The message is clear: To successfully sell a career change, remember to logically lay out a bridge explaining why you — with no prior matching experience — will be able to handle the job you seek. And take pains to assure that you, as a career changer, aren't given to snap judgments and quick reversal.

Funny stuff will happen if you say either of the following bloopers:

✔ *I saw the job posting and, what the hey, this company is in an industry that I'm willing to give a whirl.*

✔ *I'm changing careers because I can't stand what I've been doing and just need several more quarters for my social security.*

People actually say things like this in interviews. They don't realize that such rationales are akin to telling a prospective buyer that you're selling your house because the heating bill is too high.

Career change auditions

In a lot of career-changing situations, the company asks the candidate to audition for the job by doing it for a few weeks, usually at peanut wages. This gives the company the opportunity to make a minimum investment in the oyster that may or may not have a pearl in it. Similarly, the audition gives the candidate a chance to find out whether the career change choice was as great as anticipated.

Chapter 15

Star Turns for Prime-Timers

*I*f you'll never see your 20s and 30s again, you may have already run into an age obstacle that puts the brakes on your job hunt in a culture that values youth over experience.

But isn't age discrimination illegal? Of course it is. But does it happen? Sometimes or often, depending on your perspective.

From a base in Weston, Conn., Matt Bud leads The Financial Executives Networking Group, a 37,000-member national organization with local chapters. Most men and women who join The FENG do so when they must find new jobs, but once employed, they tend to stay aboard and bond with other financial professionals as a kind of safety net against future joblessness.

Understanding How Employers See the Age Issue

Based on his vast experience, Bud observes that many employers have a profile of a winning candidate in mind. A rejection decision may not be discrimination: In the employer's eyes, the candidate simply may have the wrong profile for the job being filled.

So rather than refer to age bias, this chapter covers solutions to what I call *age trouble,* whether the trouble is due to discrimination or to a wrong profile. The following segment focuses on recognizing and overcoming issues of age trouble when it stops you in your tracks.

Showing That You Improve with Age

Age trouble shows up in many guises. In this overview, I present examples of questions that may mask common unspoken age-related concerns, followed by sample responses that show you don't have an expired shelf-life date stamped on your forehead.

Age and job performance

A big chunk of age trouble is centered on doubts that you can do the work. Here are three masked put-offs and push-backs.

✔ This is stressful and demanding work. How well do you work under pressure? (*Translation:* You may lack the stamina to do the job.)

I work well in all situations, especially when I'm under pressure. I like having deadlines. Early on, I learned to set internal deadlines for myself in all my projects, breaking the projects into segments so I always knew how I was doing. I consistently brought my projects in on time and on budget. Internal deadlines are my specialty.

✔ What do you do to maintain good health? (*Translation:* You don't look too healthy to me, and you may not be around long enough to justify training costs.)

Maintaining good health is a passion with me. My body mass index is similar to or better than that of most 30-year-olds. I exercise several times a week. Once a week, I play volleyball on the beach. And I watch what I eat.

✔ What office software do you use? Do you have a smartphone? Do you have a tablet? (*Translation:* You look like you do things the old-school way, and we're into new-school thinking.)

I'm proficient with (current business software). I took a class for it on my own time last year at St. Louis Community College. My BlackBerry is with me 24/7. I make it a point to stay current with such major trends in our industry as (give one or two examples). I'm a member of the World Future Society.

Age and money

In a world impacted by business budgets, companies may see prime-timers as too pricey for value received, as the following two examples illustrate:

✔ What can you bring to this company? (*Translation:* You expect to earn more money to start than we want to pay; I can hire someone at half of what you want.)

I bring a background that includes a related degree and successful years of experience in a similar position with another company. The contacts I have already made in my previous positions will help me be productive immediately, saving costs and earning revenues. My background is an open book, showing that, by any measure, I am a bargain!

✔ What are your monetary expectations of this job? (*Translation:* You're a seasoned worker accustomed to regular raises; our firm won't be able to make that kind of commitment, so why am I wasting time interviewing you?)

Yes, I've been rewarded for my contributions to the bottom line for previous employers. Sometimes the compensation was in the form of a raise and sometimes it was a performance bonus for meeting goals. If you decide that I'm the right person for this position, I believe the monetary details won't present a problem, and I'll work with you on making that the case.

Age and attitude

Prime-timers may be perceived as living in another dimension of values and viewpoints or as set in their ways, as the following two questions and responses indicate:

The health insurance put-off

Health insurance cost for employees is a monster age-related cost bite for employers who consider hiring prime-timers. It's a tough issue to beat, says Dallas ace job connector Tony Beshara: "Boomers' inclusion in a group insurance plan drives up the cost for an average American company. Additionally, older workers are perceived to miss more work because of their own illness or that of their spouse."

So what's the answer? Other than carrying your own health insurance plan and letting the interviewer know you won't be another policy to feed, Beshara says the best you can do is look healthy: "Get in shape, dress sharply, and interview with energy."

✔ How would you go about doing this job? (*Translation:* You're accustomed to doing things your way, which may not be our way.)

Although I've been quite successful in previous positions, I don't buy the idea of resting on one's laurels. I'm always happy to learn new and better ways to do things. Before suggesting any innovations, I would first make certain that I understand company policies and ways of working. I am very excited about this work opportunity and look forward to starting to work with you as soon as possible.

✔ You look as though you've led too accomplished a life to be returning to a career now (*Translation:* You don't fit in with our young culture.)

I believe that my extensive experience in many productive settings will be of great benefit to your company because (give one or two examples). I can work effectively with people of all ages. In fact, I really like working with young people because I respect their energy and vitality and fresh look at challenges.

Outing Elephants: Address Age Issues

Have you heard the expression "If there's an elephant in the room, introduce it?" That's the topic of Chairman Matt Bud's advice to members of The Financial Executives Networking Group.

Bud warns FENG prime-timers that it's a huge mistake to avoid an age-related issue that the interviewer may be wary of bringing up directly. That's because an age zinger becomes an elephant in a small room — impossible to overlook, an obvious truth that is being ignored. Instead, get the sensitive question out in the open where you have a fighting chance to overcome the perception that you're too old for the job.

What follows is a part of what Bud counseled:

Among difficult questions an interviewer would like to ask you, a big one is age related: How much longer are you planning to work?

Close to being an illegal question even if the job is potentially long term or may involve a move, the interviewer may not ask, but the question is hanging out there, and until you get it out of the way, not much will happen during an interview.

If you choose not to address it, the interviewer may be trying to think up a way to politely ask you instead of listening to your very fine offerings about your many talents and how they could be applied to the job in question.

Radio babies and retirement reversal

Are you way over 50? If so, you may be in the generation born in the years 1930–1945, sometimes called radio babies (guess why) or traditionalists. Perhaps you decided to opt out of the workforce for a period of time and now want back in. How do you best answer the following question?

Why are you looking for a job after being retired for three years?

The effective answer is not that you need the money or that you were bored out of your mind with your job.

For a ShowStopper answer, follow this line of persuasion:

✔ Retired? Who retired? Explain that you didn't actually do the R-word. Discuss positive reasons for taking time off. Everyone needs to refresh and refill from time to time. Now you're opting back in.

✔ Discuss work with enthusiasm and declare that you're itching to get back to it.

✔ Describe how you can contribute to the company in chapter-and-verse detail.

Don't wait to be put on the defensive; that may cause you to flush red-faced or stammer. My experience has been that most folks are uncomfortable with the answers to these kinds of questions and hope they won't come up. Wrong!

Get your story out in exactly the way you want it to be heard. When an elephant is in the room blocking the doorway to your progress, it is in the best interests of both parties to get this and other difficult questions out of the way early in the interview so that more important matters can be addressed.

The interview won't move forward until you expose and conquer hidden hiring objections.

Overcoming the Overqualified Label

Overqualified can be code for one of five perceptions. Interviewers may use the term to indicate that you

✔ Have too many years' experience

✔ Have too much education

✔ Will want to be too highly paid

✔ Are too rigid with demands

✔ Are too rusted with obsolete skills

In my observation, when you're told you're overqualified for a position, you can usually chalk it up to the first perception: age trouble.

But Dallas-based Tony Beshara is a job-finding whiz who disagrees that being rated as overqualified for a position is because of age trouble, and he has strong credentials to back up his opinion. Beshara runs Babich and Associates, one of the nation's most successful job-placement firms, and he personally has connected thousands of people with employment. Beshara says:

> When a candidate of any age applies for a job one step or more below the level of his or her previous position, a hiring authority is going to be concerned that the candidate will be underemployed, depart as soon as something better turns up, and leave the authority holding the blame for a bad choice. The same overqualified tag could be applied to a 35- or 40-year-old candidate, but since the predominant numbers of people going down the career ladder are in their 50s, the overqualified experience appears to be an age thing, but it's not.

In either case, whether you're dealing with age trouble or not, why go down with the one-word punch of being rated as "overqualified"? Come back with a strong response — or a pre-emptive strike to clear the air.

Try the following tactics when you hear the "O" word:

- ✔ Clarify the interviewer's concerns. Find out whether the interviewer really thinks you're overqualified — or just overaged — and whether you'll want to earn too much money or be bored by the position.

- ✔ Enthusiastically address the interviewer's concerns, emphasizing the positive. Explain how you can grow in this position: today a clerk, tomorrow a back-up manager.

- ✔ Show how you can use your experience to benefit the company in solving long-term problems, building profit, or assisting in other departments.

- ✔ Make sure that the interviewer understands your qualifications.

- ✔ In an office full of younger people, explain how you're an anchor: experienced, calm, stable, reliable. You can provide continuity.

Here are six model responses to the overqualified put-off:

> Overqualified? Some would say that I'm not overqualified, but fully qualified. With due respect, can you explain the problem with someone doing the job better than expected?

When the boss is your kid's age

Tony G., a reader of my newspaper column, wrote to me to say that, at age 60, he had just landed an excellent position with a start-up company after being interviewed by the 33-year-old company president, who, coincidentally, is the same age as his son. The other three employees are in their late 20s, as are Tony's daughters. Tony credits his success to his lack of *neophobia* (fear of new things).

"I think I was offered the job because of my attitude during the interview. I made it clear to the young boss that I would rather work with people in 'your age bracket' because there is so much energy and new, fresh ideas. That's the environment where I want to work," Tony said with conviction.

Advising other prime-timers, Tony added, "Think young, think responsibly, and always be prepared to put something solid and attractive on the interview table."

Fortunately, I've lived enough years to have developed the judgment that allows me to focus on the future. Before we speak of past years, past titles, and past salaries, can we look at my strengths and abilities and how I've stayed on the cutting edge of my career field, including its technology?

I hope you're not concerned that hiring someone with my solid experience and competencies would look like age bias if, once on the job, you decided you'd made a mistake and I had to go. Can I present a creative idea? Why don't I work on a trial basis for a month — no strings — to give you a chance to view me up close? This immediately solves your staffing problem at no risk to you. I can hit the floor running and require less supervision than a less experienced worker. When can I start?

This job is so attractive to me that I'm willing to sign a contract committing to stay for a minimum of 12 months. There's no obligation on your part. How else can I convince you that I'm the best person for this position?

My family's grown. And I'm no longer concerned with title and salary — I like to keep busy. A reference check will show I do my work on time and do it well as a team member. I'm sure we can agree on a salary that fits your budget. When can we make my time your time?

Salary is not my top priority. Not that I have a trust fund, but I will work for less money, will take direction from managers of any age, will continue to stay current on technology, and will not leave you in the lurch if Hollywood calls to make me a star. And I don't insist that it's my way or the highway.

Mastering Top Tips for Prime-Timers

As good actors and actresses grow older, they no longer have to prove their talent, but they do have to prove that they still have what it takes to play a demanding role.

Take the following A-game hints to heart, two of which are suggested by contributing experts Liz Ryan, acclaimed speaker and writer on networking, and Tony Beshara, author of *Unbeatable Resumes* (AMACOM, 2011).

✔ Experiment with statements clarifying that contributing to the employer's goals is your first priority.

✔ Tell interesting true stories that illustrate your high energy, fresh enthusiasm, and willingness to compete.

✔ Carry yourself with a young attitude. Enter the room with pep in your step.

✔ Liz Ryan advises that you think of concrete examples of times when you overcame an obstacle, made a save, and had a breakthrough solution. Talk about how you deal with change. Work these things into the conversation before they're asked. Overcome any sense that people your age can't hustle.

✔ Tony Beshara suggests that you build rapport with an interviewer by mirroring his or her body language in the first few minutes. But as the interview develops, present yourself in an open, direct, and assertive manner. Keep your feet planted on the floor, keep your arms open at your sides or on the arms of a chair, and lean forward just enough to make good eye contact. If your body language isn't appropriate, your words may never be heard.

✔ Don't enter an interviewing room with the attitude that your experience should speak for itself. Merely listing your tasks doesn't impress employers. Instead, answer the so-what question: Explain what difference you made and how your experience translates to their needs right now.

✔ Downplay ancient history. Unless you have a compelling reason to look way back in your career, focus your comments on the past 10 or 15 years. Talk only about your past experience that relates to the job at hand.

✔ To get around being seen as a tiresome know-it-all, don't constantly say "I know." Instead, acknowledge an interviewer's statement with "That's interesting" or "You make a good point" or "I see what you mean."

✔ Don't fall into the trap of thinking "uppity child" when you're being interviewed by a younger hiring manager. Mutual respect is the right tone — even when the interviewer is young enough to be your kid.

✔ Use the question technique to avoid seeming to take charge of the interview: "Did I fully explain how I can make a difference in solving the problem we've just discussed?" or "Have I left unanswered any questions that you may have about my being the best person for this position?" When the answer indicates no reservations remain, smile, and ask, "When do I start?"

Keeping Your Career Fit

Everyone 50 and over knows that scooping up choice jobs isn't the cinch it often was when you were younger. As a prime-timer, you can greatly improve your odds of being chosen by learning new and improved job search skills, particularly the A-game interviewing techniques that determine what comes next in your life.

Greener pastures

Do you know that the federal government is the nation's largest employer, is age diverse, and has 85 percent of federal jobs located outside of the Washington, D.C., area (including Virginia and Maryland)? But acceptance into the federal workplace is complex. Find job openings on www.USAjobs.gov and on federal job boards (www.federaljobs.net/federal.htm). Then read both of the following books that excel in shepherding you through the thicket of merit hiring practices.

✔ *Federal Resume Guidebook: Strategies for Writing a Winning Federal Resume,* 5th Edition, by Kathryn Kraemer Troutman (JIST Works, 2011). This must-have book for the serious federal job hunter includes tips on mastering the behavioral interview process.

✔ *The Book of U.S. Government Jobs: Where They Are, What's Available and How to Complete a Federal Resume,* 11th Edition, by Dennis V. Damp (Bookhaven Press, 2011). This excellent guide contains an instructive chapter on federal interviewing.

Good advice

"Most two-week assignments last several months. The reason is that once a company finds someone who actually knows how to do something, they tend to find more work for them.

"Most people don't buy ¼-inch drill bits. They buy something to make ¼-inch holes. If you can lay out chapter and verse about how you are going to solve the problem represented by the job in question, it will be yours for the taking."

— *Matt Bud, Chairman, The Financial Executives Networking Group*

Part IV
Lights, Camera, Talk! Answering Questions

The 5th Wave   By Rich Tennant

"Frankly? I'd stay away from using 'plucky' as a keyword unless you're looking for a job at a chicken processing plant."

In this part . . .

Questions are the beginning, middle, and end of any interview story. How you respond to them and the questions you ask in return are the primary way interviewers get a feel for who you are and what you can do.

This part runs down the do's and don'ts of answering questions about yourself, your education, and your experience. It fills you in on answering questions about the job you hope is ahead and the jobs you've had in the past. It also covers questions about hard-to-market situations and tells you how to handle sticky questions you might not want to answer.

Chapter 16

What Can You Tell Me About Yourself?

....

In This Chapter

▶ New! Explaining away multiple online identities

▶ Separating strong from wrong answers about you

▶ Breaking a leg with a big-time branding brief

....

Questions and answers are dialogue on the stage of job interviews. This chapter illustrates response strategies that put you front and center for selection when you're asked about the kind of person you are as related to the employer's bottom line.

Working from an employer's perspective, interviewers seek to discover what's right with you and what's wrong with you. Some interviewers are experts at making that call — others not so much.

This information is central to a full understanding of how to sell yourself for any attractive job to any employer.

But First, Who Are You — Really?

Does your job search stretch across several industries, and maybe even more than one career field? If so, don't be surprised to wake up one day and be shocked to learn that your true identity is unclear — even suspect — to hiring authorities.

I'm talking not about the fearsome fraud of identity theft, but about multiple — and sometimes conflicting — online identities that can result from a broad digital job search.

The problem with multiple identities

Why is the issue of multiple online identities emerging as a dilemma for job seekers in this digital age? Why is it important to you? What can you do about it?

The answers to those questions become clearer after you review the underlying reasons a confused online identity has consequences in the job market. Here's a recap of those reasons, followed by examples.

- **Job history focus is a hiring magnet.** Employers try to minimize financial risk by hiring people who are doing, or who have recently done, the same job they're filling. Employers are less interested in taking a chance on you if you lack proven qualifications for the job.

- **Relevant industry experience is highly valued.** Even if you haven't done the exact job for which you are a candidate, are you at least in the same or industry or a closely related one? Employers want to know that you've survived the bumps in their industry for a specified number of years — or, at least, that you understand the industry's behavior in the marketplace.

- **A tailored resume is widely preferred.** Employers like you to customize your resume to show exactly how you're perfectly qualified for their job opening — not sort-of qualified, not maybe qualified, and certainly not flat-out unqualified. By contrast, generic resumes and social media profiles usually miss the mark of spelling out that you provide the exact "fit" for a specific job.

Examples of online multifaceted identities

Imagine this scenario: Suppose you have a genuine work history that includes these three main occupations and industries:

- Retail pharmacist
- Electronics manufacturing manager
- Replacement-window sales manager

You need a job, and you would work again in any of these three roles. That's why you blast three online versions of your resumes and public profiles all over the Internet.

Catch me if you can

After awhile, you receive a call to interview for a job at a hospital pharmacy. Well, the nibble seems like good news, even though your last pharmacy gig was nine years ago, right? Not so fast. Once inside the interview room, sunny skies quickly turn cloudy.

The interviewer kicks off the meeting by asking which of your three resumes and profiles best describe your real expertise. Is it You 1? You 2? You 3? Are you a butcher, baker, or candlestick maker?

Taken aback, you quickly realize the interviewer must have Googled you and discovered you seem to be three different people with three very different sets of qualifications.

Your prospects quickly go from bad to worse when the interviewer tartly says that the hospital pharmacy isn't planning to sell replacement windows or manufacture electronics, but does plan to hire a pharmacist with heavy-weight experience in the retail pharmacy industry. "So who are you, really?" the interviewer asks.

The rest of the discussion doesn't go well for you, not only because you've been away from the pharmacy industry for a number of years, but because the interviewer's directness catches you off guard — and you certainly don't want to admit you're desperate to find employment in this decade of a shaky job market. Gulp!

The Internet never forgets!

To avoid your own episodes of this simmering-under-the surface dilemma, why not merely post differing "private" versions of profiles and resumes? An obvious solution, but, alas, not much remains hidden on the Internet today.

Most hiring professionals now Google candidates and screen them on social media before inviting them to interview. Here's what they look for:

- ✔ Work history
- ✔ Education and training
- ✔ Recommendations from previous employers
- ✔ Hobbies and interests
- ✔ Activities and "likes"
- ✔ Posted comments
- ✔ Group affiliations
- ✔ Pictures and videos
- ✔ Comments and links posted by candidate's friends

Although most of what employers look up online is pretty standard information, some recruiters try to uncover more controversial stuff and contract with a new breed of social media screening and monitoring service, such as the Social Intelligence Corporation in Santa Barbara, Calif. Such a digital background-checking service can crack open even closed databases in the deep web.

(For details of how easily your life and career path can become an open book, browse for articles like "Data Mining: How Companies Now Know Everything About You," by Joel Stein.)

The challenge of presenting more than one of you

The multiple-identity pitfall is being noticed by experts who pay attention. As career-management legend John Lucht (www.ritesite.com) says, "A good rule is to assume that everything you put out online will be read — *and in the context of everything else you have put out.*"

Career authority Miriam Salpeter (www.keppiecareers.com) comments that the dilemma of multiple online identities is certainly a modern job seeker's problem and makes this observation: "Gone are the days of being able to have multiple job/career personalities in place without being found out! There is really no perfect answer, but there are some considerations."

Salpeter, who is the author of the top-rated book *Social Networking for Career Success* (Learning Express), offers a number of ways to defuse the confused online identity problem before it happens, including this tip:

"Don't post multiple versions of your resume all over the Internet. In general, posting resumes online is not a useful strategy, anyway. If you're a job seeker with several targets, it's even less constructive to plaster information that may cause someone to think you can't decide what you want to do."

Before digital days, positioning yourself as a perfectly qualified candidate for a specific job didn't used to be so steep a hill to climb as it is for some candidates today.

Putting Out Identity Fires

When you're after a choice job in a super-competitive market, the most likely outcome of your multiple-identity exposure is that you just won't be invited to interview. You may never know why you're missing out.

But in case you're called in for a closer look even though your presence online reveals two, three, or more separate professional identities, here's what you can do to boost your candidacy.

Untangle a same-name mix-up

You and another job seeker may share a common name. It happens. If you receive a screening call (see Chapter 2), sprint beyond this potential barbed-wire fence with a simple response, as this example illustrates:

I assume you checked online resources for "Karen Lee." That's me, Karen Lee the science teacher, but it's also the name of Karen Lee the photographer, and Karen Lee the retail store manager, and Karen Lee the so on, and so on. What would you most like to know about me, Karen Lee the science teacher?

Project Renaissance-quality talent

Assume that you have three professional identities. Wear your multiple abilities as a badge of honor. Explain that you are not three different people, but one person with superb skill sets that can be applied in multiple industries.

Add substance to your claim of exceptional ability in multiple areas by giving examples of famous people who often are described as "a Renaissance person." Three examples follow:

✔ Renaissance wonder Leonardo da Vinci was an artist, engineer, and inventor. We now know da Vinci as the great painter of the *Mona Lisa,* but in his time, he was sought out for his work as a military engineer. (Thanks to Joellyn Wittenstein Schwerdlin, www.career-success-coach.com, for suggesting the Renaissance strategy.)

✔ Before he was an engineer, a designer, an author, a systems theorist, and an inventor, Richard Buckminster "Bucky" Fuller invented the geodesic dome, wrote more than 30 books, and created terms like *synergetics* and *Spaceship Earth.*

✔ Woody "Renaissance" Allen, one of the most notable American film directors of the 21st century, writes, directs, and stars in his films — and, on the side, he plays a little jazz clarinet. He does it all.

Expand on your talents

Early in your interview, without seeming to be boastful, take a page from Renaissance talent and say something like this:

Luckily, I'm gifted with several strong talents. Thank you for recognizing how my ability and experience seem to be a perfect match for the requirements of your job. For example, —.

Lean in to the challenge

Display a positive attitude: "Without question, I'm highly qualified for more than one type of position." When challenged, the best defense is a good offense: Confirm the advantages earned in your diverse work history.

Yes, I was the senior vice president of marketing and sales for a giant company, as well as the CEO of a smaller one. And yes, they were in different industries. I'm a quick study. After succeeding in both positions, I believe I've demonstrated my versatility to move smoothly among various key posts that — in common — share the need for above-average competencies in management and leadership.

Doing Your Best in an Online Job Market

Because this book targets interviewing performance, I emphasize what to do and say to minimize rejection from conflicting identities *after* the problem surfaces in a meeting.

But for now, as Miriam Salpeter astutely observes earlier in this segment, there are zero perfect answers to *preventing* the problem from occurring in the first place. There are tactics to minimize your risk, but no money-back guarantees that any of your online identities will remain hidden.

Moving on, I call your attention to the bone-crusher of all job interview questions, and it usually is the interview's opening round.

Answering a Very Broad Question about Yourself

In trying to figure out whether you're the right person to hire, interviewers usually start with the parent of self-revealing questions, often phrased as a statement:

> *Tell me a little about yourself.*

No matter how the question is worded, take care to get your act together for it, because it comes early in an interview — at the very time when an interviewer is forming an initial impression of you.

A good beginning sets the stage for the halo effect to kick in (see Chapters 9 and 10). The *halo effect* happens when an interviewer is impressed with you right off the bat and may assume that if you excel in one area, you excel in others.

 When you start to tell about yourself, focus on aspects of your life that *illustrate your value as a candidate for the position you seek*. In addition to knowing that you have competencies, skills, and experience related to the potential work, employers want to feel confident that you're the sort of person who

- ✔ Can do the job
- ✔ Will do the job
- ✔ Gets along with others while doing the job

A contrarian expert speaks

In the Different-Strokes-for-Different-Folks Department: Ace placement professional Neil P. McNulty (www.mcnultymanagement.com) of Virginia Beach, Va., has made hundreds of individual placements over 25 years. McNulty is a cut-to-the-chase kind of guy who advises his candidates to stick to business. Here's McNulty's take on the Tell Me About Yourself question:

"Job hunting book experts say the question is asked because the interviewer wants to hear how you organize your thoughts, learn how you articulate your career ambitions, and see how you present yourself when under pressure. That's not always the case.

"The real reason it's asked is often because the interviewer is unprepared, doesn't know where to begin, and while you are speaking, he or she is trying to figure out what to ask you next.

"I teach candidates to give a two-minute (max) chronological rundown of their professional history — no personal information — just a list of positions held, ending the rundown with this statement: *This brings us to today. Tell me, what exactly do you want someone to do for you in this position?* The tactic gives the interviewer a direction to go and also gives the candidate a 'needs target' to shoot at as the interview develops."

Employers want to know how well you accept management direction. They want to know whether you have a history of slacking off as you get too comfortable on a job. They want to know whether — despite their lack of long-term commitment to you — you will jump ship at an inconvenient time if another employer dangles more money before your eyes.

When answering the Tell Me About Yourself question, bear the following thought in mind:

Focus on the Best You.

In sticking to the Best You theme, you may ask, "But isn't that kind of like lying?" No. Lying is a time bomb that doesn't travel well.

I know a woman who did not inflate her previous salary — instead, she did the opposite, lowering it because she didn't want to be considered overqualified for a job she wanted. After 11 months, she was fired for lying when her reference checks finally caught up with her. The week before that, she had been offered a promotion!

Always be honest about the wonderful parts of you. But don't wildly exaggerate your best traits to the extent that your performance bears no relationship to your promise — remember that the piper who lives down the road will demand to be paid, and maybe paid at a very inconvenient time.

Shade your answers to pack a punch

A careful questioner hears not only your lyrics, or content, in response to the self-defining question. The questioner also listens to your music and where you choose to turn up the volume:

- Do you focus on your competencies and skills, your education and training as they relate to the job? The interviewer is likely to conclude — *hooray!* — that you're work oriented.

- Do you focus on your hobbies? The interviewer may decide that you're more interested in your leisure hours, working only because you don't want to starve to death.

- Do you focus on your present job? The employer may think that you're still attached to your current haunts and not ready to move on. Or that you'll cynically use a job offer merely to leverage a counteroffer from your boss.

Narrow the question

You can jump right in and answer the Tell Me About Yourself question, or you can ask for prompts:

I can tell you about experience and accomplishments in this industry, or the education and training that qualify me for this position, or about my personal history. Where shall I start?

Employers typically answer that they want to hear about both your work and relevant background — or a little bit of everything.

Writing Your Marketing Pitch

The sensible way to make star tracks in responding to a request to tell about yourself is to memorize — literally memorize — a personal commercial about yourself. Your "show and sell" bit should run between one and two minutes.

Think for a few seconds about what a commercial does. It focuses on selling a product in a blink of time. It grabs your attention fast with information of interest to you. Then it tells why you should buy the product.

Your personal commercial works exactly the same way by enabling you to

- Grab employers' interest with a confident statement about yourself and your value related to the job you want

✔ Support that statement with specific facts

✔ Sell employers on why they should hire you instead of someone else

I wasn't kidding about memorizing your personal commercial. Practice until it sounds natural. Just like an actor, you need to learn your script and deliver it in character. No stumbling. No ad-libbing.

Perhaps you're not so sure about that advice. Won't all this memorization make you sound as canned as a tin of tuna? Maybe. But which would you prefer — to sound a bit stiff or to flounder about as though you have no idea why you're there, or why you're right for the job, or why you have marbles in your mouth? Duh.

Depending on your experience level and the job you're trying to land, your personal commercial can include any or all of the following information:

✔ Competencies, skills, and experience for the job

✔ Academic degree

✔ Positions of leadership

✔ Specific job training

✔ Date of expected graduation (if applicable)

✔ Honors or achievements

✔ General goals

✔ A branding brief (See the sidebar, "Cool tool: The branding brief," at the end of this chapter.)

Crafting Personal Commercials

A prospective new graduate applying for a news website start-up may use a personal commercial like this:

Your need for a web editor who can handle breaking news deadlines is just what I want and am qualified to handle. Working and attending school full time taught me to organize and prioritize for superior time-management skills — I wouldn't have succeeded without mastering these skills. Considering the demand of deadlines, I see multitasking skills as especially important in a journalism career.

I will graduate in May from the University of Kansas with a Bachelor of Arts in journalism. I was a feature writer on the school's website and the student newspaper. I would have been named editor, but I worked throughout my education to pay for 80 percent of my school expenses. At the same time, I managed to maintain a high GPA, so I expect to graduate cum laude.

A seasoned manager's personal commercial highlights accomplishments and experience. For example:

I am an experienced line manager with extensive knowledge in team building that ranges from organizing project teams to informally encouraging people to work together. I've developed solid skills in hiring and retaining employees.

I also have incorporated technological advances into a company where such advances require a significant amount of employee retraining.

Additionally, my track record is substantial in major presentations to clients, which has led to as much as an 87-percent increase in product adoption from the year I took over.

In summary, I believe I have the required skills and experience you seek for this position, as well as the technological savvy and a positive attitude toward implementing change. Is my background on the mark?

How many personal commercials should you work up for your repertory theater? The answer depends on how widely you're touring the job market.

- ✔ You can create one all-purpose personal commercial (think core commercial) and edit it on your feet to make it fit the requirements of the position you seek.

- ✔ If you're not too hot at instant editing, prepare several different personal commercials aimed at related but slightly different types of jobs. Tweak the appropriate version and rehearse before each interview.

- ✔ When, as discussed at the start of this chapter, you're presenting multiple identities online (butcher, baker, candlestick maker), rehearse a personal commercial for each identity. In advance of an interview, be certain you're not pitching your identity of baker to the candlestick maker.

Try writing your own personal commercials. Avoid seeming stiff in your presentation by adding pauses, smiles, gestures, and timing. (Try your commercial in an off-Broadway setting: Check out participation in a local chapter of Toastmasters International.)

Describe your experience, competencies, and skills that are relevant to the type of position you want. Make the information interesting and illustrated with true stories; remember to *sell* rather than *tell* employers what you've got and why they want it.

Raising the Curtain on Specific Questions about You

For the following questions in this chapter, *ShowStoppers* are answers that work for you; *Clunkers and Bloopers* are answers that work against you.

What is your most memorable accomplishment?

ShowStoppers

- ✔ Relate an accomplishment directly to the job for which you're interviewing.
- ✔ Give details about the accomplishment, as if you're telling a story.
- ✔ Describe the challenge, the action you took, and the results (known as the CAR technique).

Clunkers and Bloopers

- ✔ Give a vague or unfocused answer.
- ✔ Discuss an accomplishment with no connection to the job you want.
- ✔ Discuss responsibilities instead of results.

Where do you see yourself five years from now? How does this position fit with your long-term career objectives?

ShowStoppers

- ✔ Say you hope your hard work has moved you appropriately forward on your career track.
- ✔ Answer realistically: In a changed business world where a long-term job may mean three years, speak of lifelong education to keep abreast of changes in your field and self-reliance for your own career.
- ✔ Describe short-term, achievable goals and discuss how they will help you reach your long-term goals.
- ✔ Explain how the position you're interviewing for will help you reach your goals.
- ✔ Strive to look ambitious, but not too much so that you threaten the hiring manager.

Clunkers and Bloopers

✔ Say that you want the interviewer's job.

✔ Describe unrealistic goals.

✔ Flippantly say that you expect to see yourself in mirrors and on YouTube.

✔ State goals the company doesn't need or can't satisfy.

What is your greatest strength?

ShowStoppers

✔ Anticipate and prepare to discuss up to five strengths, such as

- Skill in managing your work schedule

- Willingness to do extra

- Ability to learn quickly

- Proficiency at solving problems

- Team-building skills

- Leadership skills

- Cool, analytical temperament under pressure

✔ Discuss only strengths related to the position you want.

✔ Use specific examples to illustrate. Include statistics and testimonials.

Clunkers and Bloopers

✔ Discuss strengths unrelated to the job you want.

✔ Fumble around, saying that you don't feel comfortable bragging about yourself.

✔ Sell yourself too hard without delivering tangible evidence to back up your claims.

✔ For women only: Bring up the fact that you're president of your child's PTA (unless you're interviewing for a job selling school supplies). Discriminatory? Yes, but studies show that moms may be seen as less committed to jobs than either childless women or men (with or without kids).

Expert contrarian discusses strengths

Virginia Beach, Va., placement pro Neil P. McNulty notes that placement experts advise you to have at least two or three significant achievements to describe, preferably in ministory format.

"That is good information," McNulty says. "What they leave out is the fact that most of the entire job-hunting populace consists simply of average, hardworking, everyday people — most of whom have not done anything of tremendous importance. I teach such candidates that I place to answer this way:

I have done many things that I consider significant, but nothing that really rocked the business world. The bottom line is that I am a hardworking, results-oriented, high-energy individual who gets the job done — and done right. My work is always on time, of correct quantity and quality, and if you hire me, you can expect nothing less, whatever the task.

My two cents: Rarely is there a job search question so universal in outcome that any given rule must always be followed. Thanks, Neil McNulty, for another slant.

What is your greatest weakness?

ShowStoppers

✔ Because of the corrective action you took, you were able to transform a starting point of failure into a success story of strength. Four examples follow:

- *Not being a natural techie, I was underperforming when I first worked with X word-processing software. So I took a class in that program at a community college on my own time, and now I'm the best administrative assistant in my office.*

- *I didn't always know what I was doing — right or wrong — when I took my first managerial position. So I took online classes in managerial techniques, read management books, and paid attention to how managers whom I admired operated. As a result, I give careful thought to the quality of guidance that I give my direct reports before launching a project. I'm not yet perfect and may never be — I'm my own toughest critic — but, as the record shows, my leadership has improved dramatically in motivating the productivity achievements of my teams.*

- *I've had trouble remembering the timing of every appointment when I had to move like lightning across town from one sales call to another sales call. But I've corrected that scheduling problem with this terrific smartphone. I haven't missed a call since I got it.*

- *I'm determined to complete whatever I start, and occasionally I can see myself getting hard-headed about it. But then I step back and recall the difference between completing a project and committing an act of stubbornness and make a course correction. Shall I tell you about the time when I —?*

✔ Cite a shortcoming you are working on, even if you haven't completely turned the weakness around — yet. Three examples follow:

- *I'm working on my time-management skills, quickly learning not to take on an overload of work if it threatens the quality of my work products. For example, I now write to-do lists and assign priorities.*

- *I'm working on cooling my tendency to be impatient. It's my nature to want to accomplish things as fast and efficiently as possible, and when others stall my progress, I lose patience. I remind myself every morning that others are busy people, too. Now I cut coworkers more slack on getting back to me before I send a friendly reminder.*

- *English is my second language. But I'm taking a class and listening to speech on TV, and my language ability is getting better every day.*

✔ Balance a weakness with a compensating strength. Three examples follow:

- *I'm not a global thinker. But being detail minded, I'm a top-notch staffer to an executive who is a big-picture guy.*

- *I don't pretend to be a gifted trial lawyer. But I'll stack my legal research and business structure skills up against any other lawyer in town.*

- *As a newcomer to this city, I can't bring a clientele to this job, but I can use my talent for public presentations to build one faster than you can say "Give me a quote." I have a plan to attract clients by quickly becoming known as a speaker at local club meetings and civic events.*

✔ Choose a weakness that doesn't matter to the job's success. An example follows:

- *I'm a very organized person, but you'd never know it by looking at my desk, which sometimes qualifies for the cover of Better Landfills magazine.*

✔ Rhetorically rephrase the question aloud to make your shortcoming seem less of a minus. One example follows:

- *Let me think . . . what attributes, when improved, would make me perform even better in this job? Hmm. . . . Then identify areas in which you want more training or guidance.*

Whacky weakness

Samuel Goldwyn spent much of his legendary life as chief of Metro-Goldwyn-Mayer, a major movie studio. He was widely known as "Mr. Malaprop" for making an amusing series of misstatements that defied the English language. When a reporter asked a young Samuel Goldwyn if he'd ever made a picture, the film executive's answer was charming:

Yes, but that's our strongest weak point.

Clunkers and Bloopers

✔ Mention a brutally honest negative, such as you're hard to work with, you're easily bored, you're lazy, you don't get along well with minority coworkers, you have a poor memory or a hot temper, or you're exhausted by stress.

✔ Fall back on clichés. Examples: You're a workaholic. (*My boss has to shove me out the door every night to make me go home.*) You're a perfectionist. (*The devil is in the time-eating details, and I sweat every one.*) But even clichés sometimes work for very young candidates.

✔ Say you have no weaknesses.

✔ Volunteer key weaknesses that were likely to go unnoticed in the hiring decision.

What are your outside interests, including sports? Do you spend much time on social networks? What books/magazine/blogs have you read recently? What movies/TV shows have you seen?

ShowStoppers

✔ Be enthusiastic.

✔ Tell why you enjoy the activities you mention.

✔ Focus on team-oriented, active hobbies — usually sports over reading.

✔ If possible, show how your hobbies or reading materials help you in your work.

✔ Focus on media that relate to personal growth.

Clunkers and Bloopers

- ✔ Say that you don't have any outside interests — just work.

- ✔ Discuss extreme solo sports, unless applicable to the job you want.

- ✔ Mention vampirelike fiction, horror, or violent media. (Stick to business and news.)

Would you rather work with others or alone? How about teams?

ShowStoppers

- ✔ Discuss your adaptability and flexibility in working with others as a leader or a follower. At heart, you're always a team player, but in certain situations, you prefer to work alone.

- ✔ Give concrete examples.

- ✔ Mention the importance of every team member's contribution.

Clunkers and Bloopers

- ✔ Appear to be overly dependent on a team to see you through.

- ✔ Let the interviewer think that you're a pushover, willing to carry the load of team members who don't contribute.

- ✔ Say you don't like to work on teams.

What is your definition of success? Of failure?

ShowStoppers

- ✔ Show that your success is balanced between your professional and personal lives.

- ✔ Relate success to the position you want.

- ✔ If you have to talk about failure, do so positively. Show how you turned a failure into a success, or discuss how and what you learned from the failure.

- ✔ Demonstrate that you're a happy person who thinks the world is more good than bad.

Clunkers and Bloopers

✔ Spend a great deal of time talking about failure.

✔ Say that you've never failed or made mistakes.

✔ Discuss success as a ruthless, take-no-prisoners shot to the top.

How do you handle stressful situations?

ShowStoppers

✔ Give examples of how you've dealt with job stress.

✔ Discuss what you do to relax, refresh, and refill.

✔ Give positive illustrations of how job stress makes you work harder or more efficiently.

Clunkers and Bloopers

✔ Say that you avoid stress. (What, me worry?)

✔ Imply that stress is usually the result of lack of preparation or knowledge.

Is there anything else I should know about you?

ShowStoppers

✔ Discuss any selling points the interview failed to uncover and relate those selling points to the job you want.

✔ Repeat the selling points you've already discussed and remind the interviewer why you're the best candidate for the job.

Clunkers and Bloopers

✔ Say "No." And not another word.

✔ Remark that you will require the first two weeks off every June for vacation because that's when your timeshare is available.

Why should I hire you?

ShowStoppers

- ✔ Prepare at least three key reasons to roll off your tongue that show how you're better than the other candidates.

- ✔ Use specific examples to illustrate your reasons. *(As a senior student, I was voted most likely to succeed in business. I want this job, and I hope I have given you reasons why you want me in this job. Are there any areas you'd like me to discuss further?)*

- ✔ Tell something unusual or unique about you that will make the interviewer remember you. You can refer to a branding brief, described in the sidebar at the end of this chapter titled, "Cool tool: The branding brief"; leave a print copy behind.

Clunkers and Bloopers

- ✔ Dance around this question *(I live nearby.)* without really addressing it.

- ✔ You would be an asset to the company bowling team; you are tired of living with your parents; your house payment is overdue; your brother needs help paying off his student debt; you need a change of scenery.

- ✔ Tell the interviewer, "You need to fill the job."

Mastering More to Tell about Yourself

Most of us have scant experience in interviewing for jobs. Contrast that with the experience of hiring authorities who interview for a living. Some human resource specialists and even hiring managers ask tricky questions that are spin-offs of "Tell me about yourself."

Be forewarned: Get the intel you need in Chapter 24, "Ten Tricky Questions to Watch Out For."

Cool tool: The branding brief

Kathryn Kraemer Troutman, executive career consultant and CEO of The Resume Place, Inc. (www.resume-place.com), in Baltimore, recommends that job seekers devise an abbreviated personal marketing message, one that she terms a *branding brief*. The length of a branding brief is 20 to 30 seconds, or about 100 words.

A similar synopsis may also be called a *mini-elevator speech, a personal branding message,* or a *profile summary;* all these terms refer to a capsule of your "story" as it relates to an employer. All are shorter than your personal commercial, which I describe earlier in this chapter.

Consider incorporating a branding brief within your one- to two-minute personal commercial for interviews, use it as a standalone statement in networking, or leave it behind after a job interview. A branding brief has more "sell" than a factual short bio and is presented in a less formal style.

A branding brief headlines what you are known for. It identifies your special characteristics and achievements of interest to an employer. You can use a branding brief to help people remember who you are, why you're memorable, and when they should seek you, Troutman explains.

"In constructing a branding brief, describe your top characteristics and how they can contribute to the mission of an organization that you hope to join. Clearly state how you can help achieve the organization's mission." Here are a few of Troutman's branding brief content examples:

- *As a kid, I listened to old radio programs that said things like, "The Shadow Knows. . . ." Right then, I developed a life-long passion for radio. In a complex media marketplace, you can count on me as a proven programming manager to target and deliver larger audiences.*

  I offer expert marketing and distribution skills that I'll stack up against anyone's in the business. As a programming chief, I've got the whole package of skills, from affiliate contract negotiation and content, to audience and technology. In short, I hope you'll agree that I know more about leading a programming effort than the Shadow ever knew . . . although the Shadow knew a lot!

- *My name is Keri Bright, and I formerly taught English at Martingale High School, where I was known for establishing community literacy programs to teach immigrants how to read and write English. My bilingual skills would be useful as an aide in the Congressman's office.*

- *I successfully worked as a library technician in the James River Free Library, with diverse accomplishments ranging from multimedia productions and program development, to speaker recruitment and publication selection for special markets.*

  After getting real library experience for six years, I invested in a library science degree program to upgrade my professional competencies and skills. Now I'm ready to begin work on blending technology, archives, and library services in efficient and affordable programs to excite library patrons.

- *My career as a logistics specialist — some people call that supply-chain specialist — is very rewarding as I work to see that important materials and resources get to the right place at the right time for the right price. I'm a perfect fit for your position, where I would continue working my magic for your customers — managing inventory, distributing goods, and monitoring the quality of materials provided.*

Chapter 17

What Do You Know about This Job and Our Company?

. . . .

In This Chapter

▶ Proving that you understand the job

▶ Showing savvy about the company

▶ Confirming that you know the industry

▶ Answering sample questions for practice

. . . .

*W*hen you're aiming for a professional or managerial job, expect a number of questions to be fired across the footlights to test your knowledge of the position, company, and industry.

Even when your aspirations are less lofty and your goal is to be hired as a supporting player, knowing something about some of the topics in this chapter can put you in the take-a-bow category of candidates.

Understanding Job, Company, Industry — and How They All Fit Together

Employers expect you to grasp what the job entails and how it fits into the overall company picture. For responsible professional jobs, they're even more impressed if you've looked into what the company does and where it stands in its industry.

An interviewer may test your knowledge with questions like this:

> *Where would you rank this company in the marketplace and why?*

Such a question requires you to go into some detail about the company's place in the scheme of things — its products, profitability, industry position, goals, and vulnerability to buyout.

An interviewer may not look at your answers for definitive details, but he is interested in how you arrived at your conclusions. You could say:

You ranked second in the industry in total earnings last year, so that's a positive. Your level of debt is a little high, but that was the result of tooling up for your next line of products due out in June. If the new line is as successful as forecast, then most of the rest of the company debt will be wiped out by new sales, leaving the company with a shot at being the most financially secure in the industry. Plus, you still enjoy an enormous potential for growth in the near future.

If you mention problems in the company's performance, offer general solutions (additional training, financial fixes, workforce restructuring, and the like). Otherwise, you appear clueless or, as some interviewers may say, *Nice cage, no bird.* Or, *all foam, no beer.* Or, *all hat, no cattle.* You get the idea.

To model credibility, you can beef up your general solutions with specifics that suggest you're doing more than merely guessing. That is, cite statistics and figures to back up the problems you note, along with your bright ideas to remedy them.

A caution: Reflect before following interviewing advice you may have read elsewhere that urges you to Superman-leap tall problems in a single bound. Certain difficulties may have eluded resolution by company managers for good reasons. On the outside looking in, chances are, you don't have all the facts on the ground.

The Questions

Look at the following questions and the strategies you can use to answer them as you gear up to show perfect casting with the job, and the company.

Choose strategies marked as ShowStoppers; avoid those indicated to be Clunkers and Bloopers.

What do you know about this position?

ShowStoppers

- ✔ From your research, discuss how the position fits into the company structure and how you would fit like a glove into that position.
- ✔ Mention how you can help the company achieve its goals.
- ✔ Confirm your understanding of the broad responsibilities of the position. Ask whether you missed any key points (thereby setting up topics to discuss your qualifications).

Clunkers and Bloopers

- ✔ Ask what the company makes.
- ✔ Use out-of-date data.

What do you know about our competition?

ShowStoppers

- ✔ Discuss the current climate of the industry and how competitors are affected.
- ✔ Add details that show you truly understand the industry and the competition.
- ✔ Analyze the impact global competition is having on industry.

Clunkers and Bloopers

- ✔ Say you know very little about the competition.
- ✔ Admit you recently interviewed with the competition.
- ✔ Reveal trade secrets from your current employer.

What are your opinions about some of the challenges facing our company?

ShowStoppers

- ✔ Show the depth of your research by discussing some of the company's upcoming projects.
- ✔ Mention several possible solutions to potential problems the company may be facing, acknowledging that you lack certainty without proprietary facts.

Clunkers and Bloopers

- ✔ Say you don't know of any challenges, but you're all ears.
- ✔ Mention problems but add no possible solutions.

What do you see as the direction of this company?

ShowStoppers

- ✔ Give a brief but somewhat detailed answer, displaying a solid grasp of the company's movement in the industry. Add how you can help.
- ✔ Support your answer with facts and figures, citing their sources.

Clunkers and Bloopers

- ✔ Make guesses because you haven't a clue.
- ✔ Offer no data to back up your comments.

Why did you apply to this company?

ShowStoppers

✔ Say that the position is a compelling opportunity and the company is a place where your qualifications can make a difference. Explain why.

✔ Relate that you heard about a new service the company is launching, which is somewhat related to a project you helped create in a (college) senior-year project; say you find the potential exciting. Ask if the interviewer would like to hear about your project.

Clunkers and Bloopers

✔ Say the company is in an industry you've always wanted to try.

✔ Say you've always wanted to live in the Southwest.

Our company has a mission statement; do you have a personal mission statement — or personal vision?

ShowStoppers

✔ In one or two sentences, give examples of your values (customer service, ethics, honor, importance of keeping one's word, and so on) that are compatible with the company's.

✔ Review the company's mission statement on its website and describe a compatible aim.

Clunkers and Bloopers

✔ Ask what a mission statement is.

✔ Ask for clarification on the meaning of values.

How will you help our company?

ShowStoppers

✔ Summarize how your key skills can help the company move toward its goals.

✔ Describe the wide circle of contacts and other intangible benefits you can bring to the company.

Clunkers and Bloopers

✔ Give a short answer with no specifics.

✔ Say you'll have to get back to the interviewer on that one.

Chapter 18

What Are Your Skills and Competencies?

With job security in today's market going the way of the ozone layer, the operative words are *skills* (what you can do) and, increasingly, a newer and broader employment concept termed *competencies* (how well you do what you do using natural talents).

The competencies concept includes skills and such related characteristics and natural abilities as motivation, industriousness, and attitudes.

In other words, the *competency-based interviewing approach* attempts to look at the whole package where you're concerned. Suppose, for example, that you're a certified expert in Java and there's no question about your skill level. Competency questions attempt to uncover whether you also have the soft skills you need to pursue successful work projects in which organization, cooperation, and communication ease are essential. (Or whether your quirky personality drives colleagues to the aspirin bottle.)

Competency-based models fall into two categories:

✔ *Work-based competencies* describe job-specific characteristics, skills, and abilities, such as fluency in the English language or the ability to read topographical maps.

✔ *Behavior-based competencies* describe all the other personal stuff you need, in addition to technical skills, to do the job well. Competencies include abilities like:

- Prioritizing and planning work
- Using time efficiently
- Planning for additional resources
- Adapting to new technologies
- Keeping technical skills up-to-date

A *competency-based interview* is highly structured and based on the premise that past success is the best predictor of future success. Many questions designed to reveal behavioral competencies begin with "Tell me about a time when. . . ." (See Chapter 5 to find out about the behavior-based interview.)

How much must you know about competency-based interviewing? That depends upon where you're interviewing. The competency-based interviewing approach is on the rise but isn't yet a mainstream interviewing method for the majority of jobs in the United States. You can expect competency-based interviewing at larger companies and with the federal government.

By contrast, small and medium-size employers (where most of the jobs are) tend to stick to skills discovery in their interview questions. Their interviewers make informal judgments about how well candidates will use their skills on the job.

Be aware that some overlap in everyday usage of terminology occurs: That is, one interviewer's *skills* is another interviewer's *competencies*. To keep it simple, in this chapter, I use the s-word — *skills*.

When you expect to be heading into competencies-based quizzing, consider reading an entire book on the approach: *Competency-Based Interviews: Master the Tough New Interview Style and Give Them the Answers That Will Win You the Job,* by Robin Kessler (Career Press, 2006).

Recognizing Questions about Your Skills

Accomplishments, like some wines, don't always travel well. You catch an employer's eye with accomplishments, but when you change jobs, you leave your accomplishments behind.

What you do pack along with you are the skills that enabled you to achieve those accomplishments: mastering the subject, meeting deadlines, and researching on the Internet, for instance.

Experienced interviewers move past the citations of what you did to discover how you did it — the essence of your skills.

Interviewers may be straightforward in trying to determine your skills through questions about specific work experiences:

> *Tell me about a time a supervisor gave you a new project when you were racing the clock to complete an earlier-assigned project.*

Or you may be tossed a pretend workplace scenario and asked how you'd handle the situation:

> *You're monitoring and integrating control feedback in a petrochemical processing facility to maintain production flow when the system suddenly goes down; what do you do?*

Other questions are less direct, going in a conversational side door to see how you react using such skills as conflict management and interpersonal relationships:

> *How would you deal with a difficult boss?*

To pull off a ShowStopper interview, learn to recognize questions that spotlight the skills you bring to a job stage.

Answering Questions about Your Skills

Use storytelling (check out Chapter 5) to comprehensively answer skills questions. Remember, too, that social, or soft, skills (people skills) play a significant role in determining the winning candidate. Take pains to convince the interviewer that you're a pleasant individual who gets along with people.

Consider that question in the previous section about how you'd deal with a difficult boss. Here's an answer, underscored with storytelling that makes you look like a reasonable and conscientious person:

> *I would first try to make sure that the difficulty isn't walking around in my shoes. Then I'd read a few books on how to interact with difficult people. I've never had a boss I didn't like, but I have had to use tact on occasion.*

> *On my last job, my boss and I didn't see eye to eye on the best software for an office application. I researched the issue in detail and wrote a short, fact-filled report for my boss. Based on this new information, my boss then bought the software I recommended.*

This answer centers on research skills but also highlights patience and acceptance of supervision.

The Questions

The sample skills questions in this chapter are generalized for wider application, although, in an interview, you should expect skills questions that relate to your career field: *What computer skills do you have? Why do you think your technical skills are a match for this job? When is the best time to close a sale? What was your most difficult auditing problem and how did you solve it? Tell me about your typical workday as a probation officer.*

Note that questions in this chapter may seem to be close relatives of the questions in Chapter 19. The difference is that those in Chapter 19 are intended to draw out your qualities as a human being; the questions in this chapter go after your skills. Is it a big goof if you mix them up? Not at all. Both are reminders to keep your self-marketing pitch up and running.

What is the toughest job problem you've ever faced?

ShowStoppers

- ✔ Recall a problem, the *skills used in your action* to deal with it, and the successful results; this is a skills-detailed version of PAR (problem, action, result).

- ✔ Explain how you can apply those same skills to the prospective job.

Clunkers and Bloopers

- ✔ Recall a problem but not an accomplishment or skill related to it.

- ✔ Say you've searched your memory and can't recall a problem you couldn't handle.

What do you like least about gathering information to deal with a problem (research)?

ShowStoppers

- ✔ Comment that, wanting to do a first-rate job, you're uncomfortable when you're uncertain that you've compiled enough research to quit and make a decision that affects the well-being of others.

- ✔ Reveal that you enjoy solving problems but become impatient with repetitive sameo-sameo answers leading to dead ends.

- ✔ Explain that you use multiple resources — websites, books, journals, and expert people — and you become frustrated when key resources aren't adequate.

Clunkers and Bloopers

✔ Dismiss researching as work for the scholars among us, and say you prefer to be an action hero. (Even bank robbers have to case the job.)

✔ Admit you prefer outdoor work and aren't sure why you're here.

How good are you at making oral presentations?

ShowStoppers

✔ Discuss how you prepare. Name presentation skills. Mention specific instances when you've given a good show.

✔ Offer to give a one-minute oral presentation on a topic you've practiced.

Clunkers and Bloopers

✔ Say that you never do them because you're terrified of speaking in front of large crowds.

✔ Admit you were roundly booed at your last political protest speech.

How would you rate your writing skills in comparison to your verbal skills?

ShowStoppers

✔ Discuss how both skills — as well as listening — are important to being a good communicator, and that while one or the other may be your strong suit, you're working to become strongly proficient at both speaking and writing. Explain how you're doing so — class work, independent study, membership in Toastmasters International or a writing group; show brief writing samples.

✔ Concretely explain a real communication situation in your past; describe how you communicated the information and the result.

✔ If you're a weak communicator, give a compensatory response that substitutes another skill for writing or verbal skills; for example, in a technical call center, problem solving outweighs the need for golden tonsils and laudable business writing.

Clunkers and Bloopers

✔ Rate your skill in one area as better than the other and clam up.

✔ Say that public speaking gives you sweaty palms and you don't like it.

How do you deal with unexpected events on the job?

ShowStoppers

✔ Discuss how you immediately reprioritize your assignments in emergencies.

✔ Mention specific instances when you were able to complete a project (or projects) on time despite unforeseen complications.

Clunkers and Bloopers

✔ Tell how you just keep doing what you are doing until you're finished.

✔ Discuss an instance when an unexpected event resulted in disaster.

How do you organize your time?

ShowStoppers

✔ Affirm that you put first things first. Each day you identify A-level tasks and get those done before moving on to B-level tasks. You return voice-mail messages once or twice daily and urgent messages immediately.

✔ Comment that you use up-to-date planning products. These include planning software such as PlanPlusOnline and PDA (personal digital assistant) hand-held devices, such as a BlackBerry. These kinds of mentions show that you are techno-current. If you organize yourself on paper, mention a formal business product such as a Franklin Planner. (Pulling out a pocket calendar is like pulling out a slide rule.) Conclude with true examples showing that you've completed multiple tasks on time.

✔ Discuss how you went through a typical day on one of your previous jobs.

Clunkers and Bloopers

✔ Say that you don't usually handle more than one task at a time.

✔ Reply that you don't wear a watch.

How do you delegate responsibility?

ShowStoppers

✔ Discuss how you involve everyone in the overall picture.

✔ Discuss specific projects that were successful because of your team effort.

Clunkers and Bloopers

✔ Reveal that you like process detail; admit your micromanaging tendencies to tell direct reports how to connect every dot.

✔ Mention your belief that a task will be done right only if you do it yourself.

What's your experience with group projects (teamwork)?

ShowStoppers

- ✔ Mention a specific project, including the group goals and your particular responsibilities.

- ✔ Discuss your positive relationship with the project supervisor; compliment coworkers.

Clunkers and Bloopers

- ✔ Don't identify your responsibilities; just say you all worked together.

- ✔ Rip your coworkers as laggards and say you're sick of doing most of the heavy lifting without credit.

Why should I hire you?

ShowStoppers

- ✔ Summarize point by point why your qualifications match the employer's needs to a tee, adding any additional competitive edge you can honestly claim. (Rehearse in advance to avoid stumbles.)

- ✔ Include accomplishments and the skills that facilitated those accomplishments, plus relevant experience and training.

Clunkers and Bloopers

- ✔ Fail to make the "perfect match" connection.

- ✔ Offer only clichés, such as "I'm honest, hardworking, and a fast learner," without factual backup illustrations.

Chapter 19

How Does Your Experience Help Us?

· ·

In This Chapter

▶ Recognizing questions that target experience

▶ Focusing your answers on an employer's needs

▶ Studying sample questions for practice

· ·

*I*n the classic adventure film *Raiders of the Lost Ark,* Karen Allen (playing Marion Ravenwood) hasn't seen Harrison Ford (playing Indiana Jones) for awhile and comments that he's not the same man she knew ten years ago. Ford's Indiana Jones has a great comeback:

> *It's not the years, honey, it's the mileage.*

And so it goes with experience. You can have ten years of skill-building experience — or you can have one year's experience with nine years of reruns. Solid experience is yet one more confirmation of your ability to do a top-notch job.

Making Your Experience Relevant

Psychologists insist that past behavior predicts future behavior. True or not, interviewers look at your yesterdays for clues on how well you'll perform in your tomorrows.

Simply reciting your experience isn't going to excite an employer. You have to make the connection between then and now. You have to show exactly how your experience-based accomplishments make you the perfect candidate for the job opening. Here's a straightforward example:

When you're technically great but quiet and shy

Some people, including those who have exceptional technical talents, are sometimes very shy during interviews and appear to be introverted and timid. Is that you?

Here's a trick around that problem from Martin Yate, author of *Knock 'em Dead: The Ultimate Job Search Guide* (Adams Media Corporation, 2012) and a raft of other best-selling job search books.

Yate says that if you reach across the desk to hand the interviewer papers, graphs, and reports from your portfolio of work samples, the interviewer will ask you questions about the samples. Your answers will keep the flow of conversation going — and you'll answer the questions and won't come across as, well, bashful.

As you'll note on my resume, I've had five years of praised experience as an instructor and training coordinator. I'd like to tell you a few details about my work as an office-work trainer for military spouses, which has a direct application to your project to retrain a portion of the company's plant workers. Would you like to hear a bit about that?

Whether you have a lot or a little experience, employers want to hire people who will continue to learn and grow to the benefit of their company. So as you answer the experience questions, focus not only on your experience, but also on how your efforts served the changing needs of your previous employer.

I started training the military wives on word-processing programs from 9 a.m. until noon three days a week. After several months, I was asked to add evening hours two nights a week to train a class on spreadsheet programs, which I myself had to quickly get up to steam on — and was glad to do so.

When you can show how you've successfully adapted in the past, convincing employers that you have what it takes to adapt your experience to their workplaces is easier.

 After the interviewing Q&A begins, what should you do if you don't understand one of the questions? Don't be afraid to ask for clarification — *I'm not sure I understand your question, and I don't want to give you an irrelevant or incorrect answer.*

The Questions

Questions that you may be asked about your work experience, along with suggested answering techniques (ShowStoppers) and definite mistakes (Clunkers and Bloopers), include the following:

What kind of experience do you have for this job?

ShowStoppers

- ✔ Gather information before answering. Ask what projects you would be working on in the first six months. Relate your experience to those projects, detailing exactly how you would go about working on them.

- ✔ Give specific examples of your success in dealing with similar projects in the past, focusing on results.

- ✔ Show how crossover (also known as transferable) skills drawn from even seemingly unrelated experience — such as waiting tables or planning events — apply to this project. You learned the value of being reliable, coordinating efforts, staying organized, and so forth.

Clunkers and Bloopers

- ✔ Say you have no experience. Next question!

- ✔ Show that your experience overreaches this particular job — unless you know your overqualification is a plus or when your real agenda is to angle for a higher-level position.

In what ways has your job status changed since you got into this field?

ShowStoppers

- ✔ Mention that you've worked in X number of positions — from small to larger employers — with increasing responsibility; this position is a logical next level in your upward track record.

- ✔ Sketch advances in your line of work over the years. Describe how you've continued your education and training to be sure you're moving forward with the technology and the times.

- ✔ Draw out hiring objections: Ask whether you failed to cover any key responsibilities. If there's a gap, show how you've handled missing responsibilities, perhaps in earlier positions.

Clunkers and Bloopers

- ✔ Omit mentioning key functions in your move upward. You'll look like you may need to catch up.

- ✔ Confirm that you've held the same job for ten years, with little change.

How long would it take you to make a contribution to our company?

ShowStoppers

- ✔ Explain how selecting you will shorten training time because your experience qualifies you as a turnkey candidate. You don't need to be brought up to speed — you've been there and done that job before. Name past challenges, actions, and results.

- ✔ Estimate how long it would realistically take you to begin producing first-class work on a particular project. Then detail how you would go about working on the project. Forecast how much time you expect each step would take. Be realistic but optimistic in your time estimates.

Clunkers and Bloopers

- ✔ Say you'll hit the ground running and smile.

- ✔ Say you can't become productive for at least four months (unless you're headed for an incredibly complex job in which a settling-in period lasting beyond three months is normal).

What are your qualifications?

ShowStoppers

- ✔ Item by item, connect your close fit between the job's requirements and your qualifications.

- ✔ Ask what specific projects or problems you may be expected to deal with and which have the highest priority.

- ✔ Identify the projects you've accomplished in the past that qualify you to work successfully on the projects the interviewer mentions.

Clunkers and Bloopers

- ✔ Assume you know what the interviewer wants to hear about, plunge in, and fail to check the interviewer's interest after a minute or so.

- ✔ When you have limited work experience, speak only of your education without weaving in nuggets of experience in your school lab work, volunteer work, or student jobs.

How did you resolve a tense situation with a coworker? Have you ever had to fire someone?

ShowStoppers

- ✔ First, discuss your analytical process for solving routine workplace problems (as advocated in conflict-resolution guidebooks). Storytell a specific example of a problem you solved.

✔ In a termination example, state the steps you took to help the fired person improve and save his job before making a termination decision.

✔ Emphasize that you follow company policy and that you're fair and tactful in dealing with employee problems.

Clunkers and Bloopers

✔ Complain that colleagues unfairly ganged up on you.

✔ Discuss an example of when you fired someone because you just didn't like the person.

✔ Focus on how horrible the problem or employee was, naming names.

Give a specific example of teamwork when you had to put your needs aside to help a coworker.

ShowStoppers

✔ Mention the importance of coworkers being able to rely on each other. Give a specific example, showing how you helped and that the reliance wasn't one-sided.

✔ Explain in the example that, although you went the extra mile for the team, your efforts did not cause you to skimp on your own duties. Perhaps you went the extra mile on your own time.

Clunkers and Bloopers

✔ Comment that you're a team player and leave it at that.

✔ Say you can't recall any examples.

What did you like best at your last job?

ShowStoppers

✔ Help the interviewer to see a match from past to future by mentioning specific work experiences you were good at and enjoyed that are likely to be present in the prospective position.

✔ Speak about opportunities to plan your own day or to think out of the box. If you've made a connection, the interviewer may encouragingly say you'll find similar opportunities in this position, and you will enthusiastically agree.

✔ Confirm that you enjoyed being visible in a high-stakes effort, knowing that your contributions directly contributed to the company's bottom line.

Clunkers and Bloopers

✔ Blast your ex-job as a loser and say that's why you're here.

✔ Explain that nothing stands out as having been especially rewarding.

Describe a time that you had to work without direct supervision. Have you ever had to make department decisions when your supervisor was not available?

ShowStoppers

✔ Discuss your level-headed decision-making process. You don't rattle easily.

✔ Show that you're self-directed and self-motivated, but are happily willing to follow others' directions or to ask for assistance when needed.

✔ Storytell: Discuss a specific example of a time you had to make a decision without supervision. Choose an instance when you anticipated company needs and finished a project ahead of time or made a beneficial decision.

Clunkers and Bloopers

✔ Whine about being forced into a decision that turned sour.

✔ Admit that you've never worked without someone looking over your shoulder or telling you what to do.

Have you ever misjudged something? How could you have prevented the mistake?

ShowStoppers

✔ Briefly discuss a specific — but minor — example of misjudgment. Say what the mistake taught you and how it led you to improve your system for making decisions or solving problems.

✔ After talking about your example and what you learned from it, ask a question to refocus the discussion on your accomplishments — "Would you like to hear about a notable win as well as that loss?"

Clunkers and Bloopers

✔ Discuss a mistake that cost your employer plenty of time and money.

✔ Pass the blame to someone else.

✔ Say you've never misjudged anything.

Has a supervisor ever challenged one of your decisions? How did you respond?

ShowStoppers

✔ Identify an example of being challenged when you listened politely but supported your decision with research or analytical data, and you won over your critical supervisor.

✔ Add that even though you justified your decision, you were open to suggestions and comments. You're confident in your abilities but not closed minded or foolishly stubborn.

Clunkers and Bloopers

✔ Castigate your supervisor for trying to micromanage.

✔ Insist that you were right even though management reversed your decision.

In your current position, what are your three most important accomplishments?

ShowStoppers

✔ Mention six of your best work accomplishment stories. Ask which ones the interviewer would like to hear more about.

✔ After describing the top three, comment that you can expand the list, and reach across the desk to hand over an accomplishment sheet with your name, contact information, and as many as ten accomplishments. (Leave your accomplishment sheet behind as a reminder of your talents.)

Clunkers and Bloopers

✔ Laughingly remark that you have so many accomplishments that it's hard to choose just three.

✔ Admit that you're not sure what counts as an accomplishment.

Your experience doesn't exactly match our needs right now, does it?

ShowStoppers

✔ Don't agree. Instead, state that you see your fit with the job through a rosier lens. Your skills are cross-functional. Focus on how you can easily transfer your experience in related areas to learning this new job.

✔ Stress that you're dedicated to learning the new job quickly. Give two true examples of how you learned a job skill much faster than usual.

> ✔ Say you don't have any bad habits to unlearn and discuss your good work habits that will help you get the job done efficiently and well.

Clunkers and Bloopers

> ✔ Agree, smile, and say nothing to compensate for the mismatch — unless, of course, you don't want the job.
> ✔ Let the door hit you on the way out.

Chapter 20

What Education Do You Have?

In This Chapter

▶ Selling educational skills and value in your job interview

▶ Capitalizing on boomers' updated workplace education

▶ Maximizing the educational punch of new college graduates

*I*nterviewers glean more from your answers about education and training than just the facts. What you say reveals your decision-making processes, your values, your ability to keep up with the times, and your willingness to adapt to a technology-driven global economy.

In addition to dealing with touchy issues that job seekers of any age or experience level may encounter — like not having a degree or other required educational credential — this chapter focuses on inquiries often directed at two specific groups:

- ✔ *Boomers,* a young-at-heart generation toting around a few extra years of experience. (See Chapter 13 for interviewing tips for people over 50.)
- ✔ *Millennials* (those born after 1980), fresh faces on the work scene and typically recent college gradates. (See Chapter 15 for interviewing tips for new college graduates.)

Right Degree, Wrong Degree, No Degree? Making the Best with What You Have

What can you do when all the jobs you want seem to require a college degree and you don't have one? Or you have an undergraduate degree, and the job requires a graduate degree? Or you have the "wrong" degree?

Your moves depend on whether you want to make a play for the degree-requiring job without additional education or make a commitment to higher learning.

Talking around an education obstacle

If you must address your lack of required education, discuss your experience and skills as education. Speak of *experience-based knowledge and skills,* for instance, and redirect the conversation to your self-teaching efforts.

Assure the interviewer that your degree-less state does not affect your ability to do the job well. Use specific examples from your experience to prove this point.

Admittedly, selling experience as education won't change anyone's mind when the education requirement is rigid — as it is in health fields, for example. But the strategy may keep your candidacy afloat when an educational requirement is simply a convenient screening device, as it often is.

You also have the choice of three more strategies that don't require returning to school:

- ✔ **Persevere.** Continue interviewing at companies too small to operate a human resources department. HR staffers are paid to exclude applicants who miss job criteria, including education.

- ✔ **Work short-term.** Seek staffing firms that will send you on temporary or contract assignments so that employers can see how good you are and offer you a regular-status job.

- ✔ **Network.** Try social networks, such as LinkedIn.com, to find a contact within your target company who will see that you're interviewed by a hiring manager. Hopefully your contact will advise the hiring manager that you're so talented that your experience is more than equivalent to a degree.

Whatever you do, don't lie about your education to get in the door. The digital explosion of online research channels makes it almost a certainty that false claims — especially false educational claims — will surface.

Heading back to school

If you enroll in a formal degree program, be sure to mention this fact, to explain that you don't have a sheepskin now but are hot on the trail of a degree.

> *My experience in the point-of-sale industry more than compensates for my present lack of a marketing degree. (Cite several examples showing you know what you're talking about.)*

> *However, I can see that a degree is important to you, and I want to mention that I'm enrolled in a degree program now, with expected graduation in 20XX.*

So you have the best of both worlds with me — heavy-duty experience, plus current academic knowledge.

But if smoothing out the scratches on your blackboard with a heavy schedule of classes at a four-year campus while pounding away at your day job is more than you can tackle right now, consider these options:

- ✔ Kick off your educational comeback in slow motion. Begin with one modestly priced community college course.

- ✔ Enroll in a distance education degree program. Costs vary considerably, from such private institutions as the University of Phoenix on the high end, to such public institutions as New Jersey's Thomas Edison State College on the low end. Scout online education at `www.geteducated. com` for the best bang for your buck.

- ✔ Take advantage of a new kind of free online "auditing" opportunity offered by some of the nation's finest colleges and universities.

   The trend started with Massachusetts Institute of Technology's *OpenCourseWare*. As of 2011, MIT freely publishes materials from virtually all of its 2,000 courses, reaching 100 million individuals worldwide.

   Joining the list of name colleges and universities offering free course materials online are Yale, Notre Dame, Bryn Mawr, University of California–Berkeley, and Stanford, to name a few. Specifics vary by school, but institutions are posting everything from lecture notes and sample tests to actual audio and video. Browse at `www.openculture. com/freeonlinecourse`.

- ✔ Sign up for lectures. Granted, lectures aren't degree-granting programs, but if you enroll in one for the joy of learning, you can legitimately mention in a job interview that you are "enrolled at MIT, [year], Physics II."

 You're probably besieged with Internet spam advertising "overnight" delivery of impressive college degrees: *Get a Harvard law degree tomorrow, only $29.95.* Don't fall for such baloney. Degree-mill documents are suitable for shredding. In this new age of instant Internet sleuthing, the truth will come out.

Boomers: High on Adaptability

Interviewers concentrate on your work experience, but you should still expect them to ask about your education or training. They want to know whether you're rusted out or ready to keep up with your industry by making the effort to learn new skills.

Education and training come in many forms. In addition to colleges and universities, vocational-technical institutions, private career schools, and military schools count heavily. And you can discuss other learning resources such as the following:

- ✔ Company training programs you've participated in and what you learned in those training programs.

- ✔ Trade or professional journals that you read regularly, online, or in print.

- ✔ Professional conferences, seminars, and workshops that you've attended recently (or plan to attend soon), especially those offering CEUs (continuing education units).

- ✔ Webinars through which you find new information; many are free.

- ✔ Technology training that you've had, are taking, or expect to take. When appropriate, use computer jargon during your interviews.

In whichever manner you address employers' questions about education and training, communicate this attitude:

You don't expect to do a job the same way tomorrow that you did yesterday.

You've continued to learn new trends and developments in your field throughout your career — and, certainly, you're always willing to learn more.

The Questions

What do you do to keep up-to-date in your job? How do you improve yourself professionally?

ShowStoppers

- ✔ Describe your participation in professional associations, seminars, meetings and activities, and Internet professional discussion groups.

- ✔ Say you study professional websites and magazines, look for technical breakthroughs, and seek certifications that document your continued skill building (describe certifications).

- ✔ Discuss classes and programs in which you're enrolled.

Clunkers and Bloopers

- ✔ Be nonspecific in saying you keep your radar up.

- ✔ Look uncomfortable and mumble that you plan to return to school soon.

Of what value do you consider academic degrees?

ShowStoppers

- ✔ Comment that, when matched with solid experience, degrees are excellent.

- ✔ Remark that degrees are essential, but emphasize that you must continue to learn throughout your life and plan to do so.

- ✔ If you have no degree, assert that work accomplishments and interpersonal skills are as important as education. Your record documents that you have the right background to succeed in this position.

Clunkers and Bloopers

- ✔ Knock the value of formal education. Say it's overrated.

- ✔ Observe that you've been too busy at home raising a family to stay current with all the things changing in the world today.

I see you've been attending a training program online. Do you believe distance education is as beneficial as sitting in a classroom?

ShowStoppers

- ✔ Say yes. Defend your education. Be positive, responding that *what* you know is the important issue — not *where* you learned it.

- ✔ Identify your institution's accreditation. Say that your study was designed by the best minds in the field. Mention any honors accorded your online program.

- ✔ Be confident, noting that some educators think online students are more committed than campus students — that their motivation is stronger. Say that, from personal perseverance, you agree.

- ✔ Add that the online learning experience immensely improved your digital skills— and be ready to explain how.

Clunkers and Bloopers

- ✔ Be defensive, lamenting that distance education was the only way you could manage to work and learn.

- ✔ Explain that your only online class was really for life enrichment or a hobby, not for work.

Boomers: Updated education is marketable

"Once we thought that you went to college or career training, graduated, and went on with your life," observes Mark S. James, CPC, president of Hire Consulting Services (www.hireconsultant.com). "Now we know that lifelong employability and enjoy-ability come with the price tag of constant vigilance in keeping your skills up-to-date."

Millennials: High on Education, Low on Experience

Education is magnificent, but today you need more than formal learning to rank as an A-list job candidate.

You have to look focused. You have to look passionate about what you want to do. You have to show how your education has prepared you for the job you target.

Whenever possible, present your education as work experience. If that seems like a reach, think of it this way:

- ✔ You have experience working with deadlines and with applying skills that you've learned throughout the years as you completed various projects and prepared for exams.

- ✔ You've probably given at least one presentation, so you've had experience preparing it, and you have experience communicating to a group of people.

- ✔ To get through school without killing yourself, you probably had to develop some type of time schedule, so you have valuable experience in time management — organizing your time for greatest efficiency.

You don't want to shortchange yourself by neglecting any of these important workplace-related experiences.

The Questions

Questions you may be asked that relate to education and training include the following:

How or why did you choose your major? What factors led to your decision to choose your major?

ShowStoppers

✔ Show that you took a deliberate, systematic approach in choosing your major, focusing on future career goals.

✔ If you studied liberal arts, respond that you sought to learn how to reason, research, and communicate, as well as to do. Explain that you put meat on academic bones with career-oriented courses, seminars, internships, co-op education programs, and extracurricular activities.

✔ Discuss the courses you've taken that are most job related and show how they can help you meet the challenges of the job.

✔ Show that your choice was logical, considering your interests and skills.

Clunkers and Bloopers

✔ Ramble or give vague answers.

✔ Say you chose the same major as the homecoming queen, based on her advice.

What was your grade point average?

ShowStoppers

When your grade point average is low, follow these tips:

✔ Give positive reasons for a poor or marginal grade point average (GPA). You had to work virtually full time to pay for your school and living expenses. For jobs working with people, you devoted much time to "real life" experiences, such as leadership positions in campus organizations.

✔ Emphasize that your grades within your major are excellent or that they improved dramatically within the last two years. Cite reasons why your grades improved.

✔ Emphasize that success in academics and on the job requires more than a high GPA. Discuss the skills you learned outside of your course work that can contribute to your success.

✔ Remark how your GPA gradually rose as you learned better study habits and say you wish you had learned them sooner, but you've got the message now.

✔ Answer the question and quickly redirect the discussion to your skills and how you can apply those skills to the job.

✔ Give specific examples of your success in job-related pursuits, outside of your GPA.

When your grade point average is impressive, use these strategies:

- ✔ Emphasize that your education extends beyond the classroom. Discuss extracurricular activities and what you learned from them that you can apply to the job.

- ✔ Explain the factors that are common to both a high GPA and success on the job, such as organizing, prioritizing, and committing to goals.

Clunkers and Bloopers

- ✔ Say you don't know why you got a low GPA.

- ✔ Confess any weaknesses, unless you can show how you have overcome them.

- ✔ Offer transparent alibis for poor grades.

- ✔ Assert that grades aren't important or be defensively arrogant.

What extracurricular activities did you participate in? What leadership positions did you hold?

ShowStoppers

- ✔ Emphasize goal-oriented activities or groups over "fun" ones. About sororities and fraternities — carefully mention only leadership and good works, not the social aspect; otherwise, nonmembers may think "party animal" and write you off.

- ✔ Discuss all leadership roles, teamwork, and self-motivation; explain how those experiences will help you do the job.

- ✔ Discuss skills you learned from the activities or groups and how those skills apply to the job.

- ✔ If you didn't participate in extracurricular activities, explain that you had to work so many hours that being active in campus groups would have left you with too little time for your course work.

- ✔ If you didn't join campus organizations until later in your education, say you wish you had joined them sooner, emphasizing what those organizations taught you.

- ✔ Mention all elected offices you held.

Clunkers and Bloopers

- ✔ Mention only good-time social activities without articulating leadership or teamwork experiences drawn from them.

- ✔ Dwell on membership in political or religious groups (unless you know you're talking to a kindred soul who shares your beliefs).

- ✔ Admit that you made a poor decision.

In what areas could your education have better prepared you for your career?

ShowStoppers

✔ Your academic studies did not include the quality of hands-on experience you hope to have here, but overall, your education superbly prepared you for this job.

✔ Explain how you made up for lack of experience with student jobs, co-op education, internships, or unpaid work with campus organizations or nonprofit organizations.

Clunkers and Bloopers

✔ Insist that you're totally prepared for your career — you could be vice president of Google tomorrow.

✔ Say that you're not sure how your degree in fine arts will translate to selling medical supplies.

Academically, what were your best and worst courses? What courses did you like best and least?

ShowStoppers

✔ For best courses, choose those that you got the best grades in that were most related to the job.

✔ For worst courses, choose those least related to the job.

✔ Discuss course content or presentation as reasons for liking or not liking a course.

Clunkers and Bloopers

✔ Name and criticize courses you did poorly in.

✔ Cite your poor academic performance — or incompetent professor — as a reason for not liking a course.

Chapter 21

What about Your Special Situation?

*T*he dream job for my next life is to out-audition Alex Trebek as host of a new version of America's top-rated quiz show, *Jeopardy!*

My vision is *Career Jeopardy!* The show would feature smart hiring professionals competing to figure out why qualified candidates don't survive interviews — and the candidates may or may not know exactly why they zoned out or how they can change future interview outcomes.

The actual reasons candidates are rejected (other than the commonly given reason of losing out to a better prepared candidate) often relate to special situations. These range from a mild to a serious stumbling block in the interviewer's perception. Sometimes the special issues are discussed, but often they remain unspoken.

Pulling Back the Curtain

Perhaps you've been in the same job too long, making you appear to be unmotivated. Maybe you have employment gaps or the opposite — too many previous jobs hanging around your neck.

Conceivably, you may be battling bias against a disability or sexual orientation. Could be that you're a woman who knows an underlying concern may be parental absenteeism — or whether you can supervise men. Or suppose you're crashing into brick walls because you're in alcohol- or substance-abuse recovery.

Sometimes you're pretty sure that you're running into rejection because you were fired for cause or demoted. Or maybe you don't know what to say because you've been convicted of a crime.

Think carefully before discussing special issues. Even a question that seems innocent may cause you to reveal things you didn't mean to tell. For nonsensitive questions, asking for more time to think about your answer is okay. But for special-issue answers, you seem more straightforward and sure of yourself when you anticipate the question and are ready with a good answer.

This chapter provides comments and response strategies to help shape your special issue to your advantage.

When You've Long Been in the Same Job

What some may consider stability, others may see as fossilization. Your chief strategy is to look industrious, ready to take on any challenge that comes your way, and adaptable to new ideas.

Because you've been with your last employer for so long, do you think you may have a hard time adjusting to a new company's way of working?

ShowStoppers

- ✔ Not at all. Give examples of how you've already learned to be adaptable — how your previous job was dynamic, provided a constantly changing environment, and shared common links with the new company. Note parallels of budget, business philosophy, and work ethics. You plan to take up mountain climbing and sky diving when you're 80 — figuratively speaking.

- ✔ Emphasize your commitment to your previous company as one of many assets you bring with you to the new position — and then name more of your assets.

Clunkers and Bloopers

- ✔ Discuss your relief at escaping that old awful job — at last!

- ✔ Simply say you're ready to try something new.

You've been in your previous position an unusually long period of time — why haven't you been promoted?

ShowStoppers

- ✔ Present the old job in modules (by clusters of skills you developed instead of by your periods of employment). Concentrate on all increases in responsibility (to show upward mobility within the position) and on relevant accomplishments. Note raises.

- ✔ Say that you're interested in this new job precisely because of the inertia of your previous position. Mention any lifestyle changes (grown kids, second family income) freeing you to make a vigorous move at this time.

✔ Agree that your career hasn't progressed much, but note that many talented people are forced to root or to accept lateral moves because few upwardly mobile job slots are available. Say your career plateau gave you time to reflect and solidify your skills set, lighting a fire under your motivation.

✔ Explain that you reached the highest position the company offered individuals in your specialty.

Clunkers and Bloopers

✔ Complain about office politics keeping you down.

✔ Say you were happy where you were and ask, "Why fix what isn't broken?"

When You've Served Prison Time

The key to dealing with prison time is to make the experience as positive as possible. Work double-time to outshine the other candidates with your positive outlook and qualifications for the job.

Here are several tips you may find useful:

✔ Find the best collection of resources that address the criminal record employment dilemma on the following website: www.exoffender reentry.com. The resources include books, DVDs, free articles, and more. An especially helpful book is *Ex-Offender's Job Hunting Guide: 10 Steps to a New Life in the Work World,* by Ron and Caryl Krannich, PhDs (Impact Publications). Inmates without access to the Internet will have to rely on family and friends to obtain these resources.

✔ Don't count on *expungement* — the court sealing of criminal records — to keep employers from knowing that you've served time in prison. Expungement is no longer a reliable strategy for ex-offender job seekers because, in this digital era, commercial databases are slow to update what courts have forgiven; expunged records now often turn up in criminal background checks ordered by employers.

✔ Job seekers with prison records should be aware of the *Federal Bonding Program* (www.bonds4jobs.com). It basically provides six months of free insurance to employers that guarantees worker honesty — an incentive to employers to hire an at-risk applicant.

✔ The U.S. military accepts enrollments from those who have served time for misdemeanors and felonies. The pathway to enlist begins with applying for a *moral waiver.* The moral waiver process varies with each military service. Ask military recruiters for more information.

Tell me about your incarceration.

ShowStoppers

- ✔ Describe how it was one of the best learning experiences you've ever had. Explain the crossover (transferable) skills and education you acquired in prison.

- ✔ Say that it helped you make changes in your life so that the behavior that got you in trouble is history. Part of your old problem was hanging out with the wrong people. In your new life, you hang out with a different group of people who do not get into trouble.

Clunkers and Bloopers

- ✔ Lie about your conviction, figuring no one will learn about it until after you've been hired. (Why risk a firing on top of your criminal record?)

- ✔ Say you're a victim of bad police work and never should have been in prison (unless technology has cleared you of all charges).

When You're Shoved out the Door

The number-one rule in explaining why you were fired is to keep it brief, keep it honest, and keep it moving. Say what you need to say and redirect the conversation to your qualifications. As for what you should say, you have two core options.

Were you fired from your last job?

ShowStoppers

- ✔ **If it wasn't your fault:**

   Explain the firing as a result of downsizing, mergers, company closure, or some other act beyond your control. Sometimes firing happens several times in a row to good people who figuratively happen to be standing on the wrong street corner when the wrong bus comes along and runs them over. So many people have been on that bus these days that being terminated is no longer a big deal. Being let go wasn't your fault, so you have no reason to feel guilty. Get on with the interview with a sincere smile on your face.

- ✔ **If it was your fault:**

   Say you learned an enormous lesson during the experience. You messed up, but you know better now, and you won't make the same mistakes again. Explain briefly how you benefited from this learning experience. Then quickly turn the interview back to the better you and go on to explain how you're the hands-down best candidate for the job.

Sidelining a series of firings

If you've been fired from a significant number of jobs, few employers will be willing to give you a second chance. Understandably, they don't want to deal with the same problems your previous employers did.

Your best strategy is to call on a third party's help. Appeal to your family and friends to step in and recommend you to people they know personally who can hire you. Make sure that the people with hiring power are aware of your past mistakes, and assure them (honestly) that you've learned from the experiences and have reformed your wicked ways.

Your other most promising options are to obtain additional education or training for a fresh start. Or consider self-employment.

Clunkers and Bloopers

- ✔ Give interviewers the impression that you're hiding something, that you're not being absolutely honest and open with them.

- ✔ Bad-mouth your former boss. Say your former coworkers were a freak show.

- ✔ Tell the interviewer that you've had personality conflicts on more than one job. That admission sets off screaming smoke detectors warning that you're a fiery troublemaker.

Have you ever been asked to resign? Why?

ShowStoppers

- ✔ Being allowed to resign (a soft firing) suggests that you may be able to work out a mutually agreeable rationale with your former employer. Do so and stick to the story the two of you come up with.

- ✔ When you have no good storyline, admit your mistake and say it was a painful lesson that caused a change in your work habits.

Clunkers and Bloopers

- ✔ Lie or give excuses to justify why you shouldn't have been treated so unfairly.

- ✔ Rip on your ex-bosses or coworkers for forcing you out.

- ✔ Give multiple examples of your interpersonal conflicts.

More answers to why you were fired

To see an additional 12 positive answers to the question "Why were you fired?", visit my website, www.sunfeatures.com. Click Columns and, at the bottom of the left screen, click Good Answers to Hard Questions.

When Sexual Orientation Is up for Discussion

A growing number of U.S. companies are expanding benefits and protections for their gay, lesbian, bisexual, and transgendered (GLBT) employees. Getting a good job as an openly gay worker is much easier than in years past.

The movement to include GLBT workers in anti-discrimination policies includes two key points:

- Offering same-sex couples the same benefits as straight couples
- Seeking out potential GLBT workers in company recruiting

Even the U.S. military is keeping pace with this trend by repealing the "don't ask, don't tell" ban on gay men and women serving openly in the military.

In a further acknowledgment of changing times, for the first time ever, the United Nations in 2011 endorsed the rights of GLBT people in a resolution hailed as historic by the United States and other backers.

Attitudes are a mixed bag

Observers of GLBT employment trends believe that the message is received not only by big companies, but by many midsize companies that already have formal nondiscrimination policies concerning sexual orientation.

Moreover, my research suggests that a generational component has played an influential role in the expansion of equality for GLBT people in the workplace. As a generality, most young interviewers seem to be flat-out neutral — not affected one way or the other by a candidate's sexual orientation.

That said, another group of interviewers — of any age — continues to form the "third rail" of interviewing for you. Because of their belief systems — or the culture that produced them — these interviewers operate with hard-wired predispositions against GLBT people, rain or shine.

Even in companies or locales where sexual orientation discrimination is forbidden, homophobic interviewers get away with it because that won't be the reason they give when you're turned down (if you ever even hear back). They find other reasons for your rejection when they have any reason to suspect your sexual orientation is one they disapprove of.

Don't be lulled into complacent mistakes because of the rapid acceleration in the GLBT equality movement. (Shockingly, being gay is not a legally recognized protected class.)

Regardless of the trend to include GLBT persons in company anti-discrimination policies and pro-gay declarations by state and local governments, discrimination is alive and well.

Be clear about your prospects

When you suspect that, for a screening interview, you've been paired with a closet homophobe whom you'll never see again, don't worry too much; that individual could be an anomaly. If the interviewer is the hiring manager to whom you'd report, worry.

As you evaluate how to move forward in your job search, note that a growing number of GLBT job seekers reject out of hand the notion of working for companies where they can't be open about their orientation. They say the effort to hide it takes a toll on their productivity, as well as their emotional and physical health.

But sometimes the need for employment takes over. When you can't find a workplace where your sexual orientation won't be used against you, and you have rent to pay, you may choose not to disclose.

Recognize when it's time to disclose

Here are suggestions to smooth away wrinkles from your interviewing experience:

- If you choose to disclose, wait until either the interviewer shows enormous interest in your qualifications and you know an offer is eminent, or the offer is actually made. Some savvy advisers recommend that you wait until you have a written offer letter in hand.

- Thoroughly research the company's culture and civil rights policies before the interview. Look for companies that proclaim a nondiscriminatory policy on sexual orientation. Look for a company that offers life partners a domestic partner benefits plan.

✔ How can you tell whether equality happy talk is real or window dressing? Ask members of GLBT support networks what they know about a company where you plan to interview. Browse for GLBT job boards and websites.

Although you won't be asked directly about your sexual orientation, an interviewer may — inadvertently or purposely — nibble around the edges with inappropriate personal questions.

ShowStoppers

Is there a special woman in your life? How's your marriage?

✔ *A nondisclosure answer:* You consider a number of women special in your life (meaning your mother, your sister, and your aunt), or just say you're not married yet.

✔ *A confirming but neutral answer:* Say you're gay, open with your family and friends, and in a stable relationship. You may also want to casually mention that your sexual orientation has no bearing on the quality of your work. Add that it's not a problem for you and that you hope it isn't a problem for the company.

(Being open suggests that you're not anxious and preoccupied about being exposed, that you have the support of your family, and that you're emotionally stable and strong.)

Clunkers and Bloopers

✔ Bluntly refuse to discuss your personal life.

✔ Ask whether the interviewer is married.

I see that when you were a college student, you were president for two years of the campus Gay-Straight Alliance Group — can you tell me about that?

ShowStoppers

✔ Note that Gay-Straight alliances are found on campuses nationwide, functioning as anti-discrimination organizations. On your campus, the Gay-Straight Alliance Group has 75 (or correct number) members. As president, you were the group's representative in student government and participated in official greeting events with visiting dignitaries. All your duties weren't so visible — you also led planning for fundraising activities, balanced the checkbook, and helped clean up after events.

✔ Explain that, after leading the Gay-Straight Alliance Group as president for two years, you received a Campus Leader Award from the university's chancellor; ask whether the interviewer would like to see it (from your portfolio).

Clunkers and Bloopers

> ✘ Answer only that it was a political action group for GLBT students.

> ✘ Say that you led angry protests at school events.

When You've Worked Everywhere

In an era of contract workers, just-in-time temporary hirings, and companies tossing employees overboard to boost already healthy profits for stockholders, I'm always surprised to hear employers object to "job hopping." I shouldn't be.

Employers favor candidates with a track record of staying a "reasonable" amount of time at previous jobs. They assume that the past predicts the future and that the candidate will stay as long as he's wanted at the company.

The kicker is the meaning of "reasonable amount of time." The current group-think narrative places a minimum stay in a job at two to three years.

This arbitrary time frame doesn't mean that you shouldn't cut your losses and leave if you're in a bad job — circumstances vary widely. It does mean you need to give plenty of thought to how you handle a job-hopper question and deal with it in a logical, convincing, and upbeat answer.

You've changed jobs more frequently than is usual — why is that?

ShowStoppers

> ✔ List accomplishments in each job that relate to the position you seek. Note that you built new skills in each job. Say that you're a person who contributes value wherever you go.

> ✔ Give acceptable, verifiable reasons why you changed jobs so frequently — project-oriented work, downsizing, dead-end positions, company sold out, or department shut down.

> ✔ Say that you've become more selective lately, and you hadn't been able to find the right job until this opportunity came along; explain your employment travels as a quest for a fulfilling job.

> ✔ If this move is a career change for you, show how your experience and skills support this change and how the position fits your revised career goals.

> ✔ If your positions were for temporary agencies, cluster the jobs by responsibility and recast them as evidence of your use of cross-functional skills in many situations. You're a Renaissance man or woman.

> ✔ Ask whether this is regular-status employment. If so, admit you've lacked some commitment in the past, but now you're ready to settle down with a good company, such as this one. If not, say a temporary job is just what you have in mind to keep your skills refreshed with experiences gained at various companies.

Clunkers and Bloopers

> ✔ Complain about what was wrong with each of your ex-employers that made you quit. Say you didn't want to waste your time working for dysfunctional people and organizations.
>
> ✔ Show a lack of focus — you just couldn't get into your jobs.
>
> ✔ Say you're looking for something that pays more.

When Gaps Drill Holes in Your History

Employers may rush to judgment when they find gaps in your job history.

If your job history has as many gaps as a hockey player's smile, try to find growth experiences (self-directed study or education by travel).

If you must blame your jobless patches on sick leave, emphasize that you have fully recovered and are in excellent health. If personal problems take the hit (ill parent or sick child), follow up with facts that indicate the personal problems are history.

When your record is spotty beyond belief, try to get on with a temporary job and then prove by your work record that you've turned over a new leaf.

Sometimes the gaps in your record are of recent vintage — you've been looking for employment without success for a very long time. In current periods of unemployment, your posture is commitment — you throw yourself heart and soul into your work and you want to be very sure to find a good fit. Explain your waiting period as a quest for a fulfilling job.

How long have you been job hunting? Wow! That's a long time — what's the problem? Why haven't you had any job offers yet?

ShowStoppers

> ✔ Say you've become more selective lately, and you hadn't been able to find the right job until this opportunity came along.
>
> ✔ If you were given a sizable severance package, explain how it financially allowed you to take your time searching for the perfect next move.

✔ Admit your career hasn't progressed as much as you'd like, but the good news is, you've had time to think through your life direction, you've reassessed your career, and you feel focused now. You're fueled up and ready to go!

✔ Explain that while you're good at building consensus (through compromise) with others, you haven't been willing to settle for a job that doesn't maximize your skills and qualifications. Say that low-end jobs are all that have turned up in this market until now. Clarify that you've taken your time to find the perfect job fit because the position is very important to you.

Clunkers and Bloopers

✔ Say you don't know what the problem is.

✔ Complain that greedy employers are beating up on the working class.

✔ Gripe abut how many opportunities you've missed out on because recruiters don't recognize your true worth.

✔ Look depressed and admit that you're becoming discouraged.

When You're Demoted a Notch

Demotion carries more negative baggage than does firing. Demotion suggests personal failure; firing doesn't, unless you're fired for cause.

Do I read this resume right — were you demoted?

ShowStoppers

✔ Your best move is to deal with demotions before you reach the interview. Ask your demoting boss for a positive reference (see my book *Resumes For Dummies,* 6th Edition) and come to an agreement about what happened that's favorable to you — assuming your boss knows you're looking around and doesn't mind helping you leave.

✔ Explain honestly and as positively as possible the reasons for your send-down.

✔ Admit that you weren't ready for the responsibility at that time, but now you are. My, how you've grown! Describe the actions you've taken to grow professionally — school courses in deficient areas, management seminars, management books, and introspection.

✔ Affirm that you're looking for a good place to put your new and improved management skills to use, and you hope that place is where you're interviewing. Quickly remind interviewers that you're qualified for the job you're interviewing for, and back that up with examples of your skills and quantified achievements.

Clunkers and Bloopers

✔ Lie or try to shift the blame to ABY (anybody but you).

✔ Accuse management of unreasonable expectations.

When People in Recovery Interview

Networking is the way many people in substance recovery get job interviews, with the result that the referring party often has revealed your background to the interviewer.

When you're sure that the interviewer is well aware of your substance history, find a way to introduce the topic on your terms: *I am a better-than-average qualified candidate for this job. As you know, I have fought the substance abuse battle and won.*

Emphasize that you are a battle-tested, proven individual who has survived a crucible, taken control of your life, and grown into a stronger person. Try not to become mired in interminable details of your recovery, but stick to your main theme of being a well-qualified applicant who overcame an illness and is now better equipped to meet new challenges than most people.

As soon as you think you've tapped in to the interviewer's sense of fairness, redirect the conversation to reasons you should be hired. But until you calm the interviewer's anxiety about your recovery, the interviewer won't truly hear anything you say about your strengths and qualifications.

Seek more advice on doing well in job interviews when you have red flags such as drug or alcohol abuse in your background. Read *Job Interview Tips for People with Not-So-Hot Backgrounds,* by Ron and Caryl Krannich, PhDs (Impact Publications.).

Head-on questions in a job interview are unlikely to be asked — *Do you drink more than you should? Do you use drugs?* But you may be indirectly questioned.

We have a drug testing policy for all employees. Do you object to that?

ShowStoppers

✔ Answer that, no, you certainly don't object. You don't use drugs or alcohol. You are very healthy, clear thinking, and reliable. You are in a 12-step or another recovery program and have been substance-free for a year (or more). Discuss your qualifications for the position.

✔ Tell the interviewer *you don't object* and add that you have no health problems that would prevent you from giving 100-percent effort on every assignment.

Clunkers and Bloopers

✔ Say you're doing your best to get your life back together; to prove it, you've attended four rehab programs in the past two years. You just need a chance at a good job to keep you clean (sober).

✔ Say you had some problems in the past, and give no details about how you kicked substance abuse.

When Women Are Put on the Spot

News flash! Young women of child-bearing age battle questions about family matters.

Research companies for family-friendly policies before you apply. For example, women's magazines regularly run stories identifying the best of national companies that promote work-life balance. Use your networks and search local newspaper stories to find similar small and midsize companies where you live.

When you have small fry and you choose to stay home with them, but you still need the pay, contemplate alternatives: working part-time, pairing up with another person to do the same job (job sharing), taking your work home (telecommuting), and rearranging work schedules without cutting productive hours (flextime).

Get quality career advice and job postings for all types of jobs by visiting Nancy Collamer's JobsandMoms.com (www.jobsandmoms.com). Is becoming a major business player more your dream than hanging out with growing kids? Lois Frankel, PhD, has long had her finger on the pulse of why women succeed or stumble. She's the author of a shelf of widely acclaimed books of what works for women who work; find her wisdom — which includes good ammo for answers to gender questions — at www.drloisfrankel.com.

In the meantime, standard responses to the subtle (or not-so-subtle) probes about the patter of little feet: Kids are way, way in the future because (say why); the lifestyle you'd like to grow accustomed to requires a two-income family; you have super-reliable child care (explain).

When cornered, try this tactic to ensure you won't become a staffing problem down the line: *Whether or not I plan to have children in the future is not central to my career. Like so many other energetic women today, I intend to work and have a career no matter what happens in my personal life.*

What are your career plans?

ShowStoppers

✔ This job meets your immediate career plan. It allows you to be a solid producer yet build on your already strong skills. You will work hard at this job to prove yourself and accept greater responsibility as it is offered. You're reasonably ambitious. You don't plan to relocate.

✔ Making career plans five years out is not realistic in today's rapidly changing job market. But you're excited about developing new green technology (or whatever), and this job is exactly what you seek. Your background makes you a perfect fit (details).

Clunkers and Bloopers

✔ You expect a promotion within a year (suggesting that you'll be unhappy if you don't quickly rise through the ranks).

✔ You don't have a particular goal in mind.

What is your management style?

ShowStoppers

✔ Explain how your management style is compatible with the company culture (you researched that culture on the company website). Incorporate contemporary management-style language (you read a few magazines and recent books on the language of business today). No marbles in your mouth when you state how you handle insubordination, motivation, serious mistakes, and other supervisory issues.

✔ Explain that you don't flinch at making tough decisions and implementing them. But you're not a bully or a screamer. Storytell: Give true examples of how you've handled past supervisory problems.

Clunkers and Bloopers

✔ Give a vague answer on management style, revealing your naiveté.

✔ Out-macho a male interviewer or seem to be too lightweight for the job.

When Disabilities Are Revealed

The Americans with Disabilities Act severely limits what interviewers can ask people with disabilities prior to offering a job. If you have a visible disability, you may benefit by giving an explanation of how you're able to do the job.

Essentially, the ADA permits an interviewer to ask you about your abilities to perform a job, but not about your disabilities. As an astute employer once said, "We are not interviewing a disability. We are not hiring a disability. We are looking to hire a person who can do the job we want done."

Suppose an interviewer asks, "How is your health?" Just explain that you're able to perform tasks that the job requires. (But if you have an obvious disability, the ADA makes the question illegal at the pre-offer stage.)

For a quick brush-up on your rights in job interviews, scour the federal Labor Department's Office of Disability Employment Policy (www.dol.gov/odep; click Frequently Asked Questions).

Examples of questions to expect include the following:

You say you can do the job. How would that work? Can you explain more?

ShowStoppers

- ✔ When practical, ask to give a demonstration — if need be, bring your own equipment.

- ✔ When a demonstration is impractical, pull an example from your last job (paid or volunteer) or educational experience. Storytell: Recount a true tale of your having been there, done that.

- ✔ Anticipate essentials to job performance (anything in the job description) the interviewer may be worried about — such as physical mobility, safety, and motor coordination. If you have vision or hearing impairment, expect some concerns that you'll miss visual or aural cues essential to job performance. Explain how you've adapted in these areas or will overcome obstacles.

- ✔ Suggest a few references (previous teachers, counselors, employers, or coworkers) who can testify to your abilities to do the job.

Clunkers and Bloopers

- ✔ Show you're offended by the question — soapbox about unspoken bias.

- ✔ Explain that your coworkers have always set aside their work to assist you with problematic tasks.

✔ Without examples to support your claims, assert you have no problems with job performance.

Because you're our first applicant with a disability, we've never dealt with accommodations before. How much are these accommodations going to cost us?

ShowStoppers

✔ Promise that your requirements are minimal and give examples of how your skills will merit the company's small investment. Get cost estimates on the Job Accommodation Network (www.jan.wvu.edu).

✔ Offer to provide some of your own equipment (you aren't required to do so, but the offer shows serious interest in contributing to the company).

✔ Offer information on accommodations, such as telephone numbers for companies that sell accommodations devices or consultant organizations specializing in accommodations.

Clunkers and Bloopers

✔ Name a costly price for all the equipment you could possibly need, assuming the company can afford the expense.

✔ Act demanding because you think that the ADA is protecting you — the interviewer on the lookout for litigious types won't hire a bad attitude.

✔ Cite the ADA requirements and threaten to sic your attorney on them. If you sue, hope you win enough money to not need a job — ever!

Chapter 22

How Should You Answer a Questionable Question?

> *Is that a Spanish name?*
>
> *What year did you graduate from high school?*
>
> *Are you a Christian?*

All these questions are foolish ones in a job interview. Every human resources specialist in America knows this. But unsophisticated interviewers who don't deal with employment issues on a regular basis often cross the line and ask personal, intrusive, discriminatory questions.

Noting Questionable Questions

Employers shouldn't quiz you about any of the following topics:

- ✔ Age
- ✔ Birthplace
- ✔ Color
- ✔ Disability
- ✔ Marital/family status
- ✔ National origin
- ✔ Race
- ✔ Religion
- ✔ Sex (gender)

Federal, state, and city laws prohibit employers from asking certain questions unrelated to the job they're hiring to fill. Questions should be job related and should not be used to pry loose personal information. Some inquiries about the off-limits topics are flat-out illegal. Others are merely borderline and inappropriate. This chapter helps you recognize both types of employment probes and suggests responses to make honey out of none-of-your-beeswax questions.

Defining Illegal Questions

An *illegal* question is one that the interviewer has no legal right to ask.

The federal government and most states and large cities have laws restraining employers from going hog-wild with intrusive questions. These laws cover civil rights — age, sex, religion, race, ethnicity, sexual orientation, and so forth. Asking illegal questions can get the interviewer called on the legal carpet.

To find out what's what in your locale, snag the facts.

- ✔ You can inquire at your state or city attorney general's office. Check out a big library for a list of questions that shouldn't be asked, especially according to state or local laws.

- ✔ At the federal level, scout the website of the U.S. Equal Employment Opportunity Commission (www.eeoc.gov; search for "Federal Laws Prohibiting Job Discrimination: Questions and Answers"). Also see the sidebar in this chapter, "Club Fed's forbidden questions."

- ✔ Browse online for "list of illegal job interview questions."

Defining Inappropriate Questions

An *inappropriate* question is one the interviewer can legally ask but probably shouldn't. Depending on whether the information is used to discriminate, inappropriate questions set up employers for lawsuits. It's a threat their corporate lawyers constantly warn against. Inappropriate questions range from civil rights and privacy issues to hard-to-classify bizarre inquiries:

Is your girlfriend white?

How would you go about making a pizza?

If you were at a departmental meeting and a coworker put his hand on your thigh, what would you do?

Club Fed's forbidden questions

Discrimination law is ever changing and complex. Contrary to popular understanding, there's no such thing as a list of questions prohibited by federal law, except for these two:

1. *Have you ever been arrested?*

An employer cannot ask about your arrest record because an arrest isn't an admission of guilt. But asking about an individual's convictions — *Have you ever been convicted of a crime?* — is okay.

2. *How's your health?*

The Americans with Disabilities Act forbids pre-employment questions asking about a candidate's health. But asking about an individual's ability to perform job-related tasks — *Can you stand for long periods of time?* — is okay.

Other than questions about arrests and health, interviewers can ask any questions they wish as far as the feds are concerned. (Of course, they ultimately may pay a stiff penalty for bias if you file a claim that sticks.)

Federal law merely notes subjects — based on disability and civil rights, such as visible and invisible impairments, race, sex, age, and so on — that can be the basis for bias complaints and prohibit discriminatory treatment on these grounds.

Interviewers in companies that have human resources departments should know better than to ask inappropriate questions. But some go on fishing expeditions, hoping that weird, unexpected questions will rattle candidates, causing them to "show their true colors."

Other interviewers are natural-born buttinskies who ask risky questions because they want the information and are willing to gamble that they won't be challenged.

Illegal questions are always inappropriate, but inappropriate questions are not always illegal.

Think First, Answer Second

What if an interviewer does cross the line and has the audacity to toss you a possibly discriminatory question? Assuming that you want the job, think through your answer before automatically flaming the transgressor with snarky responses like the following:

Is your question aimed at trying to find out how old I am? That would be illegal. Shame on you!

As you know, under Title VII, basing employment decisions on sex is illegal, and I feel that this question is discriminatory in nature.

Those passive-aggressive comebacks work only in he-said-she-said movies. It's a mistake to verbally punch out an interviewer — especially if the interview is otherwise going well and you're sensing that this job could be the right one for you.

Having said that, if a question is repugnant or blatantly discriminatory, don't answer it at all or answer it your way. For example, an answer to the question mentioned earlier in this chapter — *Is your girlfriend white?* — may be this one:

> *I don't feel that specific, intimate details of my personal life would be appropriate to discuss here. They do not affect my ability to effectively perform the duties of this position.* (Translation: Back off.)

Sometimes you have to establish your boundaries firmly. But in general, if you want the job, avoid becoming confrontational and answer all the questions to your benefit.

But what if the interviewer would be your boss and is such a jerk that you don't want the job? Utter a polite exit line and leave.

Redirect Inappropriate Questions

Another, foxier approach works better for you, especially if you think the interviewer's questions come from ignorance rather than bias. Deftly twist the offensive question. Here's an example of redirecting:

Suppose the interviewer asks a question about age:

> *I see you went to the University of Colorado. My son's there now. When did you graduate?*

The smooth candidate directly responds to the question, sort of:

> *I don't think your son and I know each other. I'm sure he's a fine young man. As for me, fortunately, I've been out of school long enough to have developed good judgment. Would you like to know a little about how my good judgment saved a previous employer $25,000?*

Another way to redirect is to answer the question you want to answer, not necessarily the question that's asked. (Politicians do so all the time.) Using the same situation, here's an example of how a smooth candidate cherry-picks the conversation:

> *You mention the University of Colorado, such a fine school. In addition to taking my undergraduate degree there, I returned last summer for an intensive executive management course that prepared me for exactly the kind of position we're discussing now. Would you like to hear more about how I'm a good match for the financial oversight functions of this position?*

You know that religion is a slippery-slope question not to answer directly. But the question may come at you sideways. Suppose, for example, you're asked whether you'll need time off to celebrate any religious holiday. Try this approach:

> *I understand your concern about the time I will need to observe my religious beliefs, but let me assure you that if this time has any bearing on my job performance at all, it will only be positive, because the inspiration of my beliefs will help me stay renewed, fresh, and mentally focused.*

My suggested answer makes no mention of specific religious holidays, it doesn't refuse to answer, and it doesn't confront the interviewer with the discriminatory nature of the question.

(Obviously, if you're interviewing at a religious organization known for restricting hiring to its faith's followers and you're one of their faithful, identify yourself.) As a rule, you win by remaining calm and outthinking an offensive questioner. A good job offer is the best interview strategy of all.

Rehearsing Dicey Questions

Table 22-1 is a playbill of inappropriate or illegal questions you hope you never hear. Decide in advance how you'll respond to nonstarters like these — just in case. When the quizzing is expressed in an appropriate version, give a straightforward answer.

Table 22-1	Questions Interviewers Shouldn't Ask	
Topic	**Inappropriate or Illegal Questions**	**Appropriate Versions**
Age	What is your date of birth?	If hired, can you furnish proof that you are over age 18?
	How old are you?	None.
Arrest and conviction	Have you ever been arrested?	Have you ever been convicted of a crime? If so, when, where, and what was the disposition of the case?
Citizenship/ national origin	What is your national origin? Where are your parents from?	Are you legally eligible for employment in the United States?

(continued)

Table 22-1 *(continued)*

Topic	Inappropriate or Illegal Questions	Appropriate Versions
Credit record	Have your wages ever been garnished? Have you ever declared bankruptcy?	Credit questions can be used if they comply with the Fair Credit Reporting Act of 1970 and the Consumer Credit Reporting Reform Act of 1996.
Disabilities	Do you have any disabilities?	Can you perform the duties of the job you are applying for?
Education	When did you graduate from high school or college?	Do you have a high school diploma or equivalent? Do you have a university or college degree?
Family	How many children do you have? Who's going to baby-sit? Do you have preschool-age children at home? What is your marital status?	What hours and days can you work? Do you have responsibilities other than work that will interfere with specific job requirements, such as traveling?
Home	Do you own your home?	None.
Language	What is your native language? How did you learn to read, write, or speak a foreign language?	Which languages do you speak and write fluently? (If the job requires additional languages)
Military record	What type of discharge did you receive?	What type of education, training, and work experience did you receive while in the military?
Organizations	Which clubs, societies, and lodges do you belong to? Are you a union member?	Are you a member of an organization that you consider relevant to your ability to perform the job?
Personal	What color are your eyes and hair? What is your weight?	Permissible only if there is a bona fide occupational qualification.
Pregnancy	Your application says that your status is married. Do your plans include starting a family soon?	None.

Topic	Inappropriate or Illegal Questions	Appropriate Versions
Religion	What is your religious denomination or religious affiliation? What church do you attend? What is your parish, and who is your pastor? Which religious holidays do you observe?	Are there specific times you cannot work?
Worker's compensation	Have you ever filed for worker's compensation?	None.
	Have you had any prior work injuries?	None.

Part V
The Part of Tens

"...faster than a speeding bullet...more powerful than a locomotive...hmm. Oh good, you type!"

In this part . . .

Here you find the short films of job interview information. I give you three quick chapters — one that leads you through ten ways to show off your star quality in an interview and another to guide you through some tricky questions that may go against a standard script. The final chapter is full of fun.

Chapter 23

Ten Tips to Avoid Rotten Reviews

*T*hink about klieg lights sweeping the Hollywood sky. Think about stretch limos pulling up to a theater entrance. Think about celebrities being interviewed by television entertainment show hosts as they make their way up a red carpet into a much-ballyhooed movie premiere. Crazy exciting, right?

Until the next morning, when the reviews appear. Uh oh. Critics rate the movie as a zero out of five stars. The film's actors are spun off center with verbal depth charges instead of hoped-for praise.

Rotten reviews affect job interviewees, too, even though shortcomings in the performances don't become public in a newspaper or on a website. When interviewees just don't hear back, they feel the same way as panned actors: awful.

Don't let that unhappy ending happen to you. Do everything you can to make your interview performance earn rich reviews. And to help, a master of job search, Joe Turner (www.jobsearchguy.com), a career coach in Phoenix, shares ten ways you can do just that.

Bring Storytelling into Prime Time

An interview is a conversation. Don't fall into an answers-only rut. Spend time learning to storytell with true prepared stories that highlight your accomplishments.

Need more encouragement? Studies suggest that people remember stories better than other forms of communication. As Mark Twain, himself no slouch as a storyteller, said, "Don't say the old lady screamed — bring her on [stage] and let her scream."

In short, an interview is a conversation. An employment conversation is a series of questions and answers. As soon as you answer a question, try following up with a question of your own.

Go in Knowing Your Lines

About 90 percent of candidates "didn't get the wiki" that their purpose in an interview is to do infinitely more than ask for a job. Not you. You got the wiki.

Your goal is two-fold: First, you want to demonstrate that you are a good "fit" for the organization — like salt and pepper, bread and butter, Jon Stewart and satire.

Second, you're looking for breaking news on whether the position is really something you want to invest a chunk of your life in.

Leave the Begging to Others

Neediness is one of the all-time deal killers in the job market. Whisper in your own ear before walking in the door: "I don't need this job. I do need air, food, and water." Keep things in perspective. Sell your strengths and your ability to do the job.

Employers don't hire because they feel sorry for you; they hire because they want you to solve *their* problems.

Share the Stage with Dignity

Generally, you want to participate in an interview as an equal, not as a subordinate of the person conducting the interview. Of course, you should still show courteous respect to the interviewer, especially if the interviewer is a general and you're a buck private.

Participating as an equal is a subtle matter of self-perception, so remind yourself of your status before the interview begins.

Remember How a Star Is Born

From the moment you walk into an interview room, demonstrate confidence. Your first impression makes a difference. Stand up straight, make eye contact, and offer an enthusiastic handshake with your interviewer. If you don't remember names well, jot down the interviewer's name on your notepad as soon as you're seated. Ditto for any other person you're meeting with.

Avoid Ad Libbing Ad Infinitum

Although you should always do your share to keep the conversational flow going, droning on loses your audience. Telling your interviewer more than he needs to know can be fatal.

Your stories should be no longer than 60 to 90 seconds, and they must — repeat, *must* — have a relevant point related to your topic. Stick with your rehearsed stories, your research, your adequate answers, and the questions you need to ask.

You're looking for an easy give-and-take in your interview without coming across as a motormouth.

Keep in Mind the Interviewer Is Not Your New Best Friend

Don't make the mistake of being overly familiar. A good interviewer is skilled enough to put you at ease within the first ten minutes of the interview. That doesn't mean the interviewer has become your best friend. Never let your guard down.

Remember that you're there to give and receive information about a position that you may want. From start to finish, treat this encounter as the professional business meeting that it is.

Know That Faulty Assumptions Equal Faulty Interviewing

Think about this scene on a stage: The leading lady is supposed to rush to the leading man as he enters stage right; for some reason, she assumes he'll enter stage left and rushes to an empty space. She looks as though she doesn't know what she's doing.

The same is true when you make a wrong guess at what your interviewer has in mind with a particular question. When in doubt, ask! You don't lose points in an interview for asking questions when you don't clearly understand a point.

Keep Emotions out of the Interview

Sure, this may be a time of stress in your life. The rent's due, the car's on the fritz, or you recently had an argument with your significant other.

Put it all behind you while you're on stage in the spotlight. Here's why: The interviewer may at times consciously attempt to provoke you into a temperamental outburst. Don't fall for it or take it personally. It may be only a part of an overambitious interviewing process.

Remember, your role is to be cool, calm, and collected — so play the part. When emotions enter an interview, failure follows.

Ask Questions That Show You Care Where You Go

You want to be sure you're getting the true picture of what this job is really about and whether you want it. Arrive with a list of several prepared questions about the company, the position, and the people who work there.

Ask questions that begin with "what," "how," and "why." Avoid simple "yes" or "no" questions. Take notes.

Most interviewers are unimpressed by a candidate who has no questions. They wonder whether you are disinterested, have no sense of curiosity, are not too bright — or think you already know everything.

Chapter 24

Ten Tricky Questions to Watch Out For

. . . .

In This Chapter

▶ Recognizing questions with hidden dangers

▶ Managing the question within a question

▶ Surviving when you don't know what to say

. . . .

*T*ricky questions look like one thing and turn out to be something very different.

A tricky question can cause you to admit something the interviewer believes to be true but isn't. As a single example, the interviewer may use the verbal construction of a "loaded question," such as the classic "Do you still beat your wife?" In this illustration, the questioner assumes that you have beaten your wife in the past.

However phrased, a tricky question may seem like slam-dunk material, but in reality, it's a double-faced probe that presents great risk to your chances of being hired. Think before talking. *Be sure you know what's really being asked.*

Spot Purpose Behind Each Question

What's the best job interview response to all questions? It's the one that adds up to "Hire me!"

As Sherlock Holmes would say, "Elementary, Dr. Watson." But recruiters report that high numbers of job seekers blab negative information without realizing they're making a farewell address to a job opportunity.

Following are ten prime-time tricky probes with hidden agendas that experienced interviewers use to separate the possible hires from the rejects.

Why've you been out of work so long? How many others were laid off? Why you?

Why is the interviewer asking you about your recent employment history when you've already said you were laid off (not fired)? This quizzing could cause you to reveal there's something wrong with you that other employers have already discovered.

The interviewer is fishing to determine whether there was a layoff of one and you were it. Or whether your former manager used the theme of recession and budget cuts to dump groups of second-string employees.

"Hire me!" answer: Explain that, after your layoff, you stopped to reevaluate where your life is headed. You began your search in earnest only a few weeks ago, when you realized your true aims. The interviewer's company and this position are of special interest to you.

An alternative explanation for not jumping into the job chase centers on a time-out event that has since resolved itself — an ill family member, for instance.

Any direct answer to why you were included in a reduction in force is risky because anger toward your former managers could pop up, raising doubt about your self-control. A better idea: Punt. Shake your head and say you don't know the reason, because you were an excellent employee who gave more than a day's work for a day's pay.

If employed, how do you manage time for interviews?

The real question is whether you are lying to and short-changing your current employer while looking for other work.

Clearly state that you're taking personal time, and that's why you interview only for job openings for which you're a terrific match. If further interviews are suggested, mention that your search is confidential and ask if it would be possible to meet again on a Saturday morning. You are not a time cheater. You are not a slacker. You are not a liar.

How did you prepare for this interview?

Translation: Is this job important enough for you to research it, or are you going through the motions without preparation, making it up as you go?

You very much want this job, and of course you researched it, starting with the company website. For other pointers, look back at Chapters 6 and 17.

Do you know anyone who works for us?

(If a company has a nepotism policy prohibiting the hiring of relatives, you'd be aware of it and not wasting everyone's time by interviewing.)

But the friend question is a two-way street. Nothing beats having a friend deliver your resume to a hiring manager, but that transaction presumes the friend is well thought of in the company. If not — ouch!

Remember the birds-of-a-feather rule: Mention a friend inside the company only if you're certain of your friend's positive standing.

Where would you really like to work? Doing what?

The real agenda for this question is assurance that you aren't applying to every job opening in sight, that you actually know what you want, and that you won't be bored stiff by the job being discussed.

Caveat: Never, ever mention another company's name or another job.

A short "Hire me!" answer is a version of: "This is the place where I want to work, and this job is what I want to do. I have what you need, and you have what I want. I can't wait to get to work here."

What bugs you about coworkers or bosses?

This not-so-subtle inquiry is a clever trap to see if you're a troublemaker or have a prickly personality.

Steer clear of this third-rail territory. Develop a poor memory for past irritations. Reflect for a few moments, shake your head, and say you can't come up with anything that irritates you. Continue for a couple of sentences elaborating on how you seem to get along with virtually everyone.

Mention that you've been lucky to have good bosses who are knowledgeable and fair, with a sense of humor and high standards. Past coworkers are able, supportive, and friendly. Smile your most sincere smile. Don't be lured into elaborating further.

Can you describe how you solved a work/school problem?

This forthright question is tricky only in the sense that most job seekers can't come up with an example on the spot that favorably reflects on their ability to think critically and develop solutions.

The answer is obvious: Anticipate a question about how your mind works and have a canned answer ready. A new graduate might speak of time management to budget more time for study; an experienced worker might speak of time management to clear an opportunity for special task force assignments.

Can you describe a work/school instance in which you messed up?

The question within a question is whether you learn from your mistakes or keep repeating the same errors. A kindred concern is whether you are too self-important to consider any action of yours to be a mistake.

Speaking of mistakes, here's a chance to avoid making one during your job interview: Never deliver a litany of your personal bad points. Instead, briefly mention a single small, well-intentioned goof and follow up with an important lesson learned from the experience.

How does this position compare with others you're applying for? Are you under consideration by other employers now?

The intent of these questions is to gather intel on the competitive job market or get a handle on what it will take to bring you onboard. Maybe the job market for your talents is flat and you can be had on the cheap. Or if your resume is parked at several companies, why haven't you been snatched up?

You can choose a generic strategy and say you don't interview and tell, that you respect the privacy of any organization where you interview, including this one. Emphasize that this company is where you hope to find a future, and ask, "Have I found my destination here?"

If you won the lottery, would you still work?

This question goes to your motivation, work ethic, and enthusiasm for work. Are you merely occupying a space until you can hang it up?

A possible answer: If you mean it, say yes, you'd retire right now. But since you need to work, this is the sort of work you prefer.

The "Hire me!" answer: While you'd be thrilled to win the lottery, you'll still seek out fulfilling work because working, meeting challenges, and scoring accomplishments are what make most people happy, including you. Say it with a straight face.

When You're Uncertain

If a hardball question comes at you out of left field, try not to panic. Take a deep breath, look the interviewer in the eyes, and comment that it's a good question you'd like to mull over and come back to. The interviewer may forget to ask again.

But if the question does resurface and your brain goes on holiday, say that you don't know the answer and that, being a careful worker, you prefer not to guess.

If you've otherwise done a good job of answering questions and confidently explained why you're a great match for the position, the interviewer probably won't consider your lack of specifics on a single topic to be a deal breaker.

Chapter 25

Tens of Lines on the Cutting Room Floor

. . . .

In This Chapter

▶ Imagining made-up wacky quotes from famous folks

▶ Laughing all the way to your next interview

. . . .

*Y*ou dutifully finished a whole book of savvy strategies and astute responses. Your big reward arrives when you get the job offer you want. But your immediate reward starts right now as you chuckle all the way to your next interview.

From the Time Machine: News You Can't Use

Here's a totally made-up collection of lines that famous figures in history, literature, and pop culture might say to a job interviewer today. The quips are the creative contribution of Jeffery R. Cox, who has a wickedly wild sense of humor. What do you think — would these quips bring home the job?

✔ **Hester Prynne** (fictional woman in *The Scarlet Letter* made to display the scarlet letter *A* on her bosom for her sin of adultery)

I offer a talent for marketing, with specific experience in branding.

✔ **William the Conqueror** (Norman general who conquered England)

I know I have reputation for hostile takeovers, but I like to think of them as friendly mergers.

✔ **Don Vito Corleone** (head of fictional crime family in *The Godfather*)

I was a good boss. I treated my employees like a family, and as you know, nothing is more important than family.

- **Zeus** (mythical Greek god-in-chief)

  I have to go through a job interview? I used to be the King of the Gods, for cryin' out loud!

- **Buffy Summers** (heroine of *Buffy the Vampire Slayer*)

  I hated my last job. Every day I felt like I was going to the gates of hell to try to keep the demons locked inside.

- **Captain Kirk** (Starfleet captain in the *Star Trek* franchise)

  I boldly took my department where no one had gone before.

- **St. Joan of Arc** (French teenage general who won great victories before being burned at the stake)

  I may look a little wet behind the ears, but I defeated the world's greatest army, liberated my country, and changed the course of history — and my last boss called me a saint.

- **Isaac Newton** (super 17th-century scientist who explained gravity after seeing an apple fall from a tree and wondering why it fell down instead of up)

  My last boss thought I took direction well. I didn't need to be hit on the head to do something.

- **David** (biblical king who defeated the giant Goliath)

  I'm not into size. When it comes to the competition, my thinking is, "The bigger they are, the harder they fall."

- **Harriet Tubman** (U.S. Civil War abolitionist who helped slaves escape through the Underground Railroad)

  My specialty is discreet outplacement.

- **Julius Caesar** (unrivaled leader of the Roman Republic who was fatally stabbed by Roman senators, including some of his pals)

  My previous job involved a lot of office politics and backstabbing. I'd like to get away from all that.

- **Cleopatra** (last pharaoh of strife-driven ancient Egypt, who died from suicide by snake bites)

  The office politics at my last job were a nightmare. I worked with a bunch of snakes.

- **Tony Soprano** (mobster boss of crime family in *The Sopranos* TV show)

  Would I go after my boss's job? Do I look like the kind of guy who would knock off his boss for a promotion?

✔ **Genghis Khan** (12th-century Mongol general who butchered entire peoples to create the Mongol empire)

My primary talent is downsizing. On my last job, I downsized my staff, my organization, and the populations of a number of countries.

✔ **Albert Einstein** (great physicist whose theory of relativity holds that time doesn't flow at a fixed rate)

I brought my major research project with me. Do you have time for a demonstration?

✔ **Pandora** (woman in Greek mythology who released all of mankind's evils by opening a box)

I think I can bring a lot to your company. I like discovering new things.

✔ **Hannibal Lecter** (serial cannibal in *The Silence of the Lambs* movies)

I was the victim of communications problems with my old boss. I had him over for dinner, and he practically disappeared after that.

✔ **Odysseus** (legendary Greek hero of *The Odyssey* who took ten years to wander home from the Trojan War)

We didn't reach our goals overnight, but we got there . . . eventually.

✔ **Michelangelo** (genius Renaissance painter and sculptor who did a lot of artistry for the Vatican)

Can we negotiate on the Sistine ceiling? I'll do the job for 50 percent less if I can use a roller.

✔ **Pharaoh Ramses II** (Egyptian ruler during biblical Exodus story)

My main accomplishment? My entire labor force walked out on me, but I still produced.

✔ **Robin Hood** (legendary British outlaw who rode through Sherwood Forest with colorful buddies)

My financial management accomplishment? Some may consider it stealing from the rich and giving to the poor, but I saw it as creative reinvestment.

✔ **Faust** (German legend who traded his soul to the devil in exchange for knowledge)

I had to make a deal with the devil, but I kept my department under budget.

✔ **Cassandra** (Greek mythological prophet whose predictions were ignored)

My greatest weakness? Perhaps it is my skill at seeing the future.

✔ **Helen of Troy** (in Greek mythology, a real babe whose abduction by her lover started Trojan War)

I'm not just another pretty face. Although I've been known to launch a thousand ships, I'd like to be known for the skills I bring to the job.

✔ **George Washington** (first U.S. president)

If I can lead a successful rebellion and a fledgling country, I'm sure I can lead your insignificant department.

✔ **Moses** (Hebrew liberator who parted the Red Sea, allowing the Hebrews to escape slavery in Egypt)

Red tape? I can part red tape to get the job done.

✔ **Christopher Columbus** (Italian explorer who, realizing the world is round, in 1492 sailed across the Atlantic looking for a shortcut to India and found America)

You bet I can open new markets for your company. Put me on the road, and I'll discover a world of opportunity, the likes of which you've never seen.

✔ **Napoleon Bonaparte** (18th-century French military giant and emperor who conquered most of Europe)

Okay, I'll start today in the mailroom, but tomorrow . . . the world.

✔ **John F. Kennedy** (American president who launched the U.S. Peace Corps, illustrating his commitment to public service)

In preparation for this interview, I asked myself not what this company can do for me, but what I can do for this company.

✔ **Joseph Guillotine** (French physician who invented a device for execution by decapitation)

I think I can give your company a head start on the competition.

✔ **William Tell** (medieval Swiss legend said to have shot an apple from the head of his son)

My last boss told me I always gave everything I did my best shot.

✔ **Othello** (stern soldier in William Shakespeare's *Othello* who forgives no supposed misdeed by anyone, including his wife, and imposes ultimate sanction across the board)

I demand performance. Even those closest to me were axed when I was told they had let me down.

✔ **Lewis & Clark** (in the early 1800s, two explorers who led an official expedition to map land acquired in the Louisiana Purchase, a big chunk of the American West)

Big land development plans? Yes, we have experience in scouting out new real estate.

✔ **Richard III** (in William Shakespeare's *Richard III,* English king whose horse is slain in battle — he pleads for another horse, for which he promises to pay dearly)

A job! A job! My kingdom for a job!

✔ **Leonidas** (Spartan king who, against all odds, led a heroic suicide mission against the Persians)

Management said there was no way my team could produce a report in time. "Nonsense!" I told them. "This is where we stand! This is where we write!"

✔ **Boris Badenov** (spy character with a heavy accent in the animated cartoon *Rocky & Bullwinkle* who repeatedly tries to knock off "moose and squirrel")

If I can make beeg trouble for moose and squirrel, I can make beeger trouble for your competitors.

✔ **King Tut** (Egyptian pharaoh in the land of the pyramids)

I understand your questioning my business practices, but where I come from, the term "pyramid scheme" has a completely different meaning.

✔ **Gollum** (a main *Lord of the Rings* character who began life as a good hobbit but — after murdering for possession of the ring — slid into slime trying to justify his actions)

Year after year, I would win our company's highest award. But fat, stupid hobbits tried to take it from me, tried to take my precious ring from me. But I didn't let them. It was mine . . . mine . . . mine . . . my precious!

✔ **Achilles** (fearless and determined warrior of Homer's *The Iliad* who was invulnerable in all of his body except his heel)

When I'm going for my goals, I never let little things stop me.

✔ **Count Dracula** (vampire in Gothic horror films)

I sucked everything I could out of my employees, but I got them to produce. No mean feat, since I could only work the night shift.

- **Maxwell Smart** (bungling Agent 86 who thwarts various threats to the world, using shoe phones and other oddities, in *Get Smart*)

  I am very versatile in the roles I can perform. Would you believe that my last assignment had me disguised as a stapler and loving it?

- **Anakin Skywalker, or Darth Vader** (fictional Jedi knight–turned–villain in the classic *Star Wars* saga)

  My boss accused me of having a dark side, but I like to think of it as commitment to getting the job done.

- **Lady Godiva** (English noblewoman on horseback who rode naked through town as political protest)

  So, this isn't what you meant by "business casual"?

Appendix

Questions by Career Fields and Industries

· ·

*P*roduction of virtually every Hollywood flick concludes with the director's "wrap party" ("That's a wrap!"). The classic event for cast and crew of a film celebrates the end of principal photography before the work goes into post-production.

Welcome to the Wrap Party

Adapting that pleasant film tradition to *Job Interviews For Dummies,* 4th Edition, I'm throwing a wrap party. Sorry, you won't find coupons here for champagne or canapés, but I do celebrate with an extra helping of a different kind of popular job interview questions. If you're wondering about the primary distinction between previous questions and those you'll find in this appendix, here it is:

- ✔ **Wide angle:** Job interview questions within this guidebook's chapters shine floodlights on information about you that can come up in any line of work.

- ✔ **Narrow angle:** Job interview questions in "The Wrap Party" shine a spotlight on information about you that can come up in a particular line of work.

Read questions even when they're out of your territory. With a little imagination, you can adapt a number of topics to your scenario.

The upcoming pages include selected job interview questions for the following categories:

Accounting

Information Technology

Administrative

Law Enforcement

Air Transportation

Legal Services

Education

Management

Engineering

Nursing

Financial Services

Sales

Hospitality

Accounting

People who work in accounting jobs help make sure that companies are run efficiently, public records kept accurately, and taxes paid properly and on time. Specific job duties vary widely among the four major fields of accounting: public accounting, management accounting, government accounting, and internal auditing.

Accountants and bookkeepers

With which accounting applications are you most familiar?

In what aspects of hands-on accounting did you participate?

Can you give me examples of the accounting reports you have prepared?

Can you describe any accounting process that you have developed or revised?

What do you consider to be the biggest challenge facing the accounting profession today?

What cost-cutting measures have you been responsible for implementing?

Can you discuss your experience in financial analysis of company/ad hoc projects?

Can you describe the expense forecasting for which you have been responsible?

What role did you play in the audit process?

Which management reports have you prepared?

Can you discuss your experience in tax planning and preparation?

How do you stay updated on all the accounting rules and techniques?

Using the Internal Revenue Service rules, what criteria differentiate a consultant from an employee?

Have you experienced handling an invoice discrepancy? If so, how did you resolve the discrepancy?

Can you tell the difference between billable and nonbillable expenses?

Can you explain the relationship between cost accounting, financial accounting, and managerial accounting?

Administrative

Receptionists, administrative assistants, and secretaries perform a variety of clerical duties necessary to make an organization run efficiently. Office and administrative support personnel are increasingly assuming responsibilities once reserved for managerial and professional staff. Extensive knowledge of computer software applications is a big plus.

Receptionists

How would you go about making a visitor feel welcome to the company?

How would you handle answering a phone caller's question with five other lines ringing?

How did our receptionist greet you? Would you have done anything differently?

Can you give an example of how you dealt with a difficult situation/caller?

Why do you think enthusiasm is an important requirement for being a receptionist?

What is the most irritating aspect of a receptionist's job?

How would you respond to the following: Upset caller? Upset supplier? Upset employee?

Give us an example of a difficult situation and how you handled it.

What three things most likely would make you angry with a caller?

How would you handle a person who has to wait a long time for a scheduled appointment?

Above all else, what character quality do you think is the most important for a receptionist?

How would you handle an interruption from a visitor with an urgent request?

How would you handle a caller while a visitor is standing before you?

What is more important to handle first — internal or external demands on your time?

How would you handle multiple demands from your managers?

Can you tell us about a time you found it necessary to be abrupt with a person to finish your task?

What is the most stressful experience you've had as a receptionist, and how have you handled it?

If your boss was working in his office and had asked not to be disturbed, what would you tell a caller asking for him?

Administrative assistants and secretaries

Are you comfortable using a phone with multiple lines and handling a high volume of telephone calls?

How would you feel supervising two or three other employees? What do you expect from a supervisor?

What did you dislike the most about working in an office environment?

This office has an official dress code. Have you reviewed our code and are you comfortable with it?

Do you have experience making national and international travel arrangements?

Were you involved in the budgeting and financial planning of the projects that you handled?

Have you handled procurement or hiring of suppliers or vendors in your previous jobs?

What process do you follow in receiving and filing incoming letters?

Can you give me an instance of an assignment, which you have recently worked on, that involved the learning of a fresh technical development?

Could your work presentation be improved by incorporating new technological knowledge and developments?

What is your experience with software used in your job? What resources do you use when faced with a computer problem?

Have you ever used software to make a work-associated presentation?

Are you acquainted with Microsoft Outlook? MS Word? MS PowerPoint? MS Excel?

What is your typing speed?

What is your knowledge with meeting planning and calendar maintenance? How do you organize and schedule a meeting?

If I asked you to plan a meeting and cover all aspects of the meeting, what would you do?

Can you name the factors to consider in determining the suitable preservation period for records?

What actions can you take to make the retrieval of records easy?

Can you tell me your experience in managing an off-site records storeroom?

What are the significant service requirements in using a contract facility for off-site records storage?

Tell me about the last job you did that concerned record keeping or bookkeeping?

How would you "file" computer files? Can you explain your knowledge of the digital filing system?

In what circumstances have you used social media? Google Plus? Twitter?

What is the reason for a records retention schedule?

What types of records would be measured as very important records for an organization?

What are the responsibilities of an executive secretary to a CEO?

Describe a situation when you had to handle multiple interactions simultaneously. What did you do?

(Also see "Information Technology" later in this chapter.)

Air Transportation

Pilots are highly trained professionals who fly airplanes or helicopters to carry out a wide variety of tasks. Most are airline pilots, copilots, and flight engineers who transport passengers and cargo. Except on small airplanes, two pilots usually make up the cockpit crew. Generally, the most experienced pilot, the captain, is in command and supervises all other crew members.

Aircraft pilots

You find your captain drinking before a flight. How will you handle this?

You are talking to the captain and you smell alcohol. Although you didn't see him drinking, what would you do?

The aircraft is loaded well beyond gross weight, but the captain tells you that he does this all the time and the aircraft will fly. What do you do?

If you were a professional pilot and had an early morning trip, how would you prepare yourself for it?

What are some of the limitations of your aircraft and yourself?

You smell smoke in the cockpit. What initial action should you take?

How would you fly this airport's SID?

Have you ever had an in-air emergency; if so how did you handle it?

What is the importance of proficiency in several languages for a pilot?

Can you obtain ground reverse/braking thrust from propellers?

What is propeller feathering, and why is it used?

How would you overtake (in the air) another aircraft at the same altitude and direction of flight?

Who has the right of way on the ground?

Can you explain stress analysis?

What is the requirement to become a professional engineer (PE) in the field of aerospace?

What is your definition of CRM (crew resource management)?

What is the pattern altitude of jet aircraft and what is the maximum speed at 10,000 feet?

Can you explain the differences between aeronautical engineering and astronautical engineering?

What is V1 (takeoff decision speed)?

Can you define balanced field length?

What would you do if you saw a passenger being abusive to a member of the cabin crew?

What do you think poses the greatest threat to airline security today?

Can you discuss the most significant business issue currently affecting the airline industry and what measures you think this airline is taking in response to its effects?

Education

If you can read this guidebook, thank a teacher. Teachers not only must be able to teach and motivate students, but they also often take on roles as advisors and mentors. American teachers who work in K–12 grades number in the millions and are found in every school district in the United States.

Teachers

What motivated you to become an educator?

How do you motivate students? What would you do if you realized that your approach wasn't working or wasn't as effective as you wanted it to be?

What have you found to be the toughest aspect of classroom management?

How do you develop curriculum? What would you do if you realized that your curriculum wasn't effective?

How do you evaluate a student's performance? How can you tell if a student is "getting" the material? Or if not "getting" the material, how would you deal with the latter?

How do you individualize learning in a classroom of students with different learning styles and needs?

How do you handle students with consistent behavior problems?

Can you describe a time that you deviated from your lesson plan for a "teachable moment"?

Do you believe that humor has value in the classroom? Is so, how do you use it to the advantage of your teaching message?

How do you give your students recognition? Do you think a student can have too much recognition?

How do you encourage students to learn?

How do you prefer to use computers in the classroom?

If a student came to you and said, "None of the other students like me," what would you say?

How would you handle a child who seems gifted but is a discipline problem?

How would you handle making a difficult phone call to a parent?

How would you work with parents who disagree with your teaching style or assessment of their child?

How do you involve parents in the learning process?

What is your view of the role of a principal (or other administrator)?

Engineering

Engineers apply the principles of science and mathematics to develop solutions to technical problems. Their work links scientific discoveries with commercial applications. Most engineers specialize in a career field (such as electrical engineering), industry (such as motor vehicles), or technology (such as turbines). Engineering technicians assist engineers.

Engineers and engineering technicians

Can you describe the most significant written technical report or presentation you had to complete?

Can you tell me about your greatest success in using the principles of logic to solve an engineering problem in your last job?

Can you give me an example of a time when you applied your ability to use analytical techniques to define problems or design solutions?

To what extent has your engineering background required you to be skilled in the analysis of technical reports or data?

Can you describe a time when you used your engineering knowledge to solve a problem for which there appeared to be no answer?

I expect the engineer who I hire for this position to be precise — detail-oriented in everything he or she does. What checks and balances do you use to avoid mistakes?

Some of the best-engineered ideas are born of an individual's ability to challenge conventional thinking. Can you tell me about a time when you were successful in doing this?

Do you have any patents? If so, can you tell me about them? If not, is it something you see yourself pursuing, and why or why not?

What factors would you consider in building an engineering department from scratch?

To whom did you turn for help the last time that you ran into a major technical wall, and why did you choose that person?

In the field of engineering, priorities often change quickly. Can you give me an example of a time when that happened? How did you handle it?

What software do you really, really know?

Are you keeping pace technically and technologically? How?

Financial Services

The financial services industry features professionals in investing, securities trading, and other activities that are "in the money." Financial analysts generally focus on trends impacting a specific industry, region, or type of product. "Buy side" analysts devise investment strategies. "Sell side" analysts help securities dealers sell stocks, bonds, and other investments.

Financial analysts and sales agents

What are the headlines in today's *Wall Street Journal*?

What do you read regularly on the industry?

What did the Dow, S&P, or NASDAQ close at yesterday?

What stocks do you follow and why? (Be prepared to discuss each stock's performance.)

What are some differences among financial consulting firms that are important to you?

What were the sales and profitability of your last financial services employer?

Are you a financial generalist or specialist? Where do you see yourself specializing?

What is an interest rate swap?

What is DCF? How do you calculate the discount rate?

How do you determine if a stock is undervalued?

How would you price the stock for an IPO?

What is the yield on a zero coupon bond trading at par with ten years to maturity?

What is working capital? Quick ratio? Free cash flow?

What do you want to do and why — M&A, capital markets, or corporate finance?

Why pick corporate finance as opposed to sales and trading?

What makes you think you can sell stocks?

Why choose selling debt vs. selling equity?

What particular markets or instruments are you interested in? Why?

What processes did you use to evaluate financial risk?

Our division is thinking of introducing a new product. How would you go about determining whether this is a good idea?

How would you value our company for a potential sale, spin-off, or liquidation?

Hospitality

Most of the people in this service industry work in hotels and restaurants. Hospitality covers a wide range of employers who sell food service and/or lodging. Travel and tourism jobs fit into this category. Although the hospitality industry employs many seasoned managers and executives, the industry is a magnet for young workers seeking entry-level employment.

Hotel and restaurant personnel

If you needed to organize a party or meeting for customers, how would you go about it?

How do you resolve conflict with customers or staff members?

Have you ever stayed/dined here? What do you think about our services and staff?

What do you know about our company?

What does customer service mean to you?

What do you understand about the term *hospitality?*

If a guest were upset, what would you do to regain the guest's goodwill?

How do you greet a high-profile customer and escort the customer to his or her restaurant seat?

How would you help build repeat business?

What steps have you taken in your previous hotel/restaurant management job for cost-cutting?

How many languages do you speak?

Cooks and food prep workers

How would you describe your style and values in cooking?

What trends/schools, if any, have influenced your development as a chef?

What, if anything, do you believe is unique about your cooking?

Tell me about experience(s) you have in designing your own dishes. How was it/were they received by diners? How do you know?

Describe a situation in which you had a cooking disaster in a restaurant or other kitchen, with hungry patrons waiting. What did you do to cope/rectify it?

Can you give me some examples of how you manage costs in your kitchen without compromising quality and freshness?

Information Technology

IT professionals are moving away from the traditional pure geeky technology emphasis to become hybrid IT/business professionals. "Technology and business skills have collapsed into each other, creating legions of these new hybrids," says David Foote, a leading IT expert. The following probes reflect a collection of industry-wide IT job interview questions.

Software engineers, programmers, and other IT specialists

What is your experience with enterprise disaster recovery?

Can you describe the maintenance and administration practices that you utilized to ensure effective performance of the corporate VOIP/WAN/IT?

Have you been responsible for the budget of company IT systems? Can you tell us how you monitored costs, business plan, and cash flow?

How do you keep yourself updated with technology?

Can you tell us about your experience in developing or maintaining an Internet site?

How can our company effectively manage our investment in personal computers and mobile devices?

Tell us about a difficult or complex programming assignment you've had. What steps did you take and how successful were you?

What techniques and tools can you use to ensure that a new application is as user friendly as possible?

How would you compare the use of a mainframe system versus a personal computer system?

What are the factors to consider in establishing a web presence?

Can you tell me about your experience with network administration?

What has been your experience in developing apps?

What various tools and measures can be implemented to secure data?

Does a business analyst need domain expertise?

Can you explain the term *system design document* (SDD)?

Let's suppose that you work for Happy City and it has recently implemented a website. Can you name some of the means by which a website may be used to improve communication with the citizens and encourage community involvement?

Have you had an experience when you, as a technical person, have had to work with nontechnical types to complete a project? Did you find the situation frustrating? If so, in what way? How did you finally work together?

You have been given the assignment to develop a training program for a new application. Approximately 30 staffers will require training. What steps will you take in developing the training?

Your assignment is to prepare the specifications to purchase a new application. What will you do?

What are some of the hot topics that technology professionals are talking about?

We need to publish a new brochure. How would you approach this task?

How would you define *SEO* and *SEM?*

What is your previous SEO history like? Can you give examples of rankings you've achieved?

Which blogs and websites do you follow daily to keep up-to-date and why?

Do you know who Matt Cutts is?

Which Google products do you use?

Which SEO tools do you prefer?

Do you use any type of web analytics?

What is a PageRank?

What is a NoFollow attribute?

How do you rate your HTML hand-coding skills?

Why is a sitemap important and how would you make search engines find it quickly?

Do you know anything about robots.txt?

How would you track the number of a website's outlinks?

Law Enforcement

Criminal justice jobs include three major fields: law enforcement, courts, and corrections. Police officers and detectives, the largest group of law enforcement officers, protect lives and property. Bilingual candidates with college training in police science or military police experience have the best chances of being hired.

Police officers

How do you feel about carrying a gun and possibly having to take someone's life in the line of duty?

What are the sources of stress in your personal and professional life? How do you manage this stress?

As a police officer, suppose you catch your friend doing something illegal. How would you handle the situation?

What is the importance of building relationships with colleagues in your professional life?

How do you handle conflict situations? Are your techniques successful?

Legal Services

The legal system affects nearly every aspect of our society. Attorneys (lawyers) form the core of this system, holding positions of great responsibility. They are assisted by court reporters and other judicial workers, especially paralegals and legal assistants. Most paralegals work for law firms and have formal training in paralegal studies.

Attorneys

Do you think your law school grades are an accurate reflection of the kind of work you will do as an attorney?

What types of cases do you usually take on, and what types of cases do you feel most passionate about?

How much preparation on files for trial do you do?

If we take a 15-minute break, can you present a closing argument based on the following x-y-z set of facts?

In your last corporate attorney leadership role, you had a large staff. Can you work without such a large staff?

How would you react if a judge threatened you with contempt of court, but your information was vital to winning your case?

What have previous employers said about your legal-writing skills?

What does *negligence* mean?

Why do you want to practice at a big firm?

How versed are you in bankruptcy law?

You've gone back and forth between plaintiff work and insurance defense. Which is your real interest?

What section of the x,y,z code would you change if you could?

Do you watch lawyer shows on TV? If so, other than entertainment value, what do you think of their presentation of a lawyer's work life? And which shows are your favorites? Why?

How would you have decided X case?

How would you placate a business client who's complaining about the firm's performance issues and threatening to leave?

Can you bring new accounts to this firm?

How would you educate a client regarding the liabilities of employment discrimination?

What would you do if a client tells you he is going to lie during his trial testimony?

How many depositions have you taken?

How many court appearances have you made?

Who was the worst client you ever had? Why?

Partway through litigation, your client decides to get another lawyer and demands you return all fees. What is your response?

Paralegals

How good are your analytical and research skills in law and legal procedures? How have previous employers rated these skills?

Can you describe an instance when you interacted with a client while the law team was busy dealing with cases and you were required to fill in?

Although you are interviewing for your first paralegal job, how has your paralegal training prepared you for it? Can you be specific, matching coursework with specific skill requirements outlined in our job post?

As a candidate for this banking paralegal position, can you describe a typical day in your previous position? Can you include common banking terms and procedures?

What area of law appeals to you?

Management

Management is getting work done through people. Recognizing that people matter, managers work to improve an organization's structure, efficiency, profits, or mission accomplishment. Changes in the business world are forcing managers to make changes in everything from regulatory and credit operations to pricing strategies and marketing changes.

Managers (in general)

How do you reinforce behavior you want repeated?

How do you develop untapped potential in your staff?

How do you build and maintain morale with your staff in a nonmonetary way?

How do you demonstrate that you value people for who they are, as well as for what they accomplish?

What are the primary management styles? Describe each. Which is your predominant style? How have you applied those characteristics? What successes and shortcomings have you experienced with your management style?

Marketing managers

Can you give us an example of a marketing brief you developed for a recent marketing project or program?

Can you give an example of how you have effectively used digital marketing tools?

Can you give me an example of a campaign that did not work out as you had planned?

What factors do you consider the most important when attempting to influence consumer behavior?

Are you familiar with our target market?

What do you use to find out if your marketing plan is working?

What do you consider the five most important aspects of successful marketing?

How do you feel about PPC (pay per click) advertising?

Do you subscribe to a particular marketing belief or methodology?

Can you describe your most successful marketing campaign?

What is the difference between marketing of service and product?

What is the important factor in service marketing?

Nursing

Millions of nurses practice nationwide, making nursing the largest workforce within the healthcare industry. There are dozens of types and levels of nurses, ranging from advance practice to bedside care. Registered nurses (RNs), licensed practical nurses (LPNs), certified nursing assistants (CNAs), and nurse aides comprise the bulk of the nursing workforce.

Nurses

Can you tell me about the last time an upset family member irritated you and how you handled it?

Can you describe what a good day of care for a hospice patient would be?

What is it about this job that excites you, and how do you relay that excitement to patients in your care?

How do you respond to crabby people in pain?

Approximately how old were you when you decided to become a nurse? Were there any defining moments that helped you decide to become a nurse?

If you encountered a patient who was uncharacteristically upset and/or difficult, what would you do?

If a patient has just expired and the family unknowingly has just arrived at the facility, how would you handle the unexpected dilemma?

Mrs. Jones is in the facility for a fractured hip. She constantly seeks attention by putting on the call light, pretending to be in pain. You pass by the room and hear her crying. What is your response?

How do you react to a sense of being overwhelmed with unfinished work ten minutes past your shift deadline when you find a new patient in need?

What would you do if you saw another nurse stealing from a patient?

How often do you think a charge nurse or director of nursing needs to be on the unit?

After an extremely demanding day with a patient who required much attention, a family member aggressively approaches you and accuses you of negligence and calls you nasty names. How do you handle this?

How would you go about making a hospital visitor feel welcome?

If needed, would you like to work another position, or would you rather not be cross-trained?

How do you make seamless transitions on shift changes?

The schedule shows eight nurses assigned, but only five show up. How does that make you feel? What would you do?

Sales

Sales is the activity of convincing prospective buyers to purchase a product or service in return for money or other required compensation. Sales workers are found in virtually all business endeavors. These questions focus first on retail sales clerks, retail department managers, and retail store managers, and are followed by sales workers in general.

Retail salespersons, department managers, and store managers

What is good customer service?

Why do customers shop at this store?

A coworker is rude to customers. What would you do?

A customer wants to pay for $15 worth of merchandise in quarters. Do you accept it?

A customer wants to return a package of food that is open and half gone. What would you do?

How do you go about familiarizing yourself with the products you sell?

How would you greet your customer? Can you give me a sample greeting?

How would you soothe an angry customer?

Sell me a product. How would you do it?

How can you increase the sales of my store?

Can you explain the importance of body language in a retail job?

I am your customer and I am asking for a product that is out of stock. Can you demonstrate how you will convey this fact to me?

I am your customer and I am asking for a discount of 10 percent, but you cannot grant more than 8 percent. How will you explain that to me?

How important is customer satisfaction to you in doing your job?

How will you remember the location of different merchandise in the store? Any ideas?

Can you describe a time when you had to handle a difficult customer?

What kind of training/induction/orientation were you given in your previous job?

What was your sales target? Were you able to achieve it?

What kind of customer complaints have you ever received? How did you handle them?

If this position requires you to handle money, are you ready to accept the responsibility? Will you sign a background screening check permission form?

How do you feel about the philosophy of the customer always being right?

How do you respond if you know the customer is wrong?

Salespersons (in general)

Are you comfortable placing cold calls to leads and existing clients?

In what ways do you maintain contacts and business relationships with clients and vendors?

Is *quota* a bad word for you? Does this word irritate or scare you?

How would you handle achieving a very high quota the first 90 days?

Can you describe your experience with corporate sales?

This job covers a large territory. How much travel time are you willing to commit to being a road warrior?

In the past, how did you expand your customer base?

How well do you know your way around the western United States?

How would you sell to a doctor who you can't meet face to face?

What have you done as a sales manager to organize a new sales force?

Index